The Quest for Theseus

The
Quest
for

An expert on Minoan and Mycenaean jewelry and work in precious metals, Dr Ward, a freelance archaeological editor, is at present engaged in research for a book on her subject.

Anne G. Ward

Associate Professor of Classics at Princeton University, where he lectures on Classical mythology, Dr Connor's publications include *Greek Orations*, which he edited, *Theopompus and Fifth Century Athens*, and contributions to learned journals.

W. R. Connor

After research at Cambridge, where her doctoral dissertation was on *Greek Legends and the Mycenaean Age*, Dr Edwards was assistant in Greek at the University of Aberdeen. She has excavated with Lord William Taylour at Skala in Laconia and at Mycenae.

Ruth B. Edwards

Mr Tidworth has made a special study of the use of mythological themes in art, music, and literature throughout the ages. He has worked for many years in academic publishing.

Simon Tidworth

With a Preface by
Reynold Higgins

Deputy Keeper of the Department of Greek and Roman Antiquities at the British Museum, Dr Higgins has published several books on Greek and Roman art, including *Greek Terracotta Figures, Jewellery from Classical Lands* and *Minoan and Mycenaean Art*.

PRAEGER PUBLISHERS

New York

Theseus

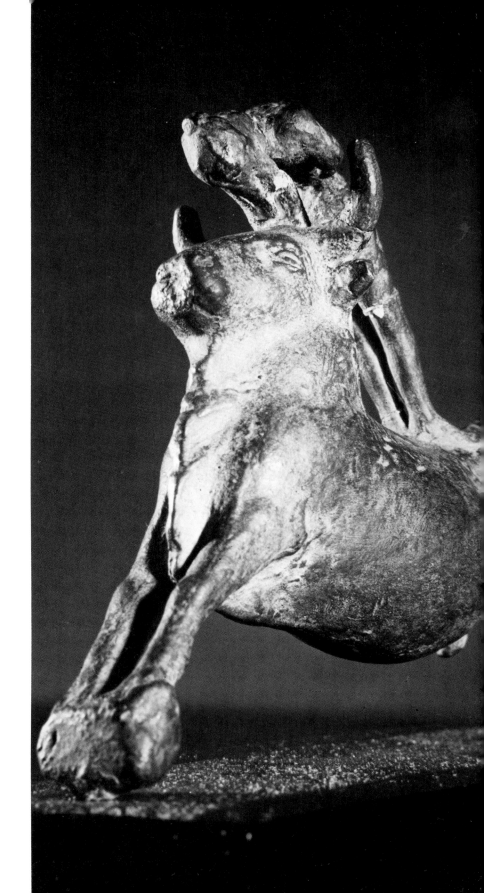

Washington · London

PUBLISHED IN THE UNITED STATES OF AMERICA IN 1970
BY PRAEGER PUBLISHERS, INC.
111 FOURTH AVENUE, NEW YORK, N.Y. 10003
ALL RIGHTS RESERVED
LIBRARY OF CONGRESS CATALOG NUMBER: 78-110285
PRINTED IN AUSTRIA

Contents

Preface

THE *Oxford Classical Dictionary* says of Theseus that 'there is no proof that any real person lies behind the legend, but that is not impossible'. Nevertheless, after reading the *Quest* one will probably come to the conclusion that if he did not exist, then it has obviously been found necessary to invent him.

An elusive hero, Theseus, surprising in his absences as in his appearances. Homer scarcely knows him, yet he was a household word to the Athenians of Pericles' day, whose bible Homer was.

This is an exhaustive enquiry. Ruth B. Edwards sets the stage with a picture of Theseus as Plutarch saw him, and follows with an account of the growth of his legend in Classical times. Anne G. Ward fleshes out the bare bones of archaeology and finds a home for our hero in Mycenaean Athens and Minoan Crete. W. R. Connor follows him into Classical Athens. Simon Tidworth traces him in the Roman and Medieval worlds, brings him through the Renaissance and into the modern world, where, not surprisingly, he seems very much at home.

Finally, Anne G. Ward sums up in all honesty. Was there a historical Theseus? The verdict is 'not proven'; but she would like us to think there was. And she and her colleagues have gone far to persuade us.

Although he had his little failings (and who hasn't?), one can't help feeling that Theseus was essentially a nice person to know; much nicer than his great rival Heracles; and a good friend in a tight corner.

REYNOLD HIGGINS

General Chronological Chart

		CHAPTERS 1, 2 GREEK LITERATURE & ART	CHAPTERS 3-7 ARCHAEOLOGY	CHAPTER 8 POLITICS & RELIGION	CHAPTERS 9-11 LITERATURE & THE ARTS
2000			Rise of Minoan palaces		
1500	BRONZE AGE		1475 Eruption of Thera 1350 Fall of Knossos 1300 1200 Mycenaean hegemony 1220 Trojan War 1120 Fall of Mycenae		
1000	DARK AGE	Composition of Homeric Poems			
500	ARCH. CLASS. HELLENISTIC	490 Marathon Fall of Athens		Pisistratus 545 Democracy in Athens 514 Cimon builds Theseus shrine Outbreak of Peloponnesian War	
BC				Catullus Virgil Ovid	Wall paintings Sarcophagi
AD	ROMAN			Seneca Pliny Plutarch *Lives* Pausanias	Labyrinth mosaics St Reparatus
500	DARK AGES				
1000					Lucca Cathedral
	MIDDLE AGES			Lambert Dante Petrarch Boccaccio Chaucer Lydgate	Illuminated manuscripts Veneto
1500	RENAISSANCE				Titian *Bacchus and Ariadne*
				Monteverdi 1608 *Arianna a Nassos* Poussin *Theseus finding his father's arms* Racine *Phèdre* 1677 Romney Handel Haydn Canova *Theseus Triumphant* 1782	
1900	MODERN		1879 Rediscovery of Mycenaean Civilization 1900 Rediscovery of the Labyrinth	Ruskin *Fors Clavigera 22, 23* Watts *The Minotaur* Frazer *Golden Bough* Jung Unamuno *Fedra* 1912 Strauss *Ariadne auf Naxos* 1912 Kazantzakis *Theseus* Picasso Renault Ayrton	

Introduction

Most people have at least heard of Theseus, legendary hero of the Classical Greeks, but for many he is no more than a childhood fairy-tale figure dimly recalled from Kingsley's *The Heroes*, barely emerging from a confused chiaroscuro of bull-monsters, centaurs, Amazons and unlikely epic feats of strength and courage, whom they have, quite understandably, relegated to the realm of legend and folktale. Others have encountered him in a more concrete form as the local hero of ancient Athens, with his shrines and his cult, founder of the Isthmian games and organizer of the political structure of Attica. In his best-known avatar as victor of innumerable encounters with superhuman enemies he seems, to say the least, highly unpromising as factual historical material. However, since the day when Schliemann located the site of Troy by placing implicit faith, in defiance of established academic opinion, in the topographical landmarks transmitted by the Homeric poems, archaeologists have been awake to the dangers of rejecting the evidence of even the most fantastic legend. In the case of Theseus, it will be shown that, paradoxically enough, it is precisely the most improbable aspects of his story which have the best historical foundation.

Agatha Christie, who is the wife of the distinguished scholar Professor Sir Max Mallowan, has described the archaeologist as 'the detective of the past'; this is a shrewd observation, for the two pursuits are based on remarkably similar principles. The object of both is to identify people and reconstruct events from the few material traces they have left behind. In both cases the technique began crudely, with all but the most obviously relevant evidence either ignored or wantonly destroyed, and each has developed into

Ill. 1. The Agora and the Acropolis, civic and religious heart of Athens, seen from the colonnade of the temple of Hephaestus.

a systematic discipline based on exhaustive comparison of all available evidence and application of the most recent methods of scientific analysis. It is true that, unlike the detective, the archaeologist is not pursuing a quarry who is consciously trying to cover his tracks; but then, Sherlock Holmes himself might well have baulked at being asked to follow a trail which had been cold for well over three thousand years, and no less a task faces the archaeologist who wishes to reconstruct the reality behind the story of Theseus.

In any problem of detection a statement of the case should come before the factual evidence is presented, and as the Theseus with whom we are familiar is the creation of the Classical Athenian poets and story-tellers, it is logical to begin by relating the legend as it was known to the ancients. There is, however, more than one version. The story developed over the course of time, gathering elaborations motivated partly by the changing demands of political propaganda and partly by alterations in current popular taste. These

4

variations, too, must be taken into account before we can form a clear picture of exactly who Theseus was and what he was believed to have done.

To the Classical Athenians he was an immediate and real figure to whom they unhesitatingly ascribed much of the best in their civic life, but at the same time he was the invincible hero whose feats endowed him with an aura somewhere between King Arthur, El Cid and Jack the Giant Killer. It is hard to accept that a pre-eminently rational people could have attributed to Theseus such sober factual activities as the organization of the political system *Ill. 1* of Attica with its detailed bureaucratic subdivisions, and at the same time found no difficulty in relating in equally prosaic and commonplace terms how he encountered a bull-headed cannibal, horse-bodied men and the earliest known monstrous regiment of women, and crowned his exploits by leaving half his posterior in the nether world—surely the most ludicrous misfortune ever to befall a national hero. In spite of these apparent contradictions the Athenians believed in him implicitly, and scholars have only recently begun to suggest that all the most practical and down-to-earth elements in his story, such as the political reforms, date to many centuries later than the Bronze Age in which the story has its setting, and were never connected with the hero in the remotest degree.

Take away these elements and the remainder apparently comprises the wilder flights of an unusually bizarre imagination. It does not do, however, to reject the myth out of hand. The example of Schliemann's experiences at Troy and Mycenae alone is enough to show the spectacular results to be obtained by taking the ancient legends at face value. A considerable number of artefacts and buildings have survived from Theseus' own day, and in the best detective tradition we must turn to these, the facts, to substantiate or invalidate the written statements of the biased witnesses of later times.

Theseus, however, was considerably more than the subject of a good story, or even a focus for Attic patriotism. He was a powerful influence in practical terms on the daily life of the Classical Athenians. He was the object of a hero cult with far-reaching moral implications, and his name was closely associated with the democratic institutions of which Athens was so proud. The legend's propaganda value was extended even beyond the borders of Attica by making Theseus an all-Ionian hero to set against the Dorian Heracles, as well as the personification of the Athenian ideal of democracy, progressiveness and philanthropy, and these practical applications of the myth are an integral factor in its development.

The story does not end with the ancient world. Each successive age has found something in the details of the myth or the personality of the hero to suit its own tastes and preoccupations, and stressed this element accordingly. For the Roman amorists such as Ovid and Catullus and the Medieval moralists, the Ariadne story tended to predominate. The Baroque period preferred the more horrific aspects of the Phaedra legend, until in the Romantic and neo-Classical ages interest returned to Theseus as the central figure. Many modern writers, painters and even psychologists are intrigued by the strange dualism of the Minotaur, and the legend is still proving a fruitful source of inspiration.

All these elements have been instrumental in shaping the myth, and we should try to bear them all in mind as, with a passing acknowledgement to the shade of the Baker Street master, we set out for the Aegean and the quest for Theseus.

As a postscript to this introduction I should like to thank the many people whose interest and assistance have helped so greatly with the production of this book. Not least among these are the staff of the Pall Mall Press for their unfailing enthusiasm, patience and ingenuity in dealing with the inevitable problems which have afflicted its progress from time to time; Dr Reynold Higgins of the British Museum for his generosity with advice and help at all stages and especially for his kind Preface; and above all, my collaborating authors, whose able contributions have added so much to the archaeological record. I should like to make it clear that each author is personally responsible only for the opinions and interpretations offered in his or her own work, and must not be held accountable for the views expressed by other contributors. Although the choice of illustrations was for the most part made by the authors, the captions, for technical reasons, are entirely the responsibility of the publishers.

Anne G. Ward

1   The Story of Theseus

Ruth B. Edwards

THESEUS WAS THE MOST FAMOUS and revered of all the heroes of ancient Athens. His achievements were depicted in numerous works of art, and told or alluded to by countless authors. It must be remembered however that there was no single or canonical form of his story in the Classical period: each writer or artist emphasized whatever aspect of the hero's various adventures was most applicable to his own particular interest and purpose. Indeed, no connected account of the Theseus legend survives earlier than those composed in Hellenistic or Roman times—most notably by Apollodorus (possibly second century BC, but more likely to be later), who compiled a handbook of mythology, and by Plutarch (*c*. AD 46—120), whose *Parallel Lives of the Greeks and Romans* included a life of Theseus. Both these Greek writers made extensive use of earlier material, and Apollodorus' version contains many interesting details, but being part of a general handbook of myths it lacks the coherent thread of Plutarch's account. For this reason Plutarch is used as the chief source for the material in this introductory outline, his account being supplemented where appropriate with details from other sources. (The relevant chapters of Plutarch are indicated in the margin at the side of each paragraph, together with some select references to other ancient writers: for further details see the Bibliography.)

Ill. 106
Ill. 4

In the north-east of the Peloponnese, less than two miles from the sea, lay the small town of Troezen. Poseidon, god of the sea, was its special patron, and it was here that there lived in the time before the Trojan War a princess named Aethra, the daughter of Pittheus, who was the son of Pelops and famed throughout Greece for his wisdom. One day a stranger came to the town to seek Pittheus' advice. He was Aegeus, the king of Athens and great-grandson of Erechtheus. He had gone to Delphi to consult the prophetess about his childlessness, and had received a cryptic oracle:

Loose not the jutting neck of the wineskin, great
 chief of the people,
Till you have come once again to the city of Athens.

Pittheus understood the oracle, but enticed or persuaded Aegeus into having intercourse with his daughter Aethra in Troezen. This Aegeus did without knowing who she was, and when he discovered that she was the king's daughter, he made plans in the event of the birth of a son. He concealed a sword and a pair of sandals beneath a great rock, and bade Aethra, if a son were born to her, to wait until he reached manhood, and then when he could lift the rock to send him to Athens with the sword and sandals as tokens of his paternity.

   In the course of time Aethra bore her son, and named him Theseus. But she kept his origin secret from him, and rumour grew up

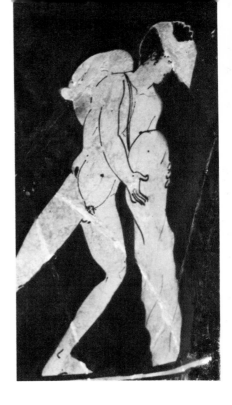

(Plu. *Thes.* 3)

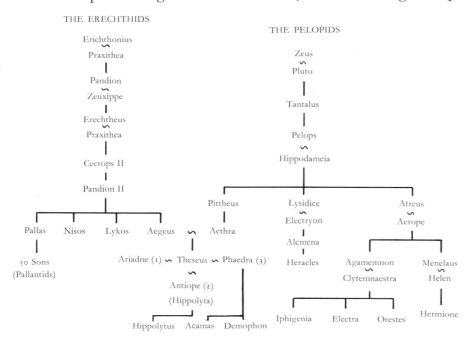

Ill. 3. Genealogical table of the houses of Erechtheus and Pelops, based on Apollodorus and other sources. There are many variants in the ancient writers about some of the precise relationships. Iphigenia, for instance, according to one tradition was the daughter of Theseus and Helen.

8

Ill. 2. Left, Theseus lifting the rock to recover his father's tokens; detail from a red-figure Attic calyx-crater of the fifth century BC. This vase is one of the comparatively rare examples of the scene in Greek art.

Ill. 4. View of the coast at Troezen, the reputed birthplace of Theseus. The tiny island of Sphairia, where in one version of the story Aethra lay with the god Poseidon, was off the coast not far from here (see *Ill. 10*).

(Plu. *Thes.* 4, 6;
Paus. I. 27. 7)

Ill. 2

Ill. 10

Ill. 3

that he was the son of the god Poseidon, a version of his birth which was given especially wide credence at Troezen, where the boy was brought up. Pausanias, a famous Greek traveller of the second century AD, tells a charming story about his childhood. When Theseus was only seven years old, Heracles came to visit the royal family. He laid aside his lion skin while at table, and the children of the nobles, thinking that it was a real lion, ran away in fear. But young Theseus snatched an axe from the servants and tried to kill it.

When Theseus had reached early manhood (Pausanias tells us it was at the age of sixteen), and had 'shown that he possessed not only physical strength, but courage and a resolute spirit, combined with good sense and intelligence', his mother led him to the rock where his father's tokens lay hidden and told him the secret of his birth. Theseus put his shoulder to the rock and raised it with ease; then taking the tokens with him he set off on the journey to Athens, despising the quick, safe route by sea and choosing to travel by land along the edge of the Saronic Gulf, a path infested by ruffians and bandits. Plutarch tells us that in his choice of the more dangerous route Theseus was inspired by the example of Heracles, to whom

9

Ills. 5—10. The exploits of Theseus on the journey from Troezen to Athens, from a red-figure kylix by the Codrus Painter of the fifth century BC. This is one of a series of red-figure cups, which provides valuable artistic evidence for these exploits. Above left: Sinis, the pine-bender; centre left: Phaia; below left: Sciron; right: the wrestling match with Cercyon and the death of Procrustes. A sixth scene represents Theseus and the bull of Marathon (*Ill. 172*). It is noticeable that the rather colourless episode of Periphetes, the club-bearer, is missing. The map shows Theseus' route and the places which were believed to be the sites of his various encounters.

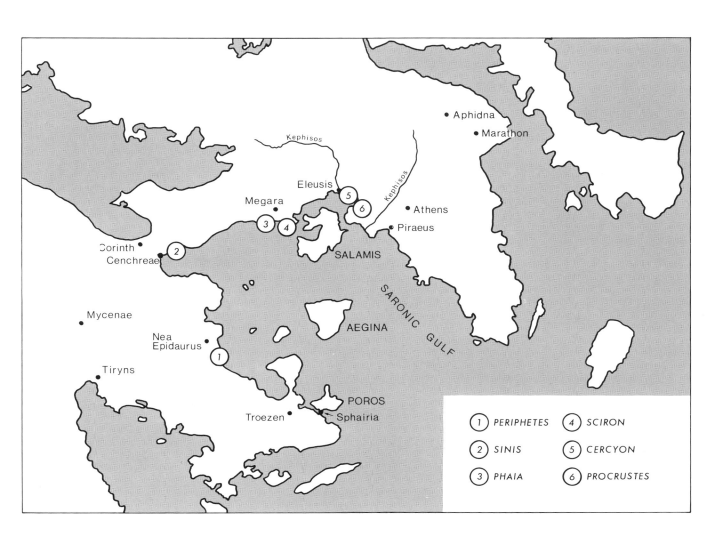

he was related (they were said to be second cousins) and who had put down many evil-doers. He certainly met with many opportunities to display his courage on the journey. First, in Epidauria, he came across Periphetes, the club-bearer, who tried to bar his way. Theseus grappled with him and slew him, and took his club as his own weapon, rather as Heracles wore everywhere the skin of the mighty lion he had slain. Then, on the Isthmus of Corinth, he met Sinis, known as Pityocamptes, 'the pine-bender', because he killed men by tying them to two pine trees which he had bent down and then letting the trees spring back. Theseus dispatched Sinis by his own cruel method, and proceeded to Crommyon, where he slew a fierce wild sow named Phaia. Plutarch here notes a variant version that Phaia was a murderous female robber.

Next on his journey along the Saronic Gulf Theseus reached the Scironian cliffs on the borders of Megara. This was a most dangerous place, where for nearly ten kilometres the narrow path passed along a crumbly ledge with an almost sheer drop down to the sea, nearly 200 m. below. The natural dangers of the cliff-path were heightened for Theseus by the presence of the robber Sciron, who intercepted travellers along the path and compelled them to wash his feet. When they bent down to perform this menial task, he kicked them over the cliff into the sea, where (in a picturesque detail not mentioned by Plutarch) a huge turtle lay in wait for them. Theseus dealt appropriately with Sciron, and likewise overcame Cercyon, the cruel wrestler at Eleusis. Then, not far from Athens, he punished another evil-doer, the notorious Procrustes,* who used to entice travellers from the path to try out his wonderful bed, which he said fitted all. In fact, he lopped off the limbs of all who were too long for it, and hammered and stretched all those who were too short. Theseus killed him in the same way as Procrustes himself had killed others and thus safely reached Athens, where he was purified of the guilt of bloodshed at the river Kephisos.

At Athens at last he encountered his father Aegeus in a strange meeting. The city was in a state of disorder, and Aegeus living in fear of his nephews, the fifty sons of Pallas. They were jealous of his kingship and had hopes of winning the throne, since Aegeus was apparently childless and was, according to some, only an adopted son of the royal house. Aegeus was also much under the influence

Ills. 5—9

(Plu. *Thes.* 6—9;
Paus. I. 27. 8, II. 1. 4;
Diod. Sic. IV. 59)

Ill. 48

Ill. 11

* i.e. 'he who beats out and stretches'. He was also known as Damastes, 'the subduer'.

(Plu. *Thes.* 10—12;
Apollod. *Epit.* I. 1—4;
Paus. I. 44. 8)

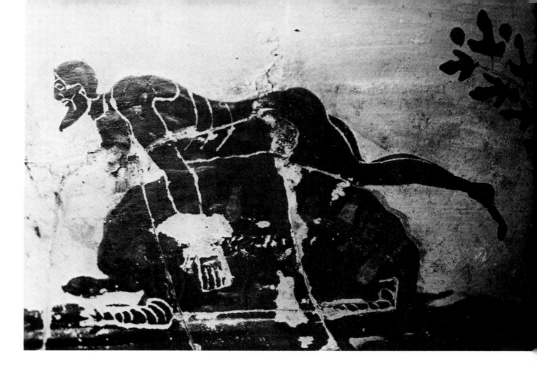

Ill. 11. Possibly a version of Theseus and Sciron's turtle, from a black-figure vase. The hero appears to be here riding on the turtle in contrast to the usual version where he avoids contact with it altogether. If he really is Theseus, he is depicted as a bearded man instead of the traditional youth of the Isthmus road adventures, and the vase would refer to a version now lost from the literary sources.

* The word used by Plutarch here (*machaira*) means a knife as well as a sword.

Ill. 12

(Plu. *Thes.* 12—14; cf. Apollod. *Epit.* I. 5—6)

Ills. 13, 14

(Plu. *Thes.* 15 Apollod. III. 1. 4)

of his foreign wife, the sorceress Medea, who persuaded him to attempt the life of the young stranger with poison at the banquet which was given in his honour. But during the meal Theseus drew his sword,* as if intending to carve; Aegeus recognized it as the one which he had left in Troezen, and dashed down the cup of poison. Theseus was acknowledged his son and heir, and when the fifty sons of Pallas rose up against him in force, he defeated their ambush and scattered them. He also displayed his bravery and skill by going out on his own initiative against yet another evil, the bull of Marathon, a savage creature which was ravaging the plain of Marathon (some 32 kilometres north-east of Athens). Theseus captured the bull alive and dedicated it to Apollo Delphinios.

He soon had to face an even greater test of his courage. A most powerful king at this time was Minos, ruler of Knossos in Crete, who controlled the seas with his navy. The story was that his wife Pasiphaë had become enamoured of a bull (some said that this was a punishment from Poseidon), and with the aid of Daedalus, a skilled craftsman from Athens, coupled with it, hidden in a wooden cow. The result of their unnatural mating was the Minotaur, a ferocious monster, part man, part bull, who fed on human flesh. Minos confined the creature in the Labyrinth constructed for him by Daedalus.

Now Minos' son Androgeos was thought to have been treacherously slain in Attic territory. In a war of revenge, Minos conquered Megara and harassed Athens. At the same time the Athenians were afflicted with divine vengeance—famine, pestilence and drought—and in their suffering they sought oracular advice. They were told to give Minos whatever satisfaction he might demand. He chose to exact a cruel tribute: every ninth year seven youths and seven maidens had to be sent to Crete, where they were thrown into the Labyrinth, either to be killed by the Minotaur or to perish, unable to find their way out of its winding passages.

(Plu. *Thes.* 15; Apollod. III. 15. 8)

Ill. 12. Aerial view of the plain of Marathon. It was here that Theseus was believed to have captured the savage bull (*Ill. 32*); and here many centuries later to have reappeared to aid the Greeks in their victory over the Persians (490 BC). The coastline has altered since the Bronze Age, but the surrounding hills still cut the plain off from Athens.

Ills. 13, 14. The coins of Knossos in the Classical period often commemorated the legend. This example from the fifth century BC shows the Minotaur on the obverse; on the reverse appears a stylized version of the Labyrinth.

When it came to the third tribute, the fathers of unmarried sons had to present them to Aegeus in order that the Minotaur's victims might be chosen by lot. Feeling against Aegeus ran high, and Theseus himself, out of pity for his countrymen, volunteered to go, in spite of all the entreaties of his father, boasting that he would slay the Minotaur and rid Athens for ever of the tribute. He promised that, if he were successful, as a sign to Aegeus he would change the black sail, with which the ship was rigged, to a white one. Plutarch adds some further details which he has taken from Hellanicus, a fifth-century logographer,* who related that a condition of the tribute was that the Athenians should carry no warlike weapon, and that if the Minotaur were slain the penalty would lapse. Moreover he gives a version whereby, instead of the victims being chosen by lot, Minos came personally to Athens to select them, and picked out Theseus first of all.

Whatever the circumstances, Theseus sailed as part of the tribute to Crete, and there Minos' daughter Ariadne fell in love with him

* i.e. writer of prose-history including the mythological period

(Plu. *Thes.* 17)

and determined to help him. She gave him the famous clew, a ball of thread, by which he could find his way out of the windings of the Labyrinth. Theseus found the Minotaur asleep, and grasping him by the forelock killed him in single combat. Then taking Ariadne with him he fled from Crete. According to Pherecydes, another fifth-century logographer, he prevented Minos' fleet from following him by scuttling his ships. As for Daedalus, because he had suggested the idea of the clew to Ariadne, Minos confined him in the Labyrinth, but he escaped and made his way to Sicily. Minos himself, when he pursued him there, was violently killed by the daughters of the local Sicilian king.

In this way Theseus escaped safely from Crete; but on his way home he abandoned Ariadne. The ancients were not agreed as to exactly what happened. Homer said that she was killed on the island of Dia at the instigation of the god Dionysus; others alleged that she killed herself. An alternative version was that when Theseus left her Dionysus made her his bride on the island of Naxos. Be that as it may, Theseus sailed to the sacred island of Delos, where he made sacrifice to Apollo and celebrated his escape from Crete with the Athenian youths and maidens in a dance, known as the Crane

Ill. 15

(Plu. *Thes.* 19; Pherecyd. frags. 148, 150; Apollod. *Epit.* I. 8—15)

Ill. 16. Right, a Classical temple ▶ near the shore on the island of Delos, where, according to Plutarch, Theseus and his friends landed to celebrate their escape from Crete.

Ill. 15. Theseus fights the Minotaur; detail from a red-figure kylix from Vulci. Young Theseus, sword in hand, attacks the Minotaur, who defends himself with a large rock. This fine vase was signed by the painter Epiktetos (*flor.* 520—500 BC).

16

Dance (*Geranos*), in which the movements of the dancers were said to imitate the windings of the Labyrinth. The dance was executed round an altar, known as the *keraton*, made up of horns (*kerata*) each taken from the left side of an animal's head. In addition, he founded games on the island, and instituted the practice of giving a palm to the victors.

(Homer *Od.* XI. 321—5;
Plu. *Thes.* 20—21;
Apollod. *Epit.* I. 9)

From Delos Theseus returned to Athens, and either in distress at the loss of Ariadne or from joy at seeing his home again he forgot to change the colour of his sails. Aegeus, who was eagerly looking out for his son's return, in despair threw himself down from a cliff and was killed. Plutarch does not say where this took place, but we learn from Pausanias that it was believed to be from the steep rock on the west corner of the Acropolis at Athens, where the little temple of Nike, or Victory, now stands.

Ill. 17

(Plu. *Thes.* 22;
Apollod. *Epit.* I. 10;
Paus. I. 22. 4—5)

On the death of his father, Theseus became king. There is no agreed order in the tradition for the events of his reign, but a great

many exploits are attributed to him. First and foremost he was famed for the so-called 'synoecism' of Attica, that is for collecting together the scattered inhabitants of the area round Athens into one capital. With this act Plutarch associates his foundation of the democracy, his naming of the town Athens, and the institution of certain festivals, notably the Panathenaia, which was the great festival of the goddess Athena. Other festivals said to have been founded by Theseus included the Oschophoria ('Carrying of Vine-branches') and the ceremonies which took place on the seventh day of the month Pyanepsion, both these festivals being connected in the popular mind with the story of his escape from Crete. He was also said to have divided the people into three classes, noblemen, husbandmen and artisans, to have struck a coinage stamped with the figure of an ox, and to have brought the territory of Megara under the control of Athens. On the Isthmus of Corinth he set up a famous pillar, bearing inscriptions to mark the frontier between

Ill. 17. View over the modern city of Athens towards the sea, from the west bastion of the Acropolis. It was from here, according to various Greek writers, that Aegeus watched for his son's return and, when Theseus forgot to change the colour of his sail, cast himself down the rock-face to his death. Some Latin sources have him fling himself into the Aegean Sea, which thus derived its name from him.

(Plu. *Thes.* 22—25;
cf. Thuc. II. 15)

the Peloponnese and Ionia, and he founded (or refounded) the Isthmian games there, in honour of his reputed father Poseidon.

Many acts of piety and patriotism were attributed to him, and he was looked upon as a friend to those in distress. Thus he kindly received in Attica the ill-fated Oedipus after he had been driven, aged, blind and destitute, from Thebes. Likewise he befriended Heracles in his time of trouble, when, afflicted by madness, he had killed his own children. In a more active way he intervened again at Thebes when its ruler Creon denied the sacred rite of burial to the Argive dead who fell in the dreadful war between the sons of Oedipus. According to the tragedian Euripides he recovered the bodies by defeating the Thebans in battle, but in other versions he secured burial by means of a truce.

(Plu. *Thes.* 29;
Soph. *Oed. Col.*;
Eur. *Heracles, Suppl.*)

Some writers added that Theseus went on the voyage of the Argo with Jason to recover the Golden Fleece from Colchis, that he helped the hero Meleager in his great hunt of the Calydonian boar, and that he joined the campaign of Heracles against the Amazons, the fierce women warriors who lived on the southern shore of the Black Sea. Another version was that he went against the Amazons on his own initiative, to carry off their queen Antiope. In revenge for her abduction, or for some other cause, the Amazonian women invaded Attica, and a battle was fought near the Acropolis of Athens itself. Plutarch tells us that this took place on the day on which, even in his own time, the Athenians celebrated the festival of Boedromia ('Running – or racing – to Help'). The war ended in a treaty, which, according to the fourth-century writer Cleidemus, was effected through Theseus' Amazonian bride, whom Cleidemus calls Hippolyta, not Antiope. As Plutarch notes, the stories of Theseus' Amazonian adventure varied a good deal, and some writers even said that Hippolyta was killed in the fighting. Certainly we later find Theseus married to another woman, Phaedra, the sister of Ariadne from Crete. Phaedra is most famous for her unrequited love for Hippolytus, Theseus' son by the queen of the Amazons; this story is discussed in the following chapter.

Ill. 18

(Plu. *Thes.* 26—29;
Apollod. I. 9. 16, I. 8. 2;
Eur. *Hippolytus*)

In many of his exploits Theseus was joined by his close friend Pirithous, king of the Lapiths from Thessaly. According to Plutarch they first became friends in Attica, and he relates the following anecdote about their meeting. Pirithous wanted to test Theseus' reputation for bravery, and so he drove away his cattle from the plain of Marathon. When he learned that Theseus was pursuing him in arms, he did not run away, but turned and faced him. On first catching sight of one another each hero was so struck by admiration for his opponent's appearance and courage that they refrained from fighting, and Pirithous held out his right hand in friendship. Theseus willingly forgave him his attempted theft, and they ratified their friendship with oaths. Later when Pirithous got married, Theseus was invited to Thessaly for the wedding. Among the guests were the centaurs, strange creatures, half horse, half man, who being unaccustomed to wine became drunk and began to lay their hands on the Lapith women. A brawl ensued on the spot, which led to a full-scale battle between the centaurs and Lapiths, and Theseus helped Pirithous to drive the centaurs from his country.

Ill. 31

Ill. 19
(Plu. *Thes.* 30)

Some of the other enterprises in which Theseus was involved with Pirithous, especially where sexual adventures were concerned, might be considered not very creditable to the pair. It has already been described how Theseus abandoned Ariadne on his way back from Crete, an action which Plutarch calls 'neither noble nor decent', and he was said to have ravished various girls, among whom were the daughters of Sinis and Cercyon. His expeditions with Pirithous included two particularly notorious acts. The first was the abduction of Helen, when Theseus was already 50 years old and Helen only a child of 10 or 12. Pirithous and Theseus travelled to Sparta together, and carried her off while she was dancing in the temple of Artemis. Because she was not of marriageable age, they left her in the town of Aphidna in Attica, while they went off elsewhere. In their absence Helen's brothers, the twins Castor and Pollux (also known as the Dioscuri, 'sons of Zeus') went to Athens and demanded back their sister, but the citizens declared that they did not know where she was. Then a certain Academus revealed her presence at Aphidna. The Dioscuri attacked Aphidna by force and captured it. They not only took back Helen to her home in Sparta, but also carried off as prisoner Theseus' mother Aethra, who had been left as a companion for the girl. Thus Aethra became a slave of Helen, and served her later at Troy.

The second of Theseus' less creditable exploits was the attempt to carry off the goddess Persephone from the underworld as a bride

(Plu. *Thes.* 29—34; cf. Herodotus IX. 73)

Ill. 18. Theseus abducting the Amazon, Antiope. This remarkably fine piece of sculpture comes from the pediment of the late sixth century BC temple of Apollo Daphnephoros at Eretria. The temple was destroyed during the Persian invasions.

for Pirithous. Such an act of impiety could hardly be expected to meet with success, and the two heroes were punished for their presumption by being imprisoned in Hades, seated on thrones of rock from which they could not rise. Pirithous was apparently kept prisoner for ever, but Theseus was rescued by Heracles. Plutarch does not tell this old story in the form we have related it, but says that the expedition was one to Epirus in the north-west of Greece, some considerable distance from Athens, and that it was to win the hand of a human girl Kore, the daughter of the local king Aidoneus (Kore was also another name for Persephone, and Aidoneus for Hades). According to his version Aidoneus let his dog Cerberus kill Pirithous, but kept Theseus closely confined. Eventually he released him at the request of Heracles.

Ills. 21, 39, 40

(Plu. *Thes.* 31, 35; Eur. *Heracles* 619; Apollod. II. 5. 12)

Ill. 19. Theseus and a centaur, from the temple of Zeus at Olympia where the fight at Pirithous' wedding feast was shown on the west pediment. Although the rest of the figure is badly preserved, the head does give some idea of Theseus portrayed as the idealized youth.

Ill. 21. Right, sixth-century shield relief from Olympia showing Heracles with Theseus and Pirithous in Hades. The descent into Hades was related in lost epic poetry, including the *Minyas* and a Hesiodic poem of which small fragments survive on papyrus.

Ill. 20. The shore and acropolis on the island of Scyros in the northern Sporades, where Theseus traditionally met his death. In one version he is pushed off the cliff by the king of Scyros but Plutarch also records a variant that Theseus accidentally slipped to his death while walking after supper.

(Plu. *Thes.* 32, 35)

Ill. 20

In his absence in Epirus or in the underworld a usurper, Menestheus son of Peteos, another descendent of Erechtheus, seized Theseus' throne at Athens and stirred up the people against their legitimate ruler. Athens became divided by civil strife, and Theseus, after sending his two sons Acamas and Demophon to safety in Euboea, sailed away to Scyros, where he had ancestral estates and expected to be well received. But the king, Lycomedes, treacherously lured him up to the highest point on the island on the pretext of showing him his estate, and then pushed him over the cliffs to his death.

Such was the end of Theseus, after which the usurper Menestheus reigned at Athens and represented the city in the Trojan War. It was not until many centuries later, around 475 BC, that the Athenians, in response to an oracle, went to Scyros to recover his bones. The expedition was led by the soldier and statesman Cimon, who had difficulty in discovering the grave and in taking away the relics because of the inhospitable character of the inhabitants of Scyros. But he captured the island by force, and, digging at a spot where he saw an eagle pecking at a mound, discovered the coffin of a body of huge size, and lying beside it a bronze spearhead and sword. The Athenians welcomed these remains with magnificent

23

ceremonies, and laid them to rest in the heart of the city. The place became a sanctuary for runaway slaves and all who were poor and oppressed, because, in Plutarch's own words, 'Theseus all through his life was the champion and helper of the distressed and always listened kindly to the petitions of the poor.'

(Plu. *Thes*. 35—36; *Cimon* 8; Diod. Sic. IV. 62. 4; Paus. I. 17. 2)

Ill. 22. Plan of the Agora at Athens in the second century AD. The shrine of Theseus is believed to have been situated somewhere in the southern part of the complex.

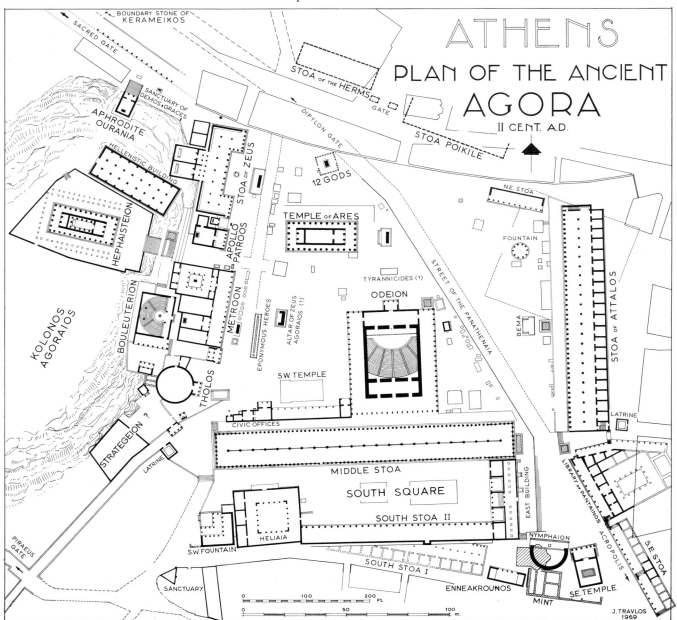

2 The Growth of the Legend

Ruth B. Edwards

THE STORY OF THESEUS is not a simple tale belonging to any one period, but a complex amalgam of different elements which arose from various causes and at different times and places. The remote origins of the legend would appear to go back to the Mycenaean age, but the story developed over hundreds of years, and its first attestation is not till the late eighth or seventh centuries BC. Even then it is known only from a few scattered references and artistic representations (not all beyond question), and it is not until the later sixth century BC that we have full evidence for it in Classical literature and art.

Ill. 23   How far can the development of the story be traced from our extant sources? Three broad phases can be distinguished: first, the Archaic period, before the last part of the sixth century BC, when the story is known only from brief and rather isolated references in poetry and a limited number of artistic representations; secondly, the Classical age, when it is very fully attested and when Theseus has clearly become the national hero of Athens; and thirdly, the period after the fall of Athens in 404 BC, when the legend lives on, a matter of interest to historians, poets and antiquarians and still a frequent subject in art.

The first of these phases is the most obscure, and for obvious reasons. Very much of early Greek literature is lost; indeed the very earliest literature inevitably perished, since it was oral poetry, transmitted by word of mouth from one generation to the next. Something of it however does survive, though probably its form differs in many ways from that in which it was first composed. Around the second half of the eighth century BC many of the old traditions were incorporated in two monumental works which we know as the *Iliad* and *Odyssey* of Homer. Not long afterwards other poems began to appear; some of these were short lyrics, composed in different metres, others were epics, similar in style to the *Iliad* and *Odyssey* and dealing with mythological subjects. The story of Theseus goes right back to these old literary sources, but since many of them exist only in fragments and often the poets merely allude incidentally to the hero, it is rather like a piece of detective work to discover what form the legend took at this early date.

Let us, however, attempt to piece together the fragmentary clues. The most striking fact to emerge is that even in this earliest phase of surviving Greek literature the legend is established in remarkable detail. Already in the Archaic period such important

Ill. 23. Chronological table to illustrate the historical, artistic and literary background to the growth of the Theseus legend.

BC		HISTORY	ART	LITERATURE	BC
			Geometric pottery	Homer: *Iliad* & *Odyssey*	
			Proto-Corinthian	Hesiod	
700	ARCHAIC				700
				ARCHAIC EPIC (7th cent. onwards)	
				LYRIC POETRY (7th to 5th cent.)	
600			Attic black-figure 625–475		600
			François Vase 570	Alcman, Sappho, Stesichorus	
		Pisistratus tyrant of Athens	Attic red-figure begins		
		Democracy established	Athenian treasury at Delphi	*Theseis* (?)	
500		PERSIAN WARS		Simonides, Pindar, Bacchylides	500
	CLASSICAL	Battle of Marathon 490			
		Athenian hegemony		LOGOGRAPHERS	
		Cimon returns Theseus' bones *c.* 475		& HISTORIANS: TRAGEDIANS:	
			Olympia sculptures *c.* 460	Pherecydes Aeschylus	
		Pericles	Hephaisteion 449–	Herodotus Sophocles	
		PELOPONNESIAN WAR	Parthenon 447–	Hellanicus Euripides	
400		Fall of Athens 404		Thucydides	400
				Isocrates & other orators	
		Alexander the Great 356–323		Cleidemus	
300	HELLENISTIC			Palaephatus, Philochorus	300
200				Callimachus	200
100		Roman sack of Corinth 146			100
AD				Diodorus Siculus	AD
100	ROMAN			Plutarch	100
200				Pausanias	200

Ill. 24. The island of Dia, seen from the north coast of Crete. This seems to be the original site of the desertion of Ariadne in the tradition.

elements are found as Theseus' expedition to Crete and slaying of the Minotaur, his descent into the underworld, his abduction of Helen, his taking part in the battle of centaurs and Lapiths, his winning of the queen of the Amazons, and probably his fight with the bull of Marathon. The most fascinating of these elements, especially when one comes to consider the possible relationship of the legend to the Bronze Age, is his Cretan expedition, and it is worth tracing its development in some detail.

The Homeric poems themselves contain reference to Minos as a king of Crete. He is said to be the ruler of the great city of Knossos, the father of fair Ariadne and, after his death, a judge among the dead. Homer does not mention his naval power, but the story of the cruel tribute of youths and maidens which Minos exacted from Athens was told by the lyric poetess Sappho, and is probably implied by one intriguing passage in the *Odyssey*. The poet is describing Odysseus' visit to the underworld and the various heroines he saw. Let us allow Odysseus to speak in his own words:

> And Phaedra I saw, and Procris, and Ariadne the fair,
> Daughter of baleful Minos, her whom Theseus once bare
> From Crete towards Athens' sacred soil—and yet did gain
> No joy thereof—by Artemis his love was slain,
> At the word of Dionysus, in Dia's sea-girt isle.

27

Ills. 25, 26. Fragment of a late seventh-century shield relief and a drawing of another shield relief *c.* 600 BC from Olympia showing Theseus fighting the Minotaur.

(Homer *Od.* XI. 321—5; see also XI. 568—71, XIX. 178—9; Sappho frag. 169)

Here we see Minos called 'baleful' or 'baneful-hearted', an epithet which contrasts sharply with other Homeric passages, where he is, for example, spoken of as 'the glorious son of Zeus'.

The passage is also remarkable for the reference to Ariadne, since it presupposes quite a different form of the story from that which later became traditional. In the most familiar version, Theseus abandoned Ariadne on the island of Naxos, and the god Dionysus made her his bride. Here, far from marrying her, Dionysus is responsible for her death. It may be that this is a reference to a version, just hinted at in late sources, in which Ariadne was the bride of Dionysus before Theseus won her love, and her death was the god's punishment for scorning him. Another interesting feature in this passage is the mention of Dia. Later authors suggested that this was an old name for Naxos, perhaps trying to reconcile two contradictory versions, but it seems likely that originally the poet intended the little island which lies off the north coast of Crete opposite Knossos, and which today, as in ancient times, bears the name of Dia.

Ill. 24

The story of Ariadne is also known in other early sources, sometimes clearly differing from the Homeric version. In the *Theogony* of Hesiod, we find reference to golden-haired Dionysus taking Ariadne as his flourishing bride and Zeus making her immortal and ageless for him. This is a poem about the gods and, like the Homeric epics, it has both oral antecedents and later accretions, which make precise dating of the passage impossible. It is safe however to assume that both this version and that of the *Odyssey* were current before the last part of the sixth century BC,

(Callim. frag. 601; Diod. Sic. IV. 61)

(Hesiod *Theog.* 947—9, frag. 298; cf. frags. 145—6)

Ill. 28. Right, late eighth-century ▶ Geometric bowl from Thebes. It has been suggested that the two large figures on the left are Theseus and Ariadne eloping from Crete.

Ill. 27. One of the earliest representations of Theseus and the Minotaur which can be identified with certainty, on a seventh-century gold ornament from Corinth.

Ill. 29

Ill. 30

and they may well be earlier. Although Theseus himself is not mentioned in the *Theogony*, in a fragment of a different poem, also ascribed to Hesiod, he is said to have deserted Ariadne for love of another woman.

In Archaic art, the slaying of the Minotaur is popular, occurring before the end of the seventh century. Several representations of Theseus and Ariadne have also been identified. Very early among these is perhaps a vase of the late eighth century depicting a man about to embark on a ship, which is vividly portrayed with its rowers and banks of oars. He clasps the hand of a woman as if about to lead her on board. While other interpretations are possible, there is much to be said for identifying the man as Theseus, particularly as the woman holds a garland, something especially associated with Ariadne. Later vases (still within the Archaic period) show a more developed form of the story with further details. Thus the famous François Vase (*c.* 570 BC) illustrates the dance of the liberated Athenian youths and maidens (traditionally placed on Delos), with Theseus, Ariadne and Ariadne's nurse. Ariadne holds her garland and ball of thread. The figures are all labelled, a characteristic which also occurs on a somewhat later vase (*c.* 540 BC), in which the youths and maidens watch the fight of Theseus and the Minotaur.

Ill. 29. Detail of the top band (side B) of the François Vase, of about 570 BC. The dance here depicted has for many years been identified as

These archaic versions of the story of Theseus and Ariadne are important because they show how radically the early accounts may differ from those popular in Classical times. Other early elements must be passed over more briefly: the sources for some of them are extremely scanty. Thus before about 525 BC the bull of Marathon appears only on a single vase, and even the interpretation of this is not beyond doubt. Similarly, as far as literature is concerned, the Amazonian adventure occurs in only one or two short epic fragments of uncertain date. But one episode does deserve fuller attention, since it is found in a number of sources and has some peculiar variants.

It is Theseus' abduction of Helen. This theme occurs early in art, being found on a remarkable vase, a proto-Corinthian aryballos (small flask), of the early seventh century BC. On it we see Helen, represented as larger than the other figures and hardly bearing out

Ill. 32

(*Theseis* in Plu. *Thes.* 28; *Nostoi* frag. 3)

Ills. 33, 34

Ill. 30. Band-cup by Archikles and Glaukytes, painted about 540 BC, which depicts Theseus killing the Minotaur. Athena, lyre in hand, is present to encourage Theseus; Ariadne holds her ball of thread, and her nurse beside her quivers with excitement. The Athenian youths and maidens are portrayed as looking on.

Theseus' 'Crane Dance' on Delos. An alternative interpretation would place the scene in Crete.

her reputation for beauty! Theseus, accompanied by his faithful friend Pirithous, grasps her by the hand; on the other side of the scene, Helen's brothers, the Dioscuri, ride up to her rescue. The variants occur in the literary versions. Certain early sources, including the lyric poet Alcman (late seventh century), say that it was to Athens that Theseus took Helen, and that the Dioscuri sacked the city to get her back. Other sources however, including the historian Herodotus and a fragment of a lost epic, assert that the place was not Athens, but Aphidna, a small town of Attica, and scholars are inclined to believe that this may have been the original place of Helen's captivity in the tradition.

(Alcman frag. 5; Herod. IX. 73; *Kypria* in Plu. *Thes.* 32)

A further point here is of interest. In the account familiar from Plutarch, Theseus did not marry Helen because she was too young, but kept her at Aphidna in the care of his mother Aethra. But an early variant tells quite another story. It is a version preserved in Pausanias and attributed by him to sources including the lyric poet Stesichorus (*c.* 640—555 BC). In this Helen became pregnant by Theseus and was delivered of a daughter at Argos, where she dedicated a sanctuary to the goddess of childbirth. The daughter was Iphigenia, who in other sources from Homer on appears as the daughter of Agamemnon and Clytaemnestra, but who was, according to Stesichorus, only their adopted daughter.

(Stesich. frag. 13 = Paus. II. 22. 6)

This must conclude our survey of the legend in the Archaic age. Although the choice of material has necessarily been selective, it is clear that the story was widely known with many details and that several striking variants existed. Theseus is already attested as a hero of Athens, a brave and adventurous warrior, who fights the centaurs, slays the Minotaur, and does not hesitate to attempt to win the hand of the Amazon queen, of Helen, or even of the goddess Persephone.

In our second period, the Classical age, we find a radical development of the legend. Though lasting little more than a century (c. 525–404 BC), these were years which saw momentous historical events for Athens. First there was her liberation from tyranny and the foundation of democracy; then her alliance with Sparta against the menace of the Persian invasions, leading to the eventual defeat of Persia, the triumph of Athens and her age of glory under Pericles; finally, in the last part of our period, the tragic war between Athens and Sparta, ending in the defeat of Athens and her fall from political greatness. It was an era of astounding artistic and literary production, and the legend of Theseus received a very full share of attention. In literature, apart from brief references in the historians Herodotus and Thucydides, it was treated at length by the lyric poets, in the works of the logographers and in drama. It was also the theme of the sculptures of several major Greek temples, and it appears on literally hundreds of vases and minor works of art. Obviously it is not possible to examine all this material here, but we can at least hope to distinguish the main lines along which the legend developed, and discuss some details of the treatment of Theseus in lyric poetry and in tragedy.

Ill. 31. Not all mythological representations on vases are readily identifiable. This scene of a man and centaur on an Attic Geometric neck-amphora, from about 700 BC, could represent Theseus, but other interpretations are possible. The centaur is a popular motif in early Greek art, and the battle between the centaurs and Lapiths at Pirithous' wedding occurs in literature as early as Homer and Hesiod.

Ill. 32. Theseus (left) captures the bull of Marathon. This detail from a black-figure amphora of the sixth century BC is one of the earliest surviving representations of this theme on vases.

Ills. 33, 34. Proto-Corinthian aryballos of the seventh century BC showing the abduction of Helen by Theseus and her rescue by her brothers, the Dioscuri.

Two main trends now stand out in the development of the story: one is the glorification of Theseus by the addition of fresh deeds of personal prowess; the other is his idealization as a patriot and national leader.

The first of these can be illustrated extensively. Perhaps the most remarkable feature is the appearance of new elements which all demonstrate the hero's valour. Before about 525 BC there are no surviving references to any of the exploits of Theseus' youth. Then towards the end of the sixth century we find that a new cycle of legend has arisen (it was possibly evolved in an epic called the *Theseis*, now lost). Theseus is now said to have been born in Troezen and to have despatched a whole string of evil-doers on his journey from Troezen to Athens. The first evidence for these adventures is artistic: they appear on a series of red-figure kylixes (cups), the earliest of which was made by the potter Kachrylion before the end of the sixth century. The fight with Sciron also appears in the sculptures of the Athenian treasury at Delphi (probably *c.* 510 BC), while several more of these adventures are later taken up in the sculptured metopes of the temple of Hephaestus at Athens (begun 449 BC).

Ills. 5—9

Ills. 35—38

Ills. 159—161

Ills. 35—38. Details of the metopes of the Athenian treasury at Delphi (probably *c.* 510 BC) showing the exploits of Theseus. Above left: Sciron; right: Theseus and the bull of Marathon; below left: Theseus and the Minotaur; right: Theseus and Antiope. Other metopes of this building depict the adventures of Heracles.

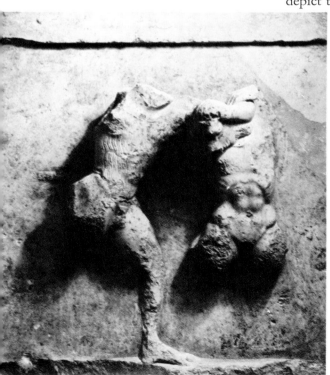

In literature the exploits on the Isthmus road are found first in the poems of Bacchylides of Keos (*c.* 505—450 BC). These were unknown, except for ancient references to them, until the discovery of a papyrus in Egypt at the end of the last century. Bacchylides' dithyramb entitled *Theseus* takes the form of a dialogue between a chorus of Athenian citizens and Aegeus, the father of Theseus, who at the dramatic point of the dialogue does not know the identity of his son. The scene is set at Athens, and the chorus are enquiring why the war-trumpet has sounded. Aegeus replies:

> Over the long Isthmus road
> A herald has newly come.
> He tells of marvellous deeds by
> A mighty man: he has killed insolent
> Sinis, strongest of mortals,
> The son of the Earthshaker,
> Poseidon the Unlooser;
> And the sow that murdered men
> Has met its death in Cremmyon's woods;
> Wicked Sciron is slain;
> Closed is Cercyon's wrestling-ring; and
> Polypemon's hammer grim
> Is cast from the hand of the Crippler,*
> Who has met with a stronger man.
> I fear how these things are to end.

*Procoptes, i.e. 'he who cuts short', is used as an alternative name for Procrustes.

(Bacch. 18 (17). 16—30)

The chorus comment on his strength, bravery and boldness. 'Some god speeds him' they say, and they ask what he is like. Aegeus replies:

> Only two attend him, it is said.
> From his glistening shoulders
> Hangs an ivory-hilted sword;
> Two polished javelins he carries; and
> A well-made Laconian cap
> Covers his red-gold hair;
> Round his chest he wears
> A purple tunic, and a thick
> Thessalian plaid. But from his eyes

Flashes a fiery flame
Like that of Lemnos. He's but a boy
In the prime of youth; yet his heart
Is filled with the joys of Ares,
War and battle, and the clash of bronze.
He makes for glorious Athens.

(Bacch. 18 (17). 46—60)

This fine description of Theseus, the earliest detailed one to survive, gives a vivid picture of him as the idealized youth, and may be aptly compared with the near-contemporary portrayal of the hero, this time fighting a centaur, in the sculptures of the temple of Zeus at Olympia.

Ill. 19

Ills. 39, 40. Details of a red-figure lekythos showing Theseus and Heracles. These two heroes were often compared in antiquity, and some of Theseus' adventures were even modelled on those of Heracles. Here Heracles, club in hand and wearing his lion skin, rescues Theseus from the throne of rock on which he was held fast in Hades.

Ill. 41. Theseus killing the Mino-taur, from a black-figure amphora from Vulci. Four of his companions are standing beside the combatants.

Ills. 39, 40

(Plu. *Thes.* 29)

Ills. 15, 41, 42

In addition to these exploits of Theseus' youth, we find glorification of his acts in other ways. There now appears for the first time evidence for the story of his overcoming the fifty sons of Pallas, of his foiling the attempt on his life by the sorceress Medea, and for his part in the stories of Meleager, Oedipus and the Theban War. Indeed he was believed to have been involved in so many heroic enterprises that it is small wonder that by Plutarch's day a proverb had arisen, 'Not without Theseus', and another, 'This man is a second Heracles', an allusion to the obvious similarity of many of their exploits.

Moreover during the Classical period many variants and fresh details are found in episodes which we know to have existed earlier in the tradition. The expedition to Crete was very popular in art, the fight with the Minotaur being shown on numerous vases. New details now appearing in the story include the ingenious notion that

Ill. 42. The centre of a red-figure cup by Aison showing Theseus dragging the dead Minotaur from the Labyrinth. His patroness, the goddess Athena, looks on.

Theseus cut holes in the bottoms of Minos' ships to prevent his fleet following him, and versions of the abandonment of Ariadne in which Theseus reluctantly leaves his bride at the command of the gods, rather as Aeneas, in the Roman epic by Virgil, deserts Dido in order that he may found a new nation in Italy. Thus, on a lekythos (oil flask) from Taranto, Theseus and Ariadne are on their bridal couch. At Ariadne's head there crouches a small winged figure of Sleep, but the goddess Athena is rousing Theseus and bidding him leave. Other vases depict the god Dionysus claiming his bride.

A new incident on the voyage to Crete is also attested. The first literary evidence is again a poem of Bacchylides, probably written *c.* 485—470 BC. He follows a version of the story in which Minos came personally to Athens to collect his victims, and tells how on the return voyage he presumed to make amorous advances to one

Ills. 43—45

(Pherecyd. frag. 150)

of the seven Athenian maidens. Theseus in indignation rebuked the king, boldly reminding him that even if he might boast that he was the son of Zeus by Europa, he, Theseus, could also claim a god—Poseidon—as his father. Minos' reply was to issue a challenge to the young hero. He prayed to his father Zeus to send a sudden flash of lightning (which he did), and then took off his gold ring and flung it into the sea, bidding Theseus leap in after it and recover it from Poseidon. Here is how Bacchylides describes the sequel (Jebb's prose translation is quoted):

So the bark sped fast on its journey, and the northern breeze, blowing astern, urged it forward. But all the Athenian youths and maidens shuddered when the hero sprang into the deep; and tears fell from their bright young eyes, in prospect of their grievous doom.

Meanwhile dolphins, dwellers in the sea, were swiftly bearing mighty Theseus to the abode of his sire, lord of steeds; and he came unto the hall of the gods. There beheld he the glorious daughters of blest Nereus, and was awe-struck; for a splendour as of fire shone from their radiant forms; fillets inwoven with gold encircled their hair; and they were delighting their hearts by dancing with lissom feet.

Ills. 43—45. Details of a red-figure lekythos from Taranto. Athena is summoning Theseus away from beside the sleeping Ariadne.

Ill. 46. The young Theseus is welcomed beneath the sea by his stepmother, the goddess Amphitrite. Dolphins indicate that the scene is under water, and a triton supports Theseus' feet; his protectress Athena stands by. Greek vases were not always made and painted by the same man: this celebrated cup, signed by the potter Euphronios, was decorated by the artist known as the Panaitios Painter.

And in that beautiful abode he saw his father's well-loved wife, the stately, ox-eyed Amphitrite; who clad him in gleaming purple, and set on his thick hair a choice wreath, dark with roses, given her of yore at her marriage by wily Aphrodite.

(Bacch. 17 (16). 90—116)

The scene is beautifully represented in the internal picture of a well-known cup by the potter Euphronios (*c.* 500 BC), and occurs also in later vase-paintings.

Ill. 46

The second trend of the Classical period was to idealize Theseus as a patriot and national leader. This is particularly noticeable in the period beginning with the Persian Wars, when Theseus was believed to have appeared in full armour at the Battle of Marathon (490 BC), and when Cimon led the expedition to bring back his bones, an act which Plutarch says endeared Cimon above all else to the Athenians. From this time onwards Theseus' exploit against the Amazons

Ill. 47

(Plu. *Cim*. 8; Paus. V. 11. 7)

takes on a new significance. Originally it seems to have been an amatory adventure: Theseus, either on an expedition of his own or, according to some versions, joining with Heracles, carries off the queen of the Amazons from the shores of the Black Sea. But around the second quarter of the fifth century the episode comes to be regarded as a patriotic act: Theseus goes against the 'barbarian' Amazons from the orient, and later leads his country's defence against them in a big battle right in the centre of Athens. Thus the scene was represented on the elaborately decorated footstool of Phidias' gold and ivory statue of Zeus at Olympia, where Pausanias, in his detailed description of this celebrated lost work, refers to Theseus' fight with the Amazons as 'the first brave deed of the Athenians against foreigners'.

At Athens itself two monumental paintings also commemorated the act. One was in the shrine of Theseus, built to house his bones after their 'return' by Cimon around 475 BC; the other was part of the decoration of an important public building, the famous Stoa Poikile or Painted Stoa (*i.e.* portico). On the paintings of this stoa, which may be dated to around 460—450 BC, Theseus' encounter with the Amazons was represented side by side with two major national events—the Trojan War and the Athenian resistance to

Ill. 47. An early red-figure amphora by Myson (*c.* 500 BC) showing Theseus and Pirithous carrying off the queen of the Amazons. Antiope is dressed in a Scythian archer's costume and carries a battle-axe. Other vases depicting the abduction show her vainly appealing to her companions for help; but Myson has here reduced the scene to the three central characters, and the other side of the vase shows a different subject.

the Persian invaders at Marathon.* Indeed, Theseus himself even appeared in this latter painting, rising from the earth to assist the Greeks to victory. Here the battle with the Amazons is clearly seen as a kind of mythological prototype of the Greek wars with the Persian invaders from the orient. These monumental paintings, now lost, had a great influence on representations of similar scenes on vases.

Theseus' role as a national leader is also illustrated by his synoecism of Attica: by the fifth century we find that he was believed to have reorganized his country, abolishing the local magistracies of the towns of Attica and centralizing the government under Athens as a political capital. (Such at least is how the historian Thucydides describes the synoecism, though Plutarch's account suggests also a movement of population.) Associated with the act was the tradition of Theseus as the first democrat and guardian of the equal rights of rich and poor. These roles were particularly emphasized by Euripides in his tragedy the *Suppliant Women*, where Theseus speaks more than once of his city's enlightened government, and proudly boasts that he has

> . . . made the land one single realm,
> A free state, with an equal vote for all.

The mention of Euripides leads to the treatment of Theseus in drama. Unfortunately most of the plays in which his story was dramatized have not survived. All three great tragedians, Aeschylus, Sophocles and Euripides, wrote plays on the theme, treating among other subjects Theseus' journey to Athens and encounter with Aegeus, his Cretan expedition and abandonment of Ariadne. Theseus does appear however in four surviving tragedies. We have already seen how, in the *Suppliant Women*, he is depicted as the ideal ruler of an idealized Athens. Elsewhere we find Theseus portrayed preeminently as a kind and generous helper of those in trouble: thus in the *Heracles Driven Mad*, also by Euripides, his role is that of comforter to that mighty hero when he recovers from the divine-sent madness which drove him to kill his own sons; and in the *Oedipus at Colonus* of Sophocles he gives his protection to the aged Oedipus, when, blinded by his own hand and exiled from his native

* A fourth painting depicted the battle between the Athenians and Spartans at Oinoe; see also page 162 below.

(Paus. I. 15—17)

(Thuc. II. 15; Plu. *Thes.* 24; Eur. *Suppl.* 352—3, 404—8)

city, he wanders to Attica. In both these plays Theseus has a real humanity: as Lesky has aptly remarked, his personality has been 'enlarged into an ideal of Athenian manhood'.

But of all the extant dramas in which Theseus is represented probably the most interesting is the *Hippolytus* of Euripides. This is one of the poet's finest tragedies, and worth studying in some detail. The play is a bold portrayal of the emotion of love: Phaedra, the young wife of Theseus, has, at the contrivance of Aphrodite, fallen in love with her step-son Hippolytus. In vain she attempts to stifle her feelings, pining away and making herself so ill that her nurse fears for her life. At last she confides her secret to the nurse, who in a mistaken attempt to be kind reveals Phaedra's passion to the young man. Hippolytus—who has devoted himself exclusively to the pursuits of Artemis, virgin goddess of the hunt, to the neglect of Aphrodite—is horrified and spurns the approaches made by the nurse. Phaedra overhears his reaction, and in despair commits suicide, leaving a letter falsely accusing Hippolytus of making love to her. At this point Theseus enters, and is filled with uttermost grief at the news of his wife's death:

> . . . Now let me die, and pass
> To the world under the earth, into the joyless dark!
> Since you, dearer than all, are at my side no longer.

On the discovery of the letter, at once convinced that his son is guilty, he curses him in his absence:

> Poseidon my father, you promised me three curses: with one of them strike down my son! If they were good curses you gave me, let him not live out this day!

Hippolytus returns, but before he can even plead his own innocence, Theseus banishes him with harsh and furious words:

(Eur. *Hipp.* 836—8, 887—90)

> The heart of man! Is there any vileness it will turn from? Will barefaced wickedness ever find its limit? If crime is to bulk bigger with each new generation, new depths of villainy be revealed age after age, the gods will need to create a second earth to house liars and lechers. Look at this man! My own son, who would pollute my marriage-bed,—and is proved guilty by the damning witness of her dead hand. Come, show your face—

foul as you are, look your father in the eyes! So you—you are the man above men who keeps the company of gods! Yours is the chaste life unsmirched with evil! . . .

Ah! Why should I fight down your defence, when her dead body blazons its evidence to my eyes? Out of this land to exile! Go, I say! Never come near the god-built walls of Athens, cross no frontier that my sword guards! I tell you, if I weaken before this outrage, the Isthmian bandit Sinis shall deny that I killed him, and call me boaster; and the sea-washed rocks where Sciron met his end shall forget the weight of my hand against evil-doers!

(Eur. Hipp. 936—49, 971—80)

As Hippolytus is leaving Troezen, driving along with his team of horses, Theseus' curse is horribly fulfilled. Poseidon sends a monstrous bull from the sea, which terrifies the horses; Hippolytus becomes entangled in the reins and is dragged almost to death. Finally the goddess Artemis reveals the truth to Theseus, and he is able to make his peace with his dying son. This tragedy perhaps, out of all those extant, shows Theseus at his most human: we see his passionate love for his wife, his intense and hasty rage against his son when he believes him guilty. Like Phaedra and Hippolytus in the same play, he is a truly tragic figure, who shows man's helpless suffering at the hands of the gods.

These four tragedies are all illuminating. They show how Theseus in the Classical age came to be firmly associated with cycles of legend from which his story once was probably quite distinct: obviously they owe a great deal to the poetic imagination of their authors, but they are fascinating for their portrayal of his character as presented in the Attic theatre. They complete this survey of the legend's development in our second period. We may sum up by saying that in the fifth century, although Theseus had his sufferings and even, to modern eyes, his faults, he has fully emerged to be the national hero of Athens and the embodiment of the Athenian ideal of manliness, bravery, patriotism and altruistic kindness.

The end of the fifth century saw the fall of Athens, and inevitably a certain decline in the legend as a living and emotional force. Nevertheless it appealed to the Attic orators, who looked back with nostalgia to Athens' heroic greatness, and even outside Athens it

Ill. 48. Right, the cliffs near the ▶ reputed site of Sciron's lair.

still occurred quite frequently as an artistic and literary theme. In the Hellenistic age it was, for example, taken up by the poet Callimachus in his miniature epic, the *Hecale*, which unfortunately survives today only in small fragments. Here, in the manner dear to Alexandrian poets, Callimachus makes the central theme not the major heroic events of Theseus' life, but a minor incident which occurred on his way to fight the bull of Marathon. Theseus was caught in a rainstorm, and took shelter with an old woman (Hecale), who received him hospitably. Callimachus lovingly describes the little details of everyday life: 'Once on a hill of Erechtheus there lived an Attic woman' . . . 'and all wayfarers honoured her for her hospitality; for she kept her house open'. When Theseus takes refuge in her cottage, he even relates how he takes off his wet clothes, and Hecale 'made him sit on the humble couch' . . . 'having at once snatched a small tattered garment from the bed'. The scene could almost be a modern household when an unexpected caller arrives!

(Dem. LX. 28; Isocrat. X. 23—38, XII. 193; Callim. *Hecale* frags. 230, 231, 240, 241)

The primary interest of the legend, however, was historical and antiquarian. In an age of doubt about the old beliefs, the story of Theseus could not be accepted at its face value, and new interpretations had to be put forward. Educated Greeks still believed that a historical basis underlay their legends, but they could not accept all the details, especially where the supernatural was involved. The usual answer to the problem was to rationalize the stories, that is to explain away the miraculous and divine elements in human terms. Thus the fourth-century sceptic Palaephatus in his little book *On Incredible Tales* attacked the story of the Minotaur for its implausibilities, arguing that the very act of a woman mating with a bull was physiologically impossible. He interpreted the Minotaur as a savage youth who roamed the hills near Knossos, and was the offspring of Minos' wife after an affair with a man named Taurus. (*Tauros* is Greek for 'bull', but it could also be interpreted as a proper name.) Another version, favoured by the Athenian historian Philochorus (*floruit c.* 300 BC), was that Taurus was an overbearing and powerful Cretan who earned Minos' disfavour by being too familiar with his wife. Theseus' defeat of him consisted of vanquishing him in the funeral games which Minos had instituted in honour of his son Androgeos. Another historian, Demon by name, imagined that to release Athens from the tribute Theseus must have had to defeat Minos in a naval battle, which he believed took place in the harbour of Knossos.

The ancient rationalizing versions are tantalizing as we cannot tell how much in them is due to the fertile imaginations of their authors and how much, if anything at all, might have arisen from independent traditions otherwise unknown. This is particularly true of the version of Cleidemus, who gives a very different account from the usual one. He tells of an expedition by Theseus against Crete after the death of Minos in Sicily. According to this version, Theseus secretly built a fleet, partly in Attica and partly in Troezen, and then sailed against Knossos. He surprised the Cretan fleet in the harbour, and then fought a battle at the Labyrinth itself, killing Deucalion, who had succeeded Minos, together with his bodyguard.

The antiquarian interest in the Theseus legend is chiefly demonstrated by his association with numerous cults and festivals, and with the founding of various institutions and games. This characteristic had already begun in the fifth century, and is to be noted not only at Athens but also further afield: on the island of Delos, for example, he was believed to have founded games, when he called there on his return voyage from Crete. We may mention here two most interesting versions, preserved by Plutarch, linking him with local cults on Cyprus and Naxos.

The Cypriot account is attributed by Plutarch to a local historian of Cyprus named Paion. According to this, Theseus and Ariadne were driven off their course on the way back from Crete and came to Cyprus. Ariadne was pregnant and very sick, and so Theseus put her ashore while he went back to see to the ship. But he was carried out to sea again and Ariadne was left alone. The local women tried to comfort her, even bringing her forged letters purporting to be from Theseus, but she died in childbirth. Theseus later returned to the island, and instituted a festival in her honour in which the young men imitated the cries and movements of a woman in labour. This story is interesting not only for linking Theseus with a local festival in Cyprus, but also for the way in which it exonerates him from blame over Ariadne.

At Naxos there were two festivals of Ariadne, one a joyful one, the other mournful. The local Naxian writers explained this as being due to the fact that there were two Ariadnes. One was the bride of Dionysus, who was honoured with joy and merrymaking; the other was the woman abandoned by Theseus, whose festival was one of sorrow and mourning. It has been conjectured that here we have a glimpse into an original role of Ariadne as a goddess of vegetation, the two Naxian festivals being originally rites of one and the same divinity.

According to Plutarch the Naxians believed that there were also two kings called Minos, a curious idea which is found in other authorities. It may have arisen partly through the discrepancies in the character of Minos from the earliest literary sources onwards, and partly through difficulties over his chronological position. In Hellenistic and later times, in spite of the doubts of sceptics about many details in the legends, there was a great interest in questions of chronography and in calculating the precise dates at which mythological events were believed to have occurred. Minos posed a real problem: on the one hand he was obviously contemporary with Theseus, who abducted Helen, the heroine of the Trojan War, in her youth; on the other he was the son of Europa, who was sought, after her abduction by Zeus, by the hero Cadmus, who according to the varying traditions lived six or more generations before the Trojan War. The idea of two kings called Minos helped to obviate the difficulty, and it was adopted in one of the best known of all Greek chronographies, the Parian Marble, where a Minos appears twice, once in the period 1462—1423 BC and once again *c.* 1294/3. It also however caused some confusions: which Minos had the famous navy? The historian Diodorus, who enthusiastically embraced the idea of two rulers named Minos, was obviously muddled. At one point in his universal history he says that the first of the Greeks to create a naval power was the younger Minos, the contemporary of Theseus, while at another point he attributes this act to the elder Minos, his grandfather!*

We have now traced the story of Theseus from its earliest attestation till the end of the Hellenistic age. It is clear that it had a complex and continuous development, which extended over many centuries. Yet it must be remembered that what we have in our surviving sources is only a fragment—though perhaps a substantial one—of its long history. We do not know what variants and

Ill. 49. Right, Dionysus sailing in a boat, its mast wreathed with vines. This superb painting of the god (who traditionally married Ariadne after her abandonment by Theseus) was painted by the sixth-century Attic master Exekias.

* Contrast especially Diod. IV. 60 and V. 78.

versions existed which have not come down to us, nor yet how long a period of transmission there was before even our oldest references. It is a matter of speculation what elements might have been present in the tradition before the Archaic age, and no amount of painstaking scholarship can determine for certain what form our legend took in this very early period—whether, for example, Theseus was originally a hero of Attica, or of Athens itself, or of some wider section of the Greek people. It is natural to wish to identify a historical nucleus; but here we must bear in mind the length of the period (some five centuries at least) between the supposed date of Theseus in the Bronze Age and our first evidence for his story in Greek literature and art; nor must we lose sight of the diverse nature of the traditions themselves, which included elements of folktale, religious myth, and ancient speculation, as well as rationalization and even political propaganda. Thus, to take only two examples, in our story the Phaedra theme is clearly an elaboration of a folktale motif, which has parallels in many cultures including the Biblical narrative of Joseph and Potiphar's wife. Similarly the tales of Theseus' prowess on the Isthmus road, like many other stories of remarkably strong men, are likely to be based on folktales which cannot be expected to relate to real events.

In spite of these very great difficulties, it should not be forgotten that for the Classical Athenians Theseus was a real person, and that for them his adventures contained historical facts. Their traditional stories constituted a vivid and detailed picture of the events and personalities of their mythological past. Today, we have not only this picture as presented to us in their surviving literature and visual arts, but also an important new source—archaeology, which enables us to see and study the physical remains of the Greek Bronze Age. These include palaces, houses, vases and wall-paintings, and even documents, which all combine to give us an insight which the ancient Greeks never had into the material culture and life of the period in which they believed that their heroes lived. Although therefore we cannot produce *history* in a strict sense, it is both possible and appropriate for us to examine this archaeological record and to attempt to set it into a relationship with the legend.

3   The World of Theseus: Bronze Age Crete

Anne G. Ward

IN ANY SEARCH FOR THE REALITY behind the Theseus legend the first question to be asked will probably be, 'When did it all take place?'. We can begin confidently enough, 'In the Bronze Age', but any attempt to narrow down this not particularly enlightening statement is liable to lead to immediate complications. There are no incontrovertible facts to work on, and it is probable that there never will be. That little is beyond the bounds of archaeological possibility, however, is proved by the expedition which set out with the almost ludicrously optimistic determination of finding the seventeen missing lines of the early Babylonian *Epic of Gilgamesh* and, contrary to every imaginable law of probability, found a tablet containing fifteen lines from the lacuna within a fortnight of its arrival in Mesopotamia. Perhaps one day archaeology will light on a dedication of 'Theseus, King of the Athenians' in a conclusive stratigraphical association with scarabs of some definitely dated Egyptian pharaoh. Meanwhile, however, in the absence of such tangible records, we can only suggest an approximate period on the grounds that it seems to fit reasonably well with the circumstances of the story. In order to do this, however, we must have a clear picture of the historical setting as a whole. Once we know exactly what was happening in Greece, Crete and the Aegean during the Bronze Age we can see which period (if any) comes closest in actuality to the details related by the legend, and pinpoint not only the precise world of Theseus, but the processes which influenced its formation and the international and domestic relations which shaped its destiny.

There is one major stumbling block in trying to reconstruct a picture of the historical evolution of the world in which Theseus

Ill. 50. Terracotta snake recently excavated at Mycenae. Emblem of the house of Erechtheus from which Theseus was descended, the snake was an important element in Bronze Age religion.

51

	CRETE		BC	MAINLAND	
MM I		Rise of Minoan Palaces	2000	Minyans arrive in Greece	MH
	MM II		1900		
			1800		
MM III		Earthquake & New Palaces built	1700		
			1600	Shaft Grave period	
			1550		
LM I A		Explosion of Thera	1500	Tholos builders	LH I
LM I B		End of Cretan hegemony	1475		LH II
		Greeks at Knossos	1450		
LM II		Final destruction of Knossos	1400		
LM III			1300		LH III
			1200	Palace & Fortress builders	
				Trojan Wars (Helen) 1220	
				Start of Dorian infiltration	
			1100	Final destruction of Mycenae	
				1120	
			1000		
	DARK AGES				

Ill. 51. Chronological table of the Aegean cultures in the Bronze Age.

lived. It was a prehistoric world in the literal sense that there was, as far as we know, no contemporary written history. Absolute dates, mostly obtained by cross-reference to the literate civilization of Egypt, are few, and though these are now beginning to be supplemented by the scientific evidence of Carbon 14 dating, the margin of error admitted by such methods is still large enough to limit their value severely. Many of the ancient references, then, are given in comparative terms—this pot is later than that one,

Ill. 51

this building was erected before that one, etc.—usually based on pottery sequences worked out with patient erudition by generations of scholars.

The Bronze Age is traditionally divided into three sections. In Crete these divisions are named after King Minos: Early, Middle and Late Minoan, each subdivided into I, II and III. In Greece similar but not exactly simultaneous periods are called Early, Middle and Late Helladic. These divisions did very well to begin with, but as knowledge of the Aegean Bronze Age expanded, the increasing scope and subtlety of the study demanded more exact references. More subdivisions were added, and there seemed no logical end to this faintly nightmarish proliferation. A new series of divisions based on the successive stages of palace building in Crete has been suggested, and this seems, in many ways, more convenient than the earlier system. Many scholars, however, still use the time-honoured chronology established by Sir Arthur Evans, discoverer and chronicler of the early Cretan civilization, out of habit and familiarity, pegging it down with a few absolute dates where they are available. The divisions are neither rigidly defined nor watertight, but, for lack of more certain knowledge, they are widely accepted.

Chronology is not the only aspect of the Bronze Age to be hotly disputed and continually modified in the light of new discoveries. There is scarcely any statement which is not subject to contradictory views, and almost every 'fact' is actually an informed conjecture based on scanty and ambiguous evidence. It would be impossible to set out all the theories with their supporting and conflicting proofs, and there is no question of offering a definitive history. What follows is simply an orthodox version based on a consensus of scholastic opinion in the present state of knowledge. In the last analysis everyone is at liberty to go directly to the facts and make up his own mind how they should be interpreted.

Bronze Age Crete

Civilization has been defined as the production of art for art's sake and, working from this hypothesis, it can be said that in comparison with the Near East, civilization was late in coming to Crete. In fact, Carbon 14 tests on recently discovered neolithic material from Knossos indicate that the human race did not appear on the island at all until just before 6000 BC. This late start can only be ascribed to the island's isolated position, as there is nothing particularly untoward in its climate or topography. In the plains the weather tends to be reasonably equable, hot in summer, it is true, but with plenty of rainfall from October to March; frost is rare and snow even rarer. Water presents something of a problem, as there is only one lake and few rivers not subject to total desiccation in an unusually dry summer, but springs are plentiful in the hills, and wells can always be dug in the lowlands where the main population centres developed. The wells at Knossos, for instance, were twelve to fourteen metres deep, but there is evidence that they produced abundant water supplies, even for the exorbitant demands of the palace population.

Much of the island is too mountainous for agriculture, but the fertile areas are very fertile indeed. It has been estimated that a Cretan olive tree produces 2.25 kg. of oil per year as against 1.7 in Greece, and even in the Bronze Age there was no lack of variety in the diet available to king and commoner alike. Olives, grapes, figs, almonds, grain, and several different kinds of pulse were eaten, and there may have been carrots, lettuce, asparagus and celery, all of which grow wild in Crete and have pre-Greek names which indicate a remote origin. Sheep, cattle, goats and pigs were kept, as well as bees to provide the only ancient sweetening agent, but no domestic fowls seem to have been known. Deer, ibex, boar, small game and birds were hunted, and a positively gourmet variety of seafood was available from an early date to the marine-minded islanders.

In the Early Bronze Age the neolithic pattern of farming villages was firmly established. The houses, mostly mudbrick, were sometimes quite well designed individually, but there was no sign of anything remotely resembling town planning. A haphazard cluster of homes was grouped together in a completely random arrangement, a characteristic which was to persist and become the dominant feature of even the most sophisticated later palaces. Fixed fireplaces, later abandoned in favour of portable braziers, were used for heating, and the fabric of the pottery is good enough to warrant the assumption that a proper kiln had superseded the rather chancy process of firing on an open hearth.

The people who lived in these villages were small and slender with dark eyes and hair, typical of the long-skulled Mediterranean type. Human remains are both scarce and fragmentary, but there are signs that towards the end of the Early Bronze Age a new element arrived in Crete. This new people, taller and shorter skulled, infiltrated in small groups along the coastline with no apparent violence. Indeed, one of the most striking features of Cretan Bronze Age history is the total absence of threat, internal or external, which was probably a powerful contributing factor to the Cretans' cheerful, inquisitive and gregarious nature, not to mention the rapid development of their peaceful evolution.

In the second Early Minoan period copper began to appear in the eastern population centres, showing an appreciable increase in both quality and quantity. The north of the island, which was later to take so decisive a lead in the political and economic life of the Bronze Age Aegean, still lagged behind, possibly because contact with the older and more developed cultures of the Near East and Egypt all took place from such eastern ports as Mochlos. Stone houses were built here at a period when some of the Cretans were still living in caves and rock shelters. A large comfortable house built on a hill at Vasiliki already showed many of the later characteristics of palace architecture, with a rather shapeless complex of rooms and corridors based on straight lines and right angles. The walls were covered with a fine quality, red lime plaster, which had the merit of encouraging the later development of fresco painting, but tended to make it too easy for the Minoan builder to get away with his besetting sin of sloppy masonry and careless construction work.

Although most of the population lived in simple two-roomed houses of the 'but-and-ben' type,* there is evidence of a startling access of prosperity in the cemetery at Mochlos. A large quantity of gold jewellery was found there, mostly of simple hammered foil but including some chains which imply fairly advanced wire making, as well as exceptionally fine stone vases made by blocking out with a tubular drill and finishing with abrasive powder. The way the colour veins of the stone have been understood and exploited in the

* A two-roomed house with an inner and an outer room.

55

shape and function of the vase shows a pronounced inborn aesthetic sense. The graves also contained a large number of beads and amulets in shell, crystal, faience, carnelian, amethyst and other semi-precious stones, and some of the earliest Cretan essays in the difficult art of seal cutting, executed in ivory and steatite. There are unmistakable signs of Egyptian, Near Eastern, Anatolian and Cycladic influence, which provide sufficient explanation of the technical superiority of this district over the more isolated central regions. Among the pottery of the period is the attractive Vasiliki ware, which has a pleasing finish of burnished red mottled with cloudy darker patches produced (perhaps originally by accident) by holding a burning branch against the side of the vase immediately after firing.

Towards the end of EM II tombs of a new type began to appear in the Mesara plain in the south. These were curious stone-built circular ossuaries in which many generations of burials were successively deposited until the end of MM I, perhaps with some honours paid to them by means of small shrines or altars outside a structure built on to the east side. Many people believe that these graves were the immediate forerunners of the vast mainland *tholos* tombs, but two main features seem to contradict this theory: the tholos is essentially an underground tomb while the Mesara ossuary was freestanding, and the tholos was closed with a huge pointed corbel vault which would have been impractical if not impossible without the counter-pressure of earth to hold the over-lapping slabs in position from the outside. However, some of the earliest Messenian tholoi were also freestanding, which strongly suggests that the mainland tombs were derived from Cretan antecedents after all, the buried vault being a later Mycenaean elaboration. Large quantities of personal ornaments were buried in the Mesara as at Mochlos, and some of these pieces show that considerable technical advances had been made. Some of the smaller objects are decorated with minute grains of gold attached to the background by the complex process known as colloid hard soldering. The secret of this technique was lost in antiquity, and for many years no one was able to reconstruct it, as the solder always flooded the joint between the grain and the background and displaced the tiny ornament. Within the present century, however, it has been

Ill. 52. Right, a sudden increase ▶ in technical skills enabled Cretan goldsmiths to make ornaments like this fine pendant from the Middle Minoan cemetery at Mallia. The details of the two bees and the honey cake between them are picked out in filigree wire and granulation.

56

discovered that such work can be executed by attaching the granule with a mixture of copper salts and organic glue. When the work is heated the salts oxidize and the glue carbonizes. The carbon then combines with the oxygen in the oxide and disperses in the form of carbon dioxide, leaving a pure copper weld attaching the grain. Since the process is chemical rather than manual there is nothing to displace the granule or spoil the complex designs which were subsequently developed.

Ill. 52

Early Minoan III was a brief, ill-defined and transitional period, but it was of paramount importance in the island's history because it saw the shift in social and economic leadership away from the eastern towns to Knossos and Phaistos in central Crete. Scarcely any homes survive from this period, and those of the previous age fell into decay. The great house at Vasiliki was deserted and the inhabitants of the district now lived in a few poor huts propped against its ruined walls. Indeed, the total absence of EM III architectural remains at Knossos has led some scholars to believe that the period never existed at all, but it is clear from the number of burials and the developments of the pottery that there must have been habitation, even if it was of so flimsy and temporary

Ill. 53. Late Minoan chest (*larnax*) painted with stylized birds and lilies. Such chests were frequently reused as coffins.

Ill. 54. One of the most important religious symbols of Minoan Crete was the double axe (*labrys*) from which the Labyrinth took its name. A votive deposit of gold double axes was found in the cave of Arkalochori in central Crete.

Ill. 53

a nature that all traces of it were completely swept away in subsequent building activities. The mottled ware was still used, but a new fabric painted in thick matt white on a dark brown or black slip began to appear alongside it, and the dead were now sometimes buried in round-cornered chests known as *larnakes* or in large jars (*pithoi*) which must often have been a horribly tight fit, even for the tiny bird-boned Minoans. The general standard of workmanship was not high, judging by the decline in quality of the stone vases, but the economy was active and outward-looking. Contact with the Cyclades had never been broken, but the increasing number of Cycladic idols, both imported and locally imitated, shows that relations were even closer. Syrian ivory was used, and the first Egyptian artefacts found in the Mesara date to the Seventh to Tenth Dynasties, contemporary with this period.

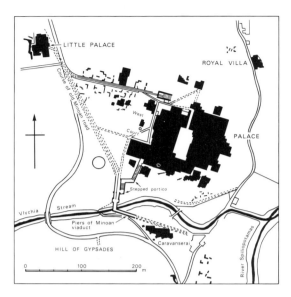

Ills. 55, 56. The palace at Knossos was not a single residence, but a whole town integrated into one building, with several handsome villas in the neighbourhood. In the Bronze Age the main approach was the road from the sea which circled the south front, crossed the ravine and entered by a stepped portico. The modern motor road (to the left in the air view) supplies a new approach via the west court.

LITTLE PALACE

ROYAL VILLA

Course of old Minoan road

West Court

PALACE

Stepped portico

Vlychia Stream

Piers of Minoan viaduct

Caravanserai

HILL OF GYPSADES

River Spiliopolanas

0   100   200 m

Ill. 57. Right, the enormous size and complex plan of the palace ▶ at Knossos clearly illustrate how the word 'labyrinth' came to be synonymous with 'maze'.

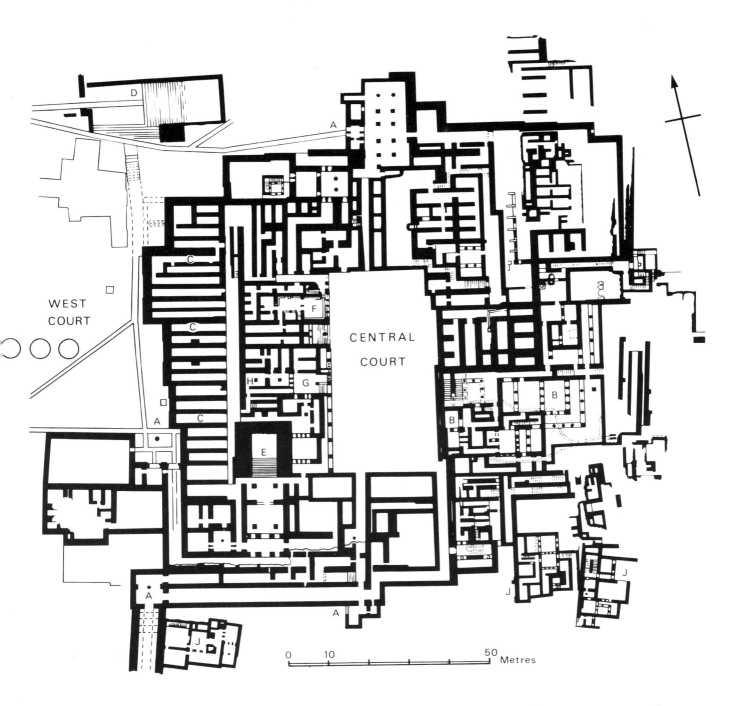

WEST
COURT

CENTRAL
COURT

A

D

C

C

H   G

C

A

E

F

B

B

B

J

J

J

A

A

0   10   50
|____|____|____|____|____|____|____|____| Metres

A   Entrances to the Palace   G   Sacral Area   D   Theatral Area
B   Domestic Quarter   H   Pillar Rooms   E   Stairs
C   Magazines   J   Private Houses   F   Throne Room

Ill. 58. Remains of the viaduct built to carry the Minoan road to the palace over the ravine.

It is possible that these intensified contacts with the older cultures paved the way for the remarkable urban revolution of MM I. All of a sudden, with no apparent intervening stages of evolution, the earliest of the great palaces rose at Knossos and the other urban centres. One of the most frequent motifs in every Cretan art form is the *labrys* or double axe, and this religious symbol is so frequent at Knossos that it is not surprising to learn that the palace was known as the 'House of the Double Axe'; in the language of the time, the Labyrinth. Knossos was always so much the largest and most imposing of the island palaces that it suggests a kingdom (or at least a voluntary alliance to begin with) led by the lord of the Labyrinth. Such a confederacy would be able to exploit the island's natural resources and foreign contacts far more efficiently than any isolated communities, and the resulting access of prosperity may have inclined the Cretans to preserve and strengthen the centralized system. Whatever the reason, the mound at Knossos was levelled down to the foundations of the neolithic houses and the first palace was built. It already embodied the basic principles of Minoan palace architecture, if so haphazard a process can be said to have any principles, and later structures were largely additions and elaborations to the original building. The heart of the palace was a spacious oblong courtyard surrounded by the different ceremonial, domestic and workshop blocks which, at this time, were isolated from each other so that the palace was in fact a group of separate buildings.

Ill. 54

Ills. 55—57

Ill. 59. Right, the central court at Knossos. Large, oblong courtyards oriented roughly north-south were one of the very few constant features of Cretan palace building from the earliest times (cf. *Ills. 134—136*).

During this period the other Cretan sites showed the same tendency for the houses to cluster sociably around the great house, even when the farms supporting them were some distance away. It is an interesting reflection on the Cretan character that neighbourliness was obviously a more important consideration than keeping a close eye on one's property or saving a long walk to work.

At Knossos, however, the work of the artisans and craftsmen lay largely within the palace, and ample accommodation was provided for them to ply their trades. The building of the palace itself must have required the prolonged participation of a veritable army of workers, for it was large and by no means a bare functional structure. For instance, there are remains of a handsome floor under the later throne room, with a sort of crazy-paving mosaic of different coloured stones neatly fitted together in a plaster bed. Later in MM I a ceremonial entrance was added to the south side of the palace where the routes from the sea and the south of the island converged. A cleverly engineered viaduct carried the road over a ravine, after which it entered an imposing stepped portico leading by devious turns to the central court. There are absolutely no defences, here or anywhere else; so confident and unsuspicious an outlook can only have been the result of many generations of harmony and prosperity both at home and abroad. A structure built of massive limestone blocks at the north entrance to the central court played the part of a guardhouse, but the soldiers were probably as purely ceremonial as the Swiss guardsmen on duty at the Vatican, and at any rate, if any attacker had already penetrated so far into

Ills. 60, 61. Cretan pottery of the Middle Minoan period ranged from fragile, eggshell-thin Kamares 'tea-cups' (left), to huge corded storage jars (*pithoi*, below), sometimes larger than a man.

the heart of the Labyrinth it would have been too late for the guards to do very much about it.

During the following period the separate blocks of the palace were joined together to form an integrated unit, the main elements of the drainage system were laid, and the intriguing circular pits known to modern archaeologists as *koulouras* were sunk in the courtyard to the west of the palace. Similar pits are known at Mallia, where they are neatly lined and have a post for a central column to support some kind of roof, but though they appear to have been a common feature of palace building, their purpose is still unknown. They may have been simple rubbish dumps, in which case the careful construction of the Mallia pits is singularly anomalous; or perhaps they were *bothroi*, shafts for the deposit of sacred objects, in which case the indifferent workmanship at Knossos is even more curious. The suggestion that the Mallia koulouras were intended for storing grain is perhaps the most satisfactory explanation.

The introduction of the fast-wheel technique of pottery making from Asia Minor brought a startling improvement in the ceramics of Knossos and Phaistos, though many other centres continued to make vases in the style of the preceding period. Kamares ware, named from the cave sanctuary of Kamares where it was first found in any quantity, is among the handsomest crockery ever made,

Ills. 62, 63. The last original achievement of Minoan pottery, the Marine style (below left), was also one of the finest. It occurs only in the period immediately before the fall of the palaces, unlike the Floral style (below right), which began earlier and continued in a modified form under the alien lords of Crete.

Ills. 64, 65. The demanding technique of fresco painting on wet plaster calls for a swift and sure touch. A master hand immortalized something of the fragile grace of the great Cretan ladies in the painting known as 'La Parisienne' (left); the Tiryns painter's lack of authority is equally captured for all time in his two-tailed bull (below).

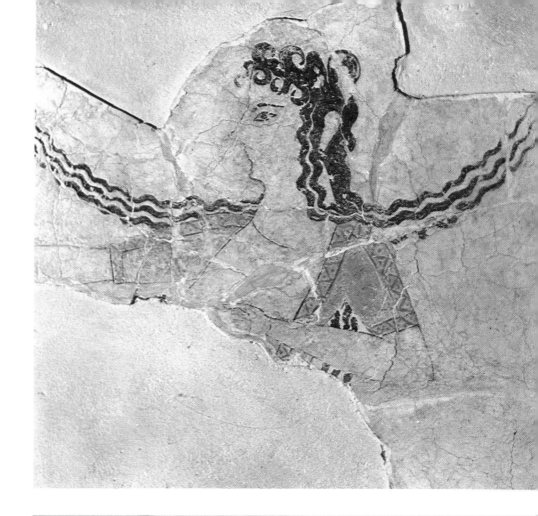

Ills. 66, 67. All the principal rooms and corridors at Knossos were adorned with paintings of the religious and ceremonial life of the court, and of the wildlife so dear to Minoan taste. Restorations of the frescoes in the Queen's Megaron (below right) have been placed in their original positions, the dancing lady (above right) with her flying curls and brilliant dress on the pier beside the colonnade, while dolphins plunge through sunny seas on a panel above the doors to the inner chambers.

Ills. 68, 69. The ornamental ladies of the Labyrinth were a favourite subject for Cretan artists, and the details of their rich and elaborate appearance have been preserved in numerous representations. A gold ring from Isopata (left) concentrates on the many-flounced dresses and open bodices to the virtual exclusion of the heads, and a gold and ivory figurine of the snake goddess (below) wears a skirt trimmed with gold ribbons and a headdress which was also once studded with gold.

and could take its place with pride in the most exclusive modern store. The fabric of the smaller pieces is eggshell thin and the shapes elegantly simple. The decoration is a natural development of the light-on-dark painting of MM I, but the patterns are no longer simple linear motifs. They are mainly based on natural forms such as leaves, flowers and marine life stylized into purely ornamental shapes which fill the field with a swirl of spiralling movement, controlled with assured skill and impressive authority. Perhaps associated with this new mastery in ceramic painting is the appearance of the earliest known Minoan fresco. Its exact period is both debatable and hotly debated, and for some time even its subject was uncertain. All that can be said is that a blueish figure known with convenient ambiguity as the 'Saffron Gatherer' is shown picking crocuses in a pleasantly impressionistic natural landscape. The figure's proportions suggest that it is not a boy, as was once thought, but a blue monkey, and it is now generally accepted as such. The fact that these fragments were found in the area of the north keep helps to underline the latter's lack of serious military purpose; it is difficult to imagine a regular soldier exercising his profession in a barracks painted with fashionable pets and flowers.

In addition to their fine table pottery the Minoans were now making huge pithoi with applied rope patterns for storing oil, grain

Ill. 70. An exceptionally fine Cretan seal shows two goats mating. It is shaped like a ring, but the hoop is too small to be worn even on a slender Cretan finger.

Ills. 66, 67

Ill. 65

and wine. These outsize vessels were sometimes considerably larger than the Cretans themselves, and they evoke an amusing picture of the diminutive palace staff struggling to handle them (though they must have been completely immovable when full), or having to climb step-ladders to ladle out the contents.

By this time the Cretans were already literate, but we can learn little from the undeciphered Linear A script except that its use seems to have been confined to the palace bureaucracies. Middle Minoan II ended—rather literally—with a bang, as a powerful earthquake struck Crete about the year 1700, radiating from the volcanic island of Santorini (Thera) which lies 120 km. north of the low-lying Knossos-Mallia coast. This was by no means the first time this had happened, as tremors of varying degrees of intensity are almost an annual occurrence, and the Cretans seem to have seized undismayed on this excuse to build bigger and better palaces than ever.

The new palaces constructed in MM III and LM I saw the finest flowering of the Minoan civilization when the island's power, prestige and wealth were at their height. The Knossos aristocracy lived a life of sophisticated ease and luxury in one of the most attractive and comfortable palaces the world has ever seen, and its influence, disseminated by its enterprising commercial fleet, reached from end to end of the Aegean. Daedalus' claim to be the architect of the Labyrinth will not stand close inspection; there is absolutely nothing of the mainland in the style, decoration and construction of the palace of Knossos at the peak of its glory. The airy halls and corridors of the palace were alive with brilliant paintings carried out in the true fresco technique on damp plaster, sometimes modelled in low relief. The rapid execution required by this demanding process may partly be responsible for the spontaneous vitality of the result, but one of the prices to be paid for such haste is that mistakes cannot be rectified. It appears, however, that the Minoan master painter did not make mistakes, unlike his Mycenaean counterpart at Tiryns, with his endearing two-tailed bull. The colour range was not large, but the shades were clear and true, and tellingly combined to produce the most varied effects. White was made from hydrate of lime, black from carbonaceous shale or slate, and red and yellow from various iron

earths; the yellow, for instance, was made from ochre, which can also produce light red, and a darker red, very common in Cretan painting, came from haematite. The Minoans' blue pigment, like the Egyptians', was compounded from a crystalline silicate of copper. The only colour they lacked was a true green. Some years later the Mycenaeans produced a pure green from ground malachite, but the Cretans had to be content with mixing blue and yellow.

The terraces of the royal family's private apartments on the east of the central court were now united by the Grand Staircase, an imposing descent at least four storeys high with one side, supported by stubby downward-tapering Minoan columns, opening on a light-well. The hall at its foot was probably intended for the menfolk of the royal family, judging from the masculine nature of its decorations. This was tactfully connected by a close but indirect route with the complex known as the Queen's Megaron, with its exquisite frescoed dancing lady and, above the doors, vibrantly lively dolphins. One end of the room was a porch opening on to a light-well which could be closed off in winter with curtains or folding doors, ensuring an equable temperature all year round. These

Ills. 71—74. Cretan jewellery is nearly all made of gold, sometimes picked out with inlaying and semi-precious stones. The pendant (above left), part of the so-called Aegina Treasure, once had lapis lazuli eyes, and the hoop earring (below right) is threaded with carnelian beads. The flower (below left) comes from a tomb in Greece but is almost certainly Cretan work. The pendant (above right) with the duck hunter shows the influence of Egypt and the Near East.

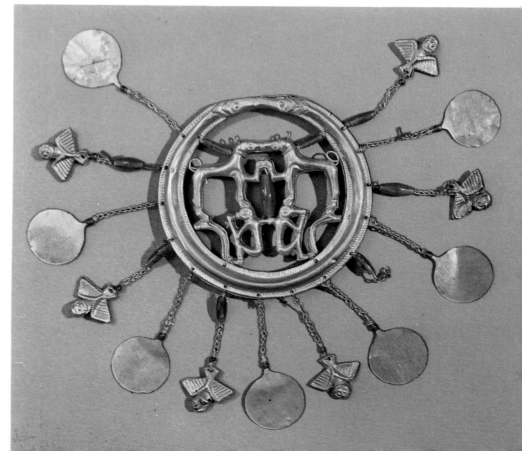

spacious, shady rooms are not the only feature of the palace which suggest that a sound grasp of creature comforts was united to the Minoans' highly developed aesthetic sensibilities. No other civilization of the ancient world until imperial Rome was to have so efficient a system of water supplies and drainage, with pipes designed on correct hydraulic principles and even effective flush lavatories. The surviving number of pottery baths appropriately painted with flowers outside and fish inside indicates that the Minoans were also personally fastidious to a rare degree.

Ill. 79
Ill. 80
Ill. 78

The furniture of these handsome rooms was sparse, and the only surviving piece is the gypsum throne (somewhat later in date, admittedly, but probably traditional in design) which still stands, a disquietingly numinous presence, in the ceremonial apartments on the west of the central court. Some of the fittings were built in, like the stone and plaster benches which occur in several parts of the palace, but comfortably cushioned folding stools are shown on frescoes and high-backed chairs with footstools on gems. A figurine of a man in a capacious armchair suggests another aspect

Ill. 76

Ill. 77

Ill. 75. Several flights of the imposing Grand Staircase which links the royal apartments on the east side of the central court at Knossos have now been restored. The Cretan column, unlike the later Classical version, tapers downwards.

Ills. 76, 77. None of the furniture of the palaces has survived apart from a few built-in pieces. The throne room (above) belongs to the period after the fall of the palaces (*c.* 1475 BC) but probably reproduces a traditional design. Other types of furnishing are known to us because they were depicted in paintings such as the fresco fragment (right) which shows a cushioned stool secured at the hinge by a knotted cord.

of the pursuit of easy living. The rooms were heated by portable braziers and lit by a considerable variety of graceful oil-burning lamps. The number and diversity of the kitchen vessels indicate that the copious raw materials were fully exploited to produce a succession of varied dishes, with the curious omission of bread; there are no known bread ovens, so flat cakes of the tortilla variety must have been eaten instead.

As to the inhabitants of the palace, they were as elegantly artificial as their surroundings. A noble lady's appearance must have required

Ills. 81—83, 85
Ills. 84, 86, 87

Ills. 78—80. The Cretans were virtually alone in the ancient world in their insistence on personal cleanliness and hygienic sanitary arrangements. Painted terracotta baths (above left) are common, and the excellent drainage system (left) indicates that the baths were regularly used. Piped water was laid on throughout Knossos, and correctly designed lavatories (right) must have added immeasurably to the comfort of life in the crowded palaces.

Ills. 68, 69

Ills. 71—73
Ill. 70
Ill. 74

Ill. 64

Ill. 88

an enormous expenditure of time, trouble and cost to keep up, and there can be little doubt that it was her main preoccupation. No fabrics have survived, and not very much jewellery in comparison with the quantity which must have been in circulation during the height of the palace culture, but there are enough fresco fragments and engraved gems to give us a good idea of Cretan court dress. The men's was minimal, but effectively designed to show off the finer points of the male form to the best advantage. Sandals bound with thongs, or bare feet, an abundance of necklaces and bracelets, a brief codpiece and a leather or metal belt pulled in as tightly as flesh and blood could bear emphasized muscular shoulders, narrow hips and trim waists, in striking contrast to the voluminous garments of the women. An hour-glass figure was evidently admired, since women also wore the tightly laced belt, with a long full skirt made in several flounces and a short-sleeved jacket open to below the breasts; they wore diadems and beads twisted in their hair, bracelets, necklaces and rings, and (if some curious pendants in the British Museum have been rightly identified) immense hoop earrings, and their clothes were stitched with ribbons and medallions of gold. They were small and slight, the men averaging about 1.56 m. and the women a diminutive 1.47 m., with attractive clean-cut features, large dark eyes, pert pointed noses, and thick black hair worn in a mass of short curls over the forehead with long ringlets over the back and shoulders. The brilliant colouring of some of the frescoes indicates that these charms were heightened by cosmetics, and it is true that a number of tweezers, razors and styluses have been found, as well as many small ornamental jars and boxes, which would be suitable for little else but paints and perfumes.

It can hardly be imagined that such exquisitely glittering, tinkling, curled and scented human butterflies can have braved the rough roads of Crete under the harsh summer sun, and indeed the evidence of frescoes and gems indicates that they were almost exclusively preoccupied with life inside the palace. Even hunting is a rare theme in Minoan art and, apart from the extraordinary ritual of the bull game (which will be fully discussed later), violence of any kind seems to have been unacceptable to them. Everything the heart could desire was gathered within the rambling complex of the Labyrinth, and they probably left its shelter as little as possible.

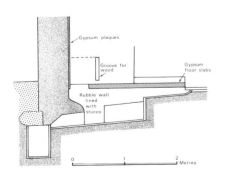

75

Ills. 81—83, 85. The Cretans used oil-burning lamps in a wide variety of shapes to light their houses. Heavy pedestals of carved stone (right) alternated with small bronze lamps (above), and one of the obviously Cretan masterpieces from Grave Circle B was a rock crystal lamp in the form of a duck (far right). The rooms were heated when necessary by portable charcoal braziers (below). Open flames and vast stocks of oil kept for cooking and lighting must greatly have intensified the final conflagration when the palaces burned down.

Ills. 84, 86, 87. The kitchens of the Cretan and Mycenaean palaces contained very much the same types of pots and pans as cooks of all ages have always used. Miniature gold scales from Mycenae (far right) are the familiar swing-balance type, and the three-handled bronze cauldron from Tylissos (left) could belong to almost any culture. The bronze cup (right) probably reproduces the appearance of the gold tableware used by the rich.

Ill. 88. Ivory cosmetic box (*pyxis*) with the figures of a charging bull and an acrobat in low relief.

When a journey was unavoidable they used open sedan chairs which were much better adapted to the bad roads than the four-wheeled wagons introduced from the Near East some time after 2000. Neither chariots nor riding horses seem to have been much used during the height of the last palace period, though both skills were later acquired from the mainland.

Ill. 89

The Minoans were much better sailors than land travellers. As early as 2000 BC they had ranged abroad in large sea-going craft steered by oars at the stern, with a high prow and a low stern fitted with a fixed, rudder-like projecting fin. At the peak of the Cretan thalassocracy the merchantmen were probably about 21 m. long by

Ill. 92

Ill. 89. Terracotta model of a sedan chair. Minoan women of fashion habitually went barefoot and were obviously unaccustomed to walking outside the shelter of the palace.

Ills. 90—92. A drawing from a jar (top), a seal stone (centre) and a clay model from Mochlos (below) preserve the main features of the ships on which Cretan power and prosperity depended. They were broad merchantmen, sometimes with an animal-head finial on the high, curving stern.

4 to 4.5 m. wide, with fifteen oars per side. The main propulsive power, however, was supplied by a single mast stepped amidships with a wide sail suspended from a heavy yard sustained by diagonal ropes. The lack of fore and aft sails suggests that they sailed before the prevailing winds south from Crete to Egypt (or from the mainland to Crete) and returned by a circuitous route via the coast of Palestine, Cyprus and the Dodecanese. Very little is known about their navigation, but the importance of the dove in Cretan art and the frequency with which the bird figures in marine contexts in Near Eastern legend (Noah, Gilgamesh and Jason all profited from its homing propensities) may be significant. Perhaps cages of pigeons were carried on shipboard. On the short runs when the ship was out of sight of land they would be released for the helmsman to follow. In view of the Cretans' comparative indifference to all things military it can probably be assumed that there was no real battle fleet as such, and that their undoubted supremacy was purely mercantile, based on their immense wealth and prosperity and only backed by the minimum of necessary force.

Innumerable representations in all the Minoan arts depict religious scenes and motifs, and with so much evidence at our disposal it is a curious paradox that the ritual still remains a mystery. Much has been written, and many explanations offered (some of them, indeed, more picturesque than believable) but no definitive answer can be found and here, above all, the absence of texts is most deeply felt. One of the few facts which can safely be stated is that the dominating figure was a goddess, either a single deity with many aspects or a whole pantheon of female divinities presiding over different activities. She was worshipped in cave and peak sanctuaries

and in the palace itself, which appears to have been the religious as well as the civic centre of the island. The function of high priest was probably interwoven with the royal power from a very early date. The goddess is shown primarily as a fertility figure, the great earth mother, but she has numerous other epiphanies associated with animals, birds, snakes, mountains, double axes and the mysterious 'horns of consecration'. Another strange facet of the cult was the worship of tree and pillar shrines. The Tree of Life is a common element of early mythology, and in a highly seismic area where the survival of the whole establishment depends on the strength and stability of the supporting columns, the pillar cult is easy enough to understand. In one of the basements of the Labyrinth stood a massive square pier belonging to the earliest days of the palace which had evidently survived the worst onslaughts of the earthquakes to become the object of a household cult.

All this power and splendour, however, were doomed to a tragic end. The volcano of Santorini had been shuddering and rumbling ominously for some years, but the Cretans were used to these manifestations and took little notice. But during the LM IB period (somewhere between 1480 and 1470, according to the most recent evidence) the whole island exploded with appalling violence. One expert writes that the noise of the eruption must have made Krakatoa sound like a damp squib in comparison, and the effect on Crete was truly frightful. Unprecedented blast-waves from the explosion toppled the palaces, spreading fire and ruin over all the population centres in the east and centre of the island and a thick layer of sterile volcanic debris blanketed the once fertile agricultural land. When the worst devastation subsided the survivors crept from their refuges to find the entire pattern of their personal lives and their island's history irrevocably changed. The palace-dwelling aristocracy must have been almost entirely wiped out, along with the bulk of its wealth, which would largely consist of perishable trade goods stored in the palace magazines, and the rich farmlands were to be largely uninhabitable for the next fifty years or more. It has been estimated that 10 cm. of volcanic fall-out is enough to render farmland unworkable for at least ten years, and up to three-quarters of a metre descended on east and central Crete. Knossos alone was able to salvage a shadow of the old life from the ruins.

Ill. 76

Perhaps the rolling country round about dispersed the volcanic debris faster than the enclosed plains elsewhere; perhaps the palace bureaucracy was so firmly entrenched that it could easily be reshaped from the few remaining remnants; and it seems that newcomers moved in to give a fresh lead to the dazed islanders. Whatever the reason, life continued at Knossos, parts of the palace were repaired and new complexes were added.

A new spirit was abroad, however. The old playful, frivolous attitude gave place to a stern militarism which is reflected in the art of the last phase of Knossos. Plant life is shown regimented in no-nonsense rows of tidily symmetrical shoots, and themes of warfare and weapons appear even on the domestic pottery. Formality and conservatism are now the keynotes where once naturalism and free-ranging imagination reigned supreme, and the graves of the period yield an unwonted amount of weapons and armour. The Cretan creative impulse had died in the eruption and thenceforward only derivative work was produced to the order of the newcomers. This influence clearly came from mainland Greece. Indeed, the palace now spoke a primitive form of Greek and kept its records in the Linear B script. No one knows how the Greeks came to Knossos. Perhaps the Cretans, sensing the need for a strong man at the head of affairs and deprived of their own nobles, had proposed a dynastic marriage, for as far as can be told amid so much devastation, the takeover was peaceful.

The new dynasty did not last very long. Shortly after 1400 a mysterious disaster overtook Knossos, and for the last time the palace burned down. Whoever was responsible for this last assault, it was apparently accompanied by circumstances of such profound horror and sacrilege that the site was avoided as haunted from that time onwards. The island civilization fell into decline, never to reach such heights again, and there is nothing to explain the final mystery. So complete was its eclipse that to the Classical Greeks a thousand years later the Labyrinth was no more than a myth. It was not until the beginning of the twentieth century that its ruined walls were uncovered again, still showing stains where thick black smoke from the burning oil jars drove before a south wind on the spring day when the Labyrinth passed from history to legend.

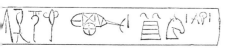

Ill. 93. In the period after the fall of the palaces the Linear B script in a primitive form of Greek was used at Knossos. Chariots and armour are listed on a clay tablet in this example of the script.

Bronze Age Greece 4

Anne G. Ward

THE MAINLAND OF GREECE is not very far from Crete in geographical terms, but the history of its development in the Bronze Age is very different from the placid, unbroken evolution of the island culture. As far as habitation is concerned it had a long start on Crete, and in northern Greece settled farming villages with a fairly civilized standard of living are known dating back as far as 6218 BC, give or take 150 years. These villages were small—the maximum was twenty wattle and daub homes—but they housed a people with a reasonably advanced way of life, using pottery, harvesting wheat and barley, keeping sheep and goats and already marking their possessions with clay stamp seals.

This development continued slowly but steadily until the fourth millennium when a new element arrived, affecting the whole country down to and including Athens (so much for the Athenians' claim to be the indigenous population!). These people are chiefly recognizable by their elaborate pottery painted with busy geometric designs. Their culture was lively and fluid with plenty of interaction, and did much to open up internal communications between the hitherto somewhat isolated village communities.

The first Early Helladic period began in the third millennium, an age of rapid advance and widespread activity in Egypt and the Near East. Perhaps the most influential of the new developments was the spread of metal working, which imposed a demand for an entirely new economy, with new trade routes, new techniques, new craftsmen and an infinity of new possibilities. The people of Greece could as yet offer nothing to compete with the contemporary splendours of Old Kingdom Egypt and Early Dynastic Mesopotamia, but they were progressing steadily. Towns were built on low hills with easy access to the sea, sometimes with an enclosing wall. The houses were mostly two-roomed with mudbrick walls on well-built foundations of distinctive herringbone stone slabs, and had tiled roofs. Seals were plentiful, and the first signs of wheel-turned pottery now appeared.

Our knowledge of EH II is largely based on one site—that of Lerna at the western corner of the bay of Nauplion. There had been a neolithic village on the site, but it had subsequently been abandoned until the EH II settlers arrived. They smoothed off the top of the mound and built a township there which persisted for the next two hundred years. In these houses the rooms were large and square with true right-angled corners set on the traditional herringbone foundations. They were grouped around a larger building of uncertain purpose in the middle of the mound. The settlement was destroyed by a violent conflagration, which must have been accidental as there appears to have been no change in the population after it. During the long slow process of recovery from this disaster the 'House of the Tiles' was built. This ambitious structure measured 25 × 12 m., with two large rooms on ground level. The floor inside and out was finished with smooth yellow clay, and the walls with rough red lime plaster. Little is known of its upper storey except that it was roofed with terracotta and blueish schist tiles laid in a clay bed. Very few artefacts were found in the house apart from a number of seal impressions. These nodules of clay were accidentally fire-hardened so as to be almost indestructible, and they show a wide variety of handsome and skilfully executed designs. There are indications that the 'House of the Tiles' was not even completed when it was attacked by a group of invaders and burned to the ground.

Some inexplicable taboo must have haunted the site, however, for the newcomers raised a mound over the ruins, encircled them with a ring of stones, and carefully avoided building there, although it was a large area of highly desirable land right in the middle of the settlement. They produced nothing to compensate for the promising culture they had so decisively destroyed. Their houses were small, straggling and irregular, and even their dead were interred with few gifts and less respect, sometimes being dumped

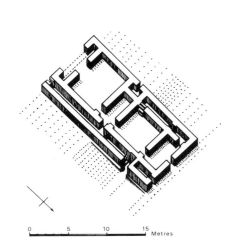

Ill. 94. Plan of the Early Helladic 'House of the Tiles' at Lerna in the Argolid.

unceremoniously down the nearest rock fissure. They made only one contribution to Greece, but it was to have a marked effect on the country's future: it was the cultivation of the vine.

The beginning of the Middle Helladic period was marked by a wave of population movements, invasions and changing fortunes all over the eastern Mediterranean and the Near East, always excepting Crete. The Hittites were making themselves felt in Anatolia; Egypt was heading for the age of eclipse which culminated in the Second Intermediate period; the once-powerful Akkadians had been humbled by the Guti, and the first of the Greeks moved down into the peninsula. The earliest signs of these people were discovered by the indefatigable Schliemann at Orchomenos, realm of the legendary King Minyas, after whom he named them Minyans. If a future archaeologist were to name all the inhabitants of Great Britain 'Arthurians' it would be just about as relevant and accurate; but the name has stuck, and time has sanctioned its use, not only for the people but for their highly distinctive pottery. This ware has sharply carinated shapes strongly reminiscent of metal prototypes, and the finish is an attractive burnished grey or yellow, slightly soapy to the touch. The culture associated with this pottery is considerably less attractive.

It took the Minyans more than two hundred years to feel fully established in their new country, and in the intervening time they were content with a somewhat temporary way of life, with very little advance. Their towns show no organization or planning, and their houses were undistinguished. There were still stone foundations, but the neat herringbone courses of the earlier period had gone, and with them the smoothly plastered walls. A fixed central hearth became customary but it would perhaps be overstraining probability to see this as the immediate forerunner of the great Mycenaean megaron. There is very little gold and silver known from this period, and few tools and weapons.

Later in the Middle Helladic period the Minyans had taken the measure of their surroundings and were looking about them. Imports from other countries suggest an increase in foreign contacts, the most significant of which is the first sign of the Cretan influence which was to have so profound an effect on the later culture of Bronze Age Greece. A Kamares jar was found in a Middle Helladic

Ill. 95. The Mycenaeans who built the citadel wall at Mycenae planned a wide curve in the fortification to incorporate the hallowed burial area of Grave Circle A.

grave at Lerna, and from this time onwards the mainland potters began to produce their own local variants on Cretan ware. Towns were mostly not yet walled, but it is worth remarking that the earliest fortified towns were those on island sites facing Crete. Were the tribute collectors already at work? Burials were not rich, although a few gifts indicate some attempt to provide for the hereafter. Children were interred in jars, often under the house floors, but adults were usually buried in shallow cists in a cemetery outside the village. There was no change in population during the period, but towards its end there was a sudden inexplicable outbreak of experimentalism, with a movement towards greater ceremony and display which may be partly due to increased contact with Crete. At this time the island was approaching the zenith of its power and wealth, and Minos seems to have been generous about sharing his trade contacts and commercial 'know-how' with his comparatively backward mainland neighbours, from whom he evidently thought he had nothing to fear. The Greeks, it would seem, learned fast.

The years which include the end of the MH period and LH I are distinguished by one of the most intriguing problems of Greek prehistory. Mycenaean archaeology began with this problem in 1876, but it has never been satisfactorily solved in all the subsequent years. We know new dynastic rulers appeared at Mycenae, burying their dead in circles of shaft graves accompanied by unimaginable splendours of gold, but we know absolutely nothing about who they were, whence they came, where they got their stupendous wealth, or what ultimately became of them. There is nothing like them anywhere else in the Aegean, and no known architecture associated with them. What little we know of them is based exclusively on their grave furnishings, and though these include an unrivalled quantity of material, its nature is bafflingly hybrid. There is purely Cretan work, objects clearly made by Cretan master craftsmen working to unfamiliar mainland requirements, Cretan motifs executed in mainland workmanship so undeveloped as to be little short of barbarous, and the hesitant beginnings of native Mycenaean styles. The materials include gold (approximately 13.5 kg. of pure bullion), silver which may have come from Anatolia although recent evidence has shown that the Classical silver mines at Laurion were already being worked in the Middle Helladic period, ostrich eggs from Nubia, lapis lazuli from Afghanistan or via Mesopotamia, alabaster and faience from Crete, ivory from Syria and amber from the Baltic.

Ill. 96

The most recent of the two grave circles was known and revered by the later Mycenaeans, for they took care to extend their fortifications to enclose it, and renovated it with handsome new stone work. This was the circle unearthed by Schliemann in 1876. Unfortunately his over-enthusiastic methods and lack of technical facilities destroyed a great deal of priceless evidence, including the human remains. He did his best to record them according to his lights by having an artist make a drawing before they disintegrated, but since this remarkable production exhibits at least thirty-two teeth although little more than half the jaw is visible its reliability is, to say the least of it, somewhat suspect. However, a fortunate discovery in recent years has made it possible to reconstruct much of the missing information. In 1951 and 1952 the Greek Antiquities Service personnel were conducting a series of repairs to the tholos known as the 'Tomb of Clytaemnestra', which lies just outside the citadel walls below Schliemann's grave circle. During these operations an arc of stone slabs was found which reminded the experts so strongly of the enclosure of the known grave circle that they thought it worth pursuing the investigation. Their efforts were rewarded by the discovery of a second circle, known as Grave

Ill. 95

Ill. 96. Inlaid dagger from Grave Circle A at Mycenae. The skill and vitality of the workmanship suggest a Cretan craftsman but the hunting theme is typical of Mycenaean taste.

Circle B to distinguish it from Schliemann's Grave Circle A, containing twenty-four tombs of various types. The first date to *c.* 1580 or earlier, some years before the beginning of Circle A, and the latest overlap it, so that they provide an invaluable check. Exactly the same stylistic tendencies can be observed, but everything is on a much more modest scale. There are fewer gifts and their quality is poorer, but the same innovations are apparent: multiple burials, goods made for purely funerary purposes, large numbers of weapons, imported Cretan and Cycladic influences and objects, and the unique portrait masks laid over the faces of the dead. A remarkable access of wealth obviously took place between the beginning of Circle B and the end of Circle A, but this dynasty was as short-lived as it was prosperous. Perhaps this very opulence, which must have marked the rulers' earthly lives as well as their dispositions for the next world, served to attract too many covetous eyes and ensured their rapid downfall. They vanished, to be superseded by a new dynasty whose achievements were expressed not so much in gold as in stone. There is little sign of conflict or interrupted life as the new princes moved in, and the old forms persisted alongside the new.

Towards the end of the shaft-grave dynasty, *c.* 1500, a new form of burial was already being practised by the élite of Messenia and the western Peloponnese. The tholos tomb was enthusiastically adopted by the new Mycenaeans, who brought it to the highest peak of perfection over the next 250 years, from 1500 to 1250. It is, however, with the earlier part of the tholos period that we are most

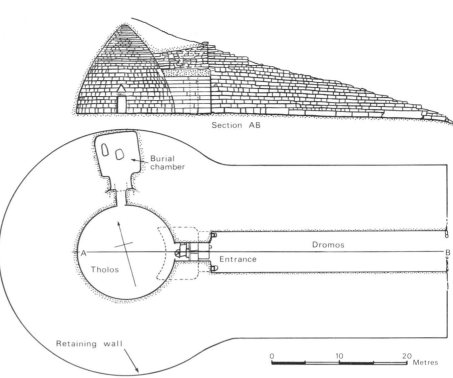

Section AB

Burial chamber

Dromos

A — Tholos — Entrance — B

Retaining wall

0   10   20 Metres

closely concerned, because the years between the last of the shaft graves and the fall of the Cretan palaces (*c.* 1500—1480/70) fit most closely with the historical elements implicit in the details of the story of Theseus. They call for close examination.

Frustratingly enough, we have only the haziest idea of the kind of home Theseus left behind when he went to Crete. Most signs of the domestic architecture belonging to the earliest tholos tombs were swept away in the subsequent upsurge of Mycenaean palace and fortress building, but even this absence of remains is enough to indicate that the houses must have been small and flimsy, perhaps with a high percentage of wood in their construction. It is surprising that these princes should have been satisfied with such undistinguished dwellings, for their tombs were among the outstanding architectural achievements of their times. These were the great tholos tombs which appear all over the mainland of Greece, but most frequently in places directly in contact with Crete. Basically they are a hole sliced into the side of a hill, lined with stone and closed with a corbel vault, but the reality is very much more impressive than so bald a statement suggests. The nine tholoi of Mycenae provide a picture of the development which is usually (but not invariably) applicable

Ills. 97, 98. The so-called 'Treasury of Atreus' has the largest known vault of the pre-Roman ancient world (above left). The plan (above right) shows how tholos tombs were constructed inside the slope of a suitable hill.

Ills. 97, 98

to this type of tomb wherever it occurs. In the earliest phase the lining was of poor quality rubble masonry and the *dromos* (the corridor leading to the façade) was sometimes not lined at all. The architects had not yet solved the problem of the enormous pressure brought to bear by the superimposed mound of earth on the lintel above the door, and it frequently cracked in the middle. In the second phase the dromos was always lined, either with rubble masonry or dressed slabs of poros, the doorways were well constructed of dressed conglomerate, and the pressure problem had been solved by leaving an empty space (the relieving triangle) above the lintel. The third stage was a logical development of the first two. The tomb was now lined throughout with beautifully smoothed ashlar masonry, the façade decorated with carved stone of different colours, the relieving triangle covered by a relief-worked slab and the whole of the interior sometimes adorned with bronze rosettes attached by metal shanks running into the stonework. The lintel, curved to fit the shape of the tomb, had acquired enormous dimensions (that of the 'Treasury of Atreus' weighs well over a hundred tons) and its transport and positioning represent a formidable feat of engineering. The largest of these tombs boasts the biggest vault in existence before the Pantheon, standing 15 m. high, and its doorway measures 6 m. to the giant lintel.

The life of the people who built these tombs was strongly martial and slightly feudal in its general tendency, with a marked aristocratic bias. The labour of a large part of the community must have been needed to raise these grandiose sepulchres, but the existence of a rich and independent trading class is attested by the number of well-stocked chamber tombs belonging to this period. The princes did not concentrate all their wealth on weapons and warfare, though these obviously absorbed a considerable portion of the budget. They extended their patronage to the local arts, encouraging the establishment of potteries and gem-cutting workshops, and their

Ill. 99   appreciation of the niceties of Minoan sophistication is unmistakable.

Ills. 142, 143   When the prince of Vapheio was buried, for instance, two Cretan gold cups were laid as close as possible to his body as if they had been his most treasured possessions—as well they might be, for they are executed in the finest style of the peak period of Cretan art, and their effect, as they stand today in the National Museum in Athens, is breathtaking. The Vapheio prince had a more direct approach to Crete than most other rulers—down the Eurotas valley to the Minoan colony at Cythera—but he was not the only one to appreciate that culturally his people had a lot to learn from the Cretans.

The art which developed during this peaceful and prosperous period was far from being a slavish imitation of island prototypes. Motifs were adopted and craftsmen imported (particularly after the fall of the palaces), but the designs did not remain static. Minoan exuberance, which the Mycenaeans must have regarded with mild disapproval as slightly untidy, was curbed, and the new styles acquired a hieratic stateliness and majesty very much in keeping with the Mycenaean character. It is not surprising that they were at their best in the matter of weapons and armour. They experimented scientifically with different designs of helmet, sword, shield and cuirass, and a grave at Dendra has yielded a full panoply of neatly overlapping plate armour which was unique until the Middle Ages. Although the armour is remarkably efficient in design, it does not require much imagination to see why the experiment was not repeated; anyone who has ever been exposed to the relentless blaze of the Greek summer sun will be more disposed to wonder what kind of a race of supermen could have supported such heat and weight at all.

Horses and light chariots seem to have been introduced by the shaft-grave dynasty as a privilege confined to the military élite. The inspiring picture of a squadron of chariots doing battle in formation, so beloved of the cinema epic, is very unlikely to have

Ill. 100

Ill. 99. The princes of mainland Greece delighted in the finest products of Cretan art, sometimes electing to be buried with treasures like the gold cup embossed with octopuses from the royal tomb at Dendra.

Ill. 100. Light chariots were used for deer hunting, as shown by a gold ring from Shaft Grave IV at Mycenae.

any foundation in fact, for the terrain away from the roads is much too bad for exercises of this nature. Chariots were probably used only to transport warriors to the battlefield, and then left in charge of a non-combatant charioteer while the owner fought on foot.

As the tholos builders improved their craft they began to add fortresses and palaces to their architectural repertoire. By the time the palace builders of Mycenae, Tiryns, Athens and Pylos were at work, the power of Crete had long since dimmed to a pathetic shadow and the Labyrinth was a deserted ruin. As the way of life of the Mycenaean palaces was probably the one transmitted by later folk-memory of the heroic age, it is well worth examination. A good deal of information about the social structure is provided by the records inscribed in Linear B script which were found in large quantities at many urban centres. The script remained tantalizingly unreadable for more than fifty years after its discovery, until its mysteries were revealed, not by an archaeologist or philologist, but by Michael Ventris, an architect with an interest in the statistical technique of code breaking. At first the archaeological world seemed to be in the position of the well-known fictional young lady who, believing that she had lighted on a priceless manuscript of Gothic confessions, found herself in possession of a prosaic laundry list, for none of the documents so far known are literary. They are all accounts and inventories kept by the palace bureaucracies. It is probable, however, that more can be learned about any civilization from its laundry lists than from the finest Gothic tale ever to stand its reader's hair on end, and doubtful and conjectural though many of the readings may be, they have still added immeasurably to our knowledge of social conditions. From them we learn, among many other things, that at the head of the social hierarchy was the king, and below him a war-lord who was presumably responsible for military organization. A succession of feudal lords apparently owed allegiance to the king and received his protection in return. A free population of craftsmen and workers supplied the economic foundation of the system, and at the bottom of the scale came the slaves.

The broader political groupings are not so well documented. There are indications of good connections between the major centres (roads of beaten earth edged with stones, often wide enough for two chariots to pass each other), but the separate cities largely

followed their own individual lines of development without reference to the rest of the country. The tablets do not give the slightest hint that the lord of Pylos even knew of Mycenae's existence. It is virtually certain that he did, but the fact was considered too irrelevant to mention. Each king seems to have established a sphere of influence beyond his immediate domains, however. In Boeotia and the Argolid some form of confederacy possibly existed, headed by Thebes and Mycenae respectively, and, in Attica, Eleusis, Marathon, Spata, Thorikos and Perati were perhaps all united in a league with Athens. Unfortunately we have no way of knowing whether these leagues were voluntary alliances; it is just as likely that they were a form of ancient 'protection racket' imposed by the strongest city, in which tribute was exacted in return for military defence in time of trouble.

Ill. 101. The remains of the central hall (megaron) of the palace at Pylos. The circular hearth with four columns surrounding it is a characteristic feature of the Mycenaean palace.

It would not have been very difficult to impress the local peasantry with the royal power to protect. Early in the thirteenth century distant echoes of approaching danger were already reverberating around the mainland and preparations were made for possible attack.

Ill. 105

The fortress walls built in the middle of this century are no mere symbols of prestige, but stone ramparts so massive that the later Greeks believed they could only have been raised by a race of giants. Within the enclosing walls preparation was made for siege by the construction of granaries and storehouses, and deep tunnels were sunk to reach subterranean water supplies. Such costly and elaborate precautions were by no means superfluous, for the Mycenaean kings had much to protect.

A wide-ranging commercial bourgeoisie extended its trading interests all over the Mediterranean, and the palaces give the impression that they were not so much the sort of heroic officers' mess painted by the epic poems as a cross between a town hall and a department store. One room at Pylos, for instance, contained 2,853 drinking cups. As this seems far too many for even the most Homeric of individual requirements, it may rather be interpreted as a trade deposit. To serve the needs of formal occasions the palace included a ceremonial reception hall, the famous Mycenaean megaron. The distinguishing characteristic of this building was an oblong arrangement of rooms consisting of a pillared porch, an anteroom and an inner chamber. The palaces were not large by Minoan standards (Pylos, one of the biggest, is hardly a quarter the size of the Labyrinth) and they did not have more than two storeys at the most, while Knossos may have had as many as five in places. These buildings were constructed of timber ties and braces filled with rubble masonry faced with ashlar work, which had the merit of providing a firm but elastic structure strong enough to withstand a moderate earthquake. The amount of wood in this style of building, however, inevitably constituted a fire hazard, and this was to be the ultimate fate of most of the Mycenaean palaces. The inner chamber of the megaron where the actual receptions and the public functions of the royal family took place was a square room with a round

Ill. 101

hearth covered with a coat of painted plaster in the middle. On the right of the hearth looking from the doorway was a dais for the throne, and round the hearth were four columns which supported

Ills. 102—104.
Gold rings from Tiryns (right) show that the Cretan dress style was adopted by Mycenaeans on their ceremonial occasions. The Tiryns smith's accuracy has been confirmed by an obsidian chalice (left) found at Zakro which exactly resembles the cup held by the seated figure (above right).

a lantern roof to let the smoke out, above the balconies of the second floor. The rooms had carved dadoes and friezes of coloured stone, alabaster and blue glass inlays, bronze-plated doors, and every available surface was coated with smooth lime plaster and painted. Even the floors were squared off into a chessboard pattern and a different motif painted in each square, producing a bewildering onslaught of colour and detail. For all this splendour, the ground-floor rooms cannot have been comfortable to live in, for they were not very well lighted or ventilated, and it seems probable that the major part of the Mycenaeans' daily lives was passed on the upper storeys, which were open, airy constructions with pleasant balconies. Bathrooms were plentiful, but they lacked the Cretans' piped running water and drainage, and no provision was made for indoor sanitation.

The Mycenaeans borrowed many elements of their ceremonial life from the Minoans, always subject to a degree of adaptation to their own needs and tastes. A Cretan form of dress seems to have been adopted for ritual occasions, but such fantastic and

Ills. 102—104

94

elaborate garments were evidently not acceptable for everyday life, or for the more energetic and athletic pastimes favoured by the mainland people. Men allowed their beards to grow and wore short brightly-coloured tunics belted at the waist and edged with contrasting braid, while the women wore a full-length version of the same garment. Both sexes were no less lavishly bejewelled than their Cretan counterparts, and it is difficult to avoid a suspicion that they were apt to mistake quantity for quality in the matter of personal and domestic adornment.

Such kingdoms as these, equally founded upon commercial wealth and military might, carried the seeds of their own destruction. So many fiercely independent warrior kings living in dazzling splendour and bristling with armaments within easy striking distance of each other along the excellent Mycenaean roads were bound to come to blows sooner or later. When the inevitable hostilities broke out the decline was appallingly swift. From *c*. 1250 onwards, when most of the great siege works were built, there are signs of attack at almost all the mainland centres. These assaults could not have been the work of invaders from beyond the peninsula, for there is no trace whatever of foreign influence. Furthermore, the Trojan War took place towards the end of the thirteenth century, and it is hardly likely that the mainland kings would have formed an alliance for the purpose of denuding their homeland of all its fighting men if there were barbarian invaders already at the gates. The legends relating the return of the kings from Troy paint a depressing and probably accurate picture of a land racked by internal strife and warring factions. The administration and economy were hopelessly disrupted, and when the first bands of Dorians began their gradual infiltration, they can have met with little effective resistance from the weakened and decadent Mycenaean cities.

The Dorians were not altogether the inexorable iron-clad destroyers of popular fancy. It is true that some sites were destroyed and others abandoned at their approach, but at many centres they settled down alongside the former inhabitants and assimilated much of their way of life. A continuous tradition can be traced in these areas from the great Mycenaean kingdoms through the Dark Ages, and the persisting spirit of the Bronze Age played an active part in the formative stages of the Classical world.

The high citadel of Mycenae was sacked and burned for the last time about 1120, and it is convenient to accept this date as the end of the Mycenaean age. The decline and destruction of a great civilization is always a saddening spectacle, so perhaps it is as well that in the case of the Mycenaean culture this process took place so long after the main events with which we are concerned that it would be irrelevant to describe it in detail. It is enough to say that although the rest of the mainland succumbed in time to the attacks of the Dorians, the Acropolis of Athens was never conquered (hence the Athenians' boast that they were the autochthonous stock), and it provided a refuge for many hard-pressed neighbours. Entirely surrounded as the Mycenaean survivors were by the newcomers, a gradual process of absorption and assimilation was inevitable, and by the time the epic poems were composed, the kings of the Trojan War were a folk-memory, and Theseus and his deeds a convenient peg on which to hang local Attic propaganda.

Ill. 105. Reconstructed view of the citadel at Mycenae. The palace occupies the crown of the hill which is additionally protected by a sheer ravine to the south-east.

5 In the Footsteps of a Hero

Anne G. Ward

Ill. 106

SUCH, THEN, WAS THE WORLD OF THESEUS: a world of eventful splendour and a certain degree of heroic enterprise when great empires were forged and fell again, and the whole of the eastern Mediterranean was alive with the spirit of innovation and expansion. It is not an unworthy, nor an unlikely setting for a career like that of Theseus, once shorn of its supernatural elements, and it would be reasonable to expect some traces in the lands where he performed his greatest feats to indicate the time of his passing.

There are several clues woven into the fabric of the legend itself. Many of the elements seem to point towards the closing stages of the Bronze Age when internal strife between the mainland kingdoms so weakened the administration and impoverished the economy that the oncoming invaders found little difficulty in overrunning these vulnerable people. Indeed, the hazards of the Isthmus crossing where brigandage was rife and no traveller expected to arrive unscathed, Aegeus' lifelong battle with his own relatives for control of his kingdom, and Theseus' own struggles with the invading Amazons and the rebellious subjects who finally drove him into retirement on Scyros all find echoes in the upheavals which, from small beginnings in the mid-thirteenth century onwards, culminated in the total dissolution of the Mycenaean world. The Homeric Catalogue of Ships, too, lists a successor of Theseus as the leader of the Athenian contingent at the Trojan War, which also tends to place the legend in the later Bronze Age.

The core of the story, however, is not these peripheral episodes, for they merely provide the overture and afterpiece for Theseus' greatest feat, his voyage to Crete and his victory over the Minotaur,

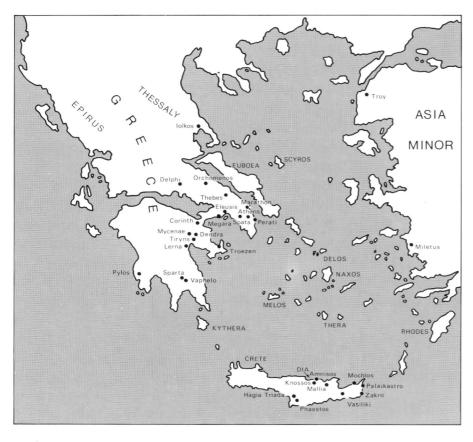

Ill. 106. Map of the Aegean.

and it is impossible to reconcile this element of the myth with the historical situation of Crete at the close of the Bronze Age. When the time came for the drawing of the lots, the islanders sent one solitary slave ship to collect their outrageous tribute, and though there is no mention of any force to back these demands, it never entered any of their victims' heads for an instant to refuse to obey or offer rebellion. The most Theseus could do for his fellow countrymen at this stage was to offer to go to Crete with them. Such a contemptuous assumption of obedience indicates that Crete must have wielded immense and unquestioned powers throughout the length and breadth of the Aegean, and there is nothing in the circumstances of Theseus' escape from Crete to suggest that the death of the Minotaur had altered the relative positions of the mighty islanders and the backward mainland, which was clearly regarded as little more than a docile source of slave labour. By the late thirteenth century, however, Crete had been a backwater for nearly two hundred years: not unprosperous, and still preserving a certain lively individuality, but none the less a backwater. Stagnation had set in at the time of the great eruption, and though the Greek rulers of Knossos had provided the impetus for a last flicker of creative enterprise, by the time of the first incursions into the mainland there was no king at Knossos, and the Labyrinth was no more than a heap of haunted ruins rapidly vanishing under encroaching vegetation and the accumulating debris of the passing years. That the humble survivors of the great days of Crete could have challenged the king of Athens in his mighty fortress at all, let alone forced him to accept their dreadful terms, is completely out of the question.

There was, however, a significant change in the position of Crete during the lifetime of Theseus. At the time of his flight from the island Minos' power was at its height. Various explanations are offered for the king's subsequent failure to follow Theseus and his own errant daughter and wreak vengeance, but there is no suggestion that the runaways doubted his ability to do so. Twenty years or so later the picture was very different. The Cretans were not only willing to forgive and forget Theseus' rebellion, the slaughter of the Minotaur and the heartless seduction and desertion of their princess Ariadne, they were only too glad to marry off another princess of the royal house, Ariadne's sister Phaedra, to the author of these intolerable outrages. Theseus had killed the Minotaur, but he did not personally overthrow the might of Crete, so some other agency must have brought about this rapid disintegration. These circumstances point unmistakably to the period in the first half of the fifteenth century when the Minoan palaces were destroyed by fire and earthquake following the eruption, and the balance of power in the Aegean swung from Crete to the mainland.

It has also been suggested that the 'Minos' of the legend may have been the Mycenaean ruler of Knossos in the period immediately following the eruption of 1480/70, and it is true that the aggressive character of the mythical Cretan king is much more Mycenaean than Minoan; moreover, this era when Crete was still a power to be reckoned with and Athens had not yet fortified the Acropolis seems to fit the circumstances of the legend as well as any.

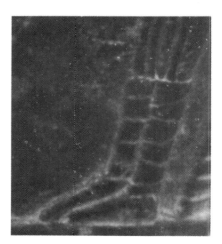

Ill. 107. Left, the stone near Troezen known as the 'Theseus Rock' where Aegeus is said to have deposited the tokens for his son.

There are, therefore, several periods at least two hundred years apart which can each put forward powerful reasons to be accepted as the historical setting of the Theseus story. They cannot all claim this distinction, and one or the other must give way, so common sense decrees. In dealing with these apparent contradictions, however, the process of formation of a legend must be borne in mind: only the most memorable episodes are handed down from one generation to another, only the most glorious (or disastrous) ages remembered. We have already seen that the period immediately before the fall of the Cretan palaces was a comparatively undistinguished time of moderate prosperity and quiet peace on the mainland. There was little at that time to fire the imagination of story-tellers, apart from the glories and terrors related by the few who had actually visited Crete and seen the brilliant palace culture with their own eyes. The great days of the Mycenaean fortresses, however, many of which were still standing as reminders of past splendours, and the endless power struggles that involved their occupants were probably much more vividly present in the folk-memories from which Classical poets drew their materials.

The making of the Theseus legend was powerfully influenced by yet another factor: for the Classical Athenians, he was good propaganda. Except for Theseus, the men of Bronze Age Attica had left no traditions comparable with the martial and domestic splendours of Mycenae 'rich in gold' to add to the status of their

Ills. 108, 109. The sword retrieved by Theseus from beneath the rock could have been an object of considerable value. An example from Mycenae (above) has a gold hilt with lion-head terminals. Typical Bronze Age sandals are worn by a soldier on a Cretan cup from Hagia Triada (above left).

Classical descendants. As a national folk-hero he was someone to be set up in competition with Jason, Perseus, Odysseus, the mighty war-lords of the Trojan campaign, and, above all, that irritatingly ubiquitous hero of a hundred ancient cliff-hangers, Heracles. As the legend passed from mouth to mouth over the generations, exploits and attributes (particularly those of Heracles) must have been borrowed from many other sources and personalities to add to the glories of the local hero, and one episode in particular casts an ironic light on the consequent telescoping of the centuries. If Theseus fought the Cretan bull before the 1480/70 eruption, and then abducted the twelve-year-old Helen, for whose beauty the Trojan War was fought at the end of the thirteenth century, she must have been nearly three hundred by that time and one can only say, with Jane Austen's Mr Bennet, that, 'In such cases a woman has not often much beauty to think of.' It is more likely that the myth has simply sought to embellish the hero's reputation by selecting the most glamorous woman of the ancient world as the object of his affections, with a fine sweeping disregard for chronology.

There is, then, no period which can definitely be pinpointed as the historical setting of the legend, and we should not be surprised to find completely incongruous elements from several different ages occurring side by side in the story.

Theseus' birthplace at Troezen is, disappointingly enough, a complete blank. The most that can be said is that it was inhabited in the Bronze Age, since Early Helladic sherds have been found on the Asklepion hill near Troezen itself. The large stone shown to the public as the 'Theseus Rock', from beneath which he retrieved his father's tokens has, no doubt, quite as good a claim to this distinction as any other rock in that exceedingly rocky neighbourhood, but certainly no better. The site of Troezen has hardly been investigated at all, and as it is close to the area which was most thickly populated in the Mycenaean period, the possibility of future discoveries cannot be dismissed. The tiny island of Sphaeria east of Poros seems less likely to have been Aethra's island than Poros itself, which has yielded unequivocal signs of Bronze Age activity, with sherds from below the temple of Poseidon and a tomb on the road from the town of Poros to the temple at Kalauria.

Ills. 107—109

Although there is no evidence to substantiate the childhood of Theseus, the story of the Isthmus crossing and its attendant adventures is supported by the nature of the landscape itself. Within the last decades a motor road has been cut along the cliffs and the knife-edged gash of the Corinth Canal now makes an island of the Peloponnese, but the route of the old road can still be seen, and the advantages of this terrain as a bandit stronghold are manifest. The legend is verified by the absence of Bronze Age habitation on the inhospitable stretch from Megara to Eleusis, and for much of the way the road clings precariously to sheer cliffs. The place near Megara where Sciron kicked his hapless victims into the sea is not recorded to be the haunt of man-eating turtles, but a rock roughly shaped like a turtle in the sea at this point would deal an equally certain and far more credible death to anyone who fell off the road.

Ill. 111

Ill. 110

Theseus' troubles, however, began long before he reached the Isthmus. His encounter with Periphetes of the great club is said to have occurred at Epidaurus, but the site is not very promising as the scene of a robber's lair. Mycenaean tombs south-west of the port of Palaia Epidaurus and grey Minyan pottery from the headland south of the harbour where the Classical town stood are evidence of Bronze Age activity, but a much more likely scene for Periphetes' lair is to be found at Vassa (Nea Epidaurus). There was a substantial settlement there, on the ridge above the road from Nea Epidaurus to Dimaina, which had the added advantage of dominating the

Ill. 110. The road from Corinth to Athens clings precariously to the side of the cliff as it winds along the shore, providing ideal conditions for bandit strongholds.

coast road from Epidaurus. The habitations cover the ridge and the slopes which fall away to the ravine below, and include Cyclopean fortification walls which give the whole establishment a decidedly martial air.

Cenchreae offers no noteworthy evidence of the meeting with the Pine-bender. Pottery remains from the small site on the promontory show that the area was inhabited throughout the Bronze Age, but unless the climate and vegetation have changed radically, Sinis' method of disposing of his victims must have put him to a good deal of trouble, since the headland is bare and virtually treeless.

Having traditionally given Periphetes, Sinis and Sciron a taste of their own respective medicines and dealt with the great sow of Crommyon, Theseus moved on up the Isthmus, and evidently had no more trouble until he reached Eleusis, where, with the involuntary assistance of Cercyon, he invented wrestling. The existing remains at Eleusis are far from suggesting any athletic antecedents for the

site. On the contrary, there is strong evidence that the most sacred place of Classical Greek religion had inherited this character from at least the Middle Helladic period. Immediately below the Archaic Telesterion built by Pisistratus, excavations in the 1930s revealed remains of at least two substantial buildings of the LH II period. They are similar to the megaron in outline, but some of the accompanying details suggest that they were never used as living quarters. There is no central hearth in the inner chamber, nor any sign of bases for the four traditional columns, and the location

Ill. 111. The whole story of Theseus' exploits from Troezen to Athens and from Marathon to Crete is told by a red-figure kylix by the Codrus Painter. Reading clockwise from the top, he encounters Cercyon, Procrustes, Sciron, the Marathon bull, Sinis and Phaia (*see Ills. 5—9, 172*). In the central medallion he is dragging the dead Minotaur out of the Labyrinth.

on the slope (rather than the top) of the mound is awkwardly chosen for a palace site. The curious projecting platform in front of one of the buildings is unique in Mycenaean architecture, and the fact that it answers exactly to Demeter's specification for her temple, as quoted in the *Hymn to Demeter* (v. 270) must surely be significant.

As Eleusis was obviously an important religious centre it might, perhaps, be logical to suggest that Theseus' purification before entering Athens took place here rather than at the place where the Sacred Way crossed the river Kephisos near the later site of Plato's Academy, particularly as the ceremony was traditionally performed by the Phytalidae, who were hereditary priests of Demeter. There was, however, one more peril to be overcome between Eleusis and Athens (the meeting with Procrustes on Mount Korydallos), so any effective purification would necessarily have to take place after this, unless the ceremony was only required for Sinis, who was related to Theseus through his father Poseidon; the others, not being his kin, were perhaps regarded as unimportant.

Ill. 112   A gold ring from Mycenae showing a curious religious scene perhaps depicts some elements of the rite of purification. A young man is shown kneeling by a small shrine, grasping the stem of a fig tree (Demeter's gift to Phytalis) which grows on it. A larger-than-life female figure stands behind him in an oddly ritualistic attitude, and another bows her head over a nearby table. Perhaps we see a suppliant, the goddess and an interceding priestess in this strange

Ill. 112. A gold ring from Mycenae shows a youth kneeling at a tree-shrine in the presence of two larger-than-life female figures. Its precise meaning is unknown, but the attitudes suggest that he is a mortal man invoking the mercy of the goddess.

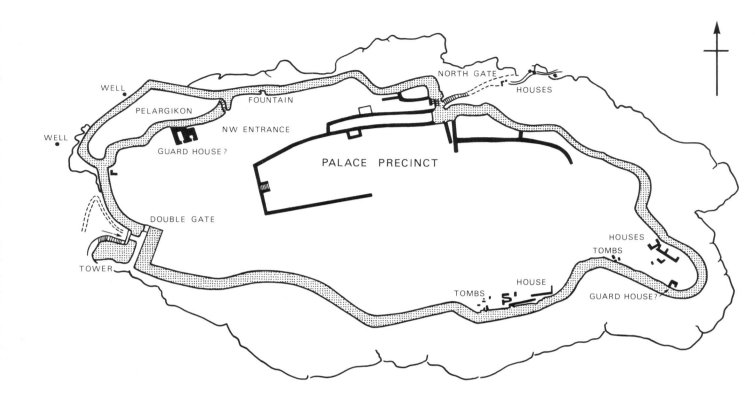

WELL

PELARGIKON

FOUNTAIN

NW ENTRANCE

WELL

GUARD HOUSE?

NORTH GATE

HOUSES

PALACE PRECINCT

DOUBLE GATE

TOWER

HOUSES

TOMBS

HOUSE

TOMBS

GUARD HOUSE?

representation. As to the site of the purification, the old bridge over the Kephisos was once in the Classical precinct of Aphrodite, but it disappeared many years ago and even the watercourse has moved, as the river now flows through an artificial canalized bed.

After so much nebulous or negative evidence, we are on firmer ground once the story reaches Athens. There are immense, sometimes insuperable difficulties attending any reconstruction of the Bronze Age city of Athens, as the site has been continuously inhabited since the neolithic period, and many of the remains lie beneath priceless Classical masterpieces or complex modern developments which cannot possibly be endangered to retrieve them. Patient search and informed conjecture have, however, been able to reassemble enough evidence to show that the 'strong house of Erechtheus' and the city of Aegeus were no myth. Cecrops is reputed to have established a settlement on the Acropolis in 1581, and it is true that potsherds and a small house belonging to the LH I period have been found near the later Erechtheum. Soon after the final collapse of the Cretan palaces a burst of building

Ill. 113. Plan of Mycenaean Athens showing the Acropolis and the immediately surrounding areas.

Ill. 113

Ill. 114. The Bronze Age city of Athens was a flourishing centre grouped round the natural fortress of the Acropolis. A substantial cemetery has been located on the slopes of the nearby Areopagus.

Ill. 114

activity occurred at Athens. Conditions must have been relatively peaceful, because some of the houses were built on exposed sites at the foot of the rock where water supplies were more easily reached. It is tempting to see this period as the time of calm when the Pallantids had been suppressed and Minos' tribute galleys were no longer to be feared, but the war with the Pallantids is probably a folk-memory of the later period towards the end of LH III, when the first upheavals had temporarily settled and the peninsula was experiencing a last cultural flowering before the final eclipse of the Mycenaean culture. The cemetery in the present Agora has yielded much fine pottery from the LH I building period, and one of the few Marine-style vases to be found in Greece (from a chamber tomb in Varkiza) must have been a souvenir brought home by an Attic sailor, which may be significant in indicating direct contact between Athens and Crete at the crucial period immediately before the fall of the palaces. At first the Acropolis was not even fortified, and its entrance was, as now, a winding ramp south of the present Propylaea with an open space at the

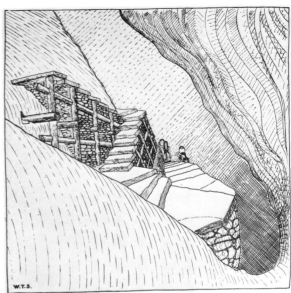

Ills. 115, 116. Increasing fear of attack in the Late Bronze Age caused the rulers of Athens to prepare the Acropolis for a siege. A spring chamber was sunk through the rock and equipped part of the way with wooden steps to ensure access to adequate water supplies.

foot for animals and vehicles, which could not be taken up the steep ascent. There were at least two other entrances: a flight of stairs approached the caves below the northern cliffs, and an easier descent led down to the Agora from the north side of the palace. Much has been made of the houses along this route, and indeed, when evidence is so scanty, full use must be made of the most trivial object, but they are in no way comparable to the rich merchants' houses outside the citadel at Mycenae. The Athenian houses were small and poor, and when the inhabitants were later forced to abandon them the removal cannot have cost very much.

In the mid-thirteenth century the whole of the Acropolis area was completely overhauled and redesigned. The top of the rock was entirely enclosed within a massive Cyclopean wall between 3 and 6 m. wide, perhaps as much as 10 m. high, and about 700 m. in circumference. A palace was built close to the present Erechtheum

Ill. 117

Ills. 115, 116

site, and a high tower and a double gate on the same lines as the Lion Gate at Mycenae were built at the south-western approach, while the other two entrances were strongly fortified. Water was plentiful at the foot of the rock, but the mounting nervous tension of the time is reflected in the construction of a fountain house in the thickness of the north wall. The shaft descended 36.5 m. to the plastered cistern, the lower part of it driven through solid rock, with eight flights of stone and wooden steps—a dark and slippery journey in the course of which many a careless Athenian lady appears to have lost her water jar, judging by the quantity of debris at the bottom. This complex piece of engineering did not benefit the inhabitants very long. The damp inside the shaft soon caused the wooden steps to rot, and when the flights fell in about fifty years after their construction they were not replaced. Later ages only knew of the first two flights down to the caves below the northern cliffs, as the whole of the shaft was quickly filled with rubbish and forgotten.

At the end of the thirteenth century it was no longer safe to live outside the walls, and the inhabitants moved up to the Acropolis. A group of houses was built for them at the south-east end, and a guard-tower added to the fortifications at that point. The easy

Ill. 117. A huge fortification wall once encircled the whole top of the Acropolis with a guard-tower beside the east entrance. Part of it still survives at this point, where the east pediment of the Parthenon can be seen above the massive blocks of Cyclopean masonry.

descent to the Agora was now felt to be a dangerously weak point in the defences, and a thick wall was built to close it off. The citadel of Athens was perhaps the most invulnerable of all the Mycenaean centres because of its natural advantages, and it resisted all the assaults of the troubled eleventh century. With the death of the last king, however, the rock was gradually abandoned to the gods, and the Greeks never again used it for human habitation.

The traditional site of Hecale's home, where Theseus spent the night before going on to Marathon, has not yielded any remains to substantiate the story, and Marathon itself now bears little resemblance to the plain as Theseus saw it. The shore-line here has altered considerably since the famous Battle of Marathon, and probably even more since the Bronze Age. The evidence from this district is oblique and allusive rather than direct, and seems at first glance to have little connection with the legend, for the surviving remains indicate a long-standing cult centre. It should, however, be remembered that bulls were an integral part of ancient Aegean religion, and if there was a cult at Marathon there were probably bulls too. Interpreted as a religious ceremony, perhaps a sacrifice, the bull episode is easier to understand, for Marathon was unquestionably the site of a shrine which, in Classical times, was connected with the herd-god Pan, and the association may have survived from an earlier period. A cave on the east side of a hill on the road from Marathon to Marathon Lake was always identified as Pausanias' 'Cave of Pan' until another cave was discovered in 1958 on the northern incline of the same hill. This second cavern was obviously more ancient and venerable, and its identity was established beyond question by the discovery of a Classical stela near the entrance naming it specifically as the Cave of Pan. At least 100 m. long and containing six or more caverns full of stalagmites and stalactites, the caves nearest the entrance yielded numerous intact offerings of pottery, figurines and jewellery dating from the neolithic period to the end of the Mycenaean age. The cave was abandoned during the Geometric and Archaic periods and reopened by the Classical Greeks, who used all the chambers for a variety of votive deposits, which continued throughout the Roman occupation into early Christian times, when the cave was forgotten. In the same district but much closer to the shore is a tholos tomb built during LH II

Ill. 12

Ill. 118. The practice of animal sacrifice is clearly attested in the dromos of the Bronze Age tomb at Marathon, where two horses were buried at the time of the first interment.

Ill. 118

(roughly contemporary with the fall of the Cretan palaces) which has the unique distinction of being provided with a recognizable animal sacrifice. Two horses were killed and neatly arranged in the dromos before the tomb was closed; it was reopened for use in LH III, but the earlier sacrifice was not disturbed. The connection with Theseus is tenuous, but the importance of the Marathon district as the centre of a cult where animal sacrifice was practised seems to be established.

If the folk-memory through which the legend was transmitted recalled the fortified Acropolis best, there is only one place where Aegeus could have stood to watch the departure and return of the black-sailed ship. Since a high wall surrounded the top of the rock in the later Bronze Age, his vantage point must have been somewhere above the battlements, facing south-west, and the obvious place is the guard-tower on the bastion by the gate. The horizon towards the sea is often dim nowadays, but Aegeus' view would not have been obscured by the industrial haze of the modern city, and from the Mycenaean tower he would have a good view, and a long drop.

6　　The Cretan Adventure

Anne G. Ward

Ill. 120. A section of the Admiralty Chart of Crete shows the rapid shelving of the sea bed on the coast round Amnisos.

◄ *Ill. 119.* Left, foreigners approaching the Labyrinth by the main road from the sea must have been sharply reminded of the bull of Minos by the massive stucco horns crowning the south façade of the palace. All the arts of Crete are haunted by the bull motif, which clearly made a profound impression on visiting mainland Greeks.

IF THE MINOAN GALLEY timed its sailing to avoid the spring south winds, it probably made good time to Amnisos, the harbour town of Knossos. The coastline of Crete has sunk here, and the water now laps among the remaining stones of the houses, but it must once have been deep. Even today the sea bed falls away very quickly from 3 to 32 m. round the headland on which most of the Minoan ruins are located. Indeed, deep water was necessary for Minoan merchantmen, for the Mediterranean custom of beaching ships cannot have been practicable in the case of a large vessel loaded heavily with fragile merchandise such as pottery. The Cretans liked to establish their harbours on deep-water headlands so that ships could be moored on the sheltered side whichever way the wind was blowing. The present-day sandy beach at Amnisos does not seem to fit these specifications very well, but there is no way of assessing how much it has altered since the Bronze Age. The harbour lies on a stretch of coast which must have been exposed to the worst ravages of the Santorini eruption, and this alone must have changed it considerably. There are plenty of remains to indicate a thriving settlement, linked to Knossos by one of the oldest roads in Europe. On the west of the hill are substantial ruins of the town where the employees of the harbour authorities once lived, and on the east is the villa where perhaps the harbour master consoled himself for his absence from Knossos by having the walls of his home painted with charming floral motifs, executed by one of the most skilful of the palace fresco painters. The harbour works are submerged, and this might well be an area which would repay attention from a sub-aqua club by producing invaluable

Ill. 121. Because of subsidence in the coastline, the tideless waves of the Mediterranean now wash among the stones of the harbour town of Amnisos. It was once a flourishing port with a busy commercial area and an aristocratic villa.

Ill. 122. It is small wonder that Greeks from the mainland were bewildered by the size of the Labyrinth. The plan of the Middle Helladic houses at Lerna (below) shows the modest type of domestic architecture to which they were accustomed.

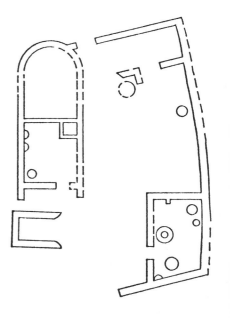

information on the little-known subject of Minoan port installations. After all, there is an admirable precedent in Theseus' dive for the gold ring, although there is little hope that the aqualung diver would have the hero's luck in lighting on Amphitrite's palace. The ways of sea nymphs are obscure, but it is doubtful if she would do anything so unwise as to establish her home in the insalubrious waters immediately below a thriving commercial dock, so it must be assumed that Theseus dived from the ship during the voyage, as Bacchylides and others have it, rather than when he arrived in Crete.

As Theseus approaches the Labyrinth and the crowning adventure of his career, his story approaches its zenith (or perhaps nadir) of improbability. Archaeology is asked to account for a maze in which bewildered youths and maidens from the mainland were ritually immolated by a frightful bull-monster; not for the first time, it has risen heroically to the occasion. We have already glanced at the simple houses of the Bronze Age mainland, with their basic two rooms and a porch, rarely more than two storeys high. It is hardly surprising that mainland visitors, faced with the 10,000 square

Ills. 123, 124. Terraces, stairs, corridors, halls, cellars and courtyards followed each other to make up the rambling complex of the Labyrinth. Now that it lies open to the sky (above) the plan is clear, but in the Bronze Age it must have presented a terrifying problem to strangers.

Ill. 125. The bulls of Crete are splendidly exemplified by a magnificent serpentine rhyton in the shape of a bull's head, the eyes and muzzle realistically inlaid with rock crystal, obsidian and shell. The gilded horns are a modern restoration.

Ills. 123, 124
metres of rambling walls, rooms, stairs, courts, terraces, cellars and corridors which make up the palace at Knossos, never told their children that 'Labyrinth' simply meant 'House of the Double Axe', and used the word to define an enormous complex designed with deliberate malevolence to confuse and perplex, in which the unwary visitor was bound to end up hopelessly lost. When the palace was no longer standing, they soon forgot that it had ever been the comfortable, well-appointed home of a large number of perfectly ordinary human beings, remembering only (as well they might) the devastating impact of its immense size and apparent total lack of integrated plan.

Although archaeology has triumphantly succeeded in producing a labyrinth, a bull-monster would seem to be a much taller order. However, the truth oversteps any bounds which even the most audacious story-teller might set for himself in this case, too. Cretan art tells the fantastic facts too clearly to be misunderstood. There *Ill. 126* are bulls everywhere: on frescoes and gems, figurines and reliefs, *Ill. 125* tableware, jewellery and sacred vessels, and the roof of the south *Ill. 119* approach of the Labyrinth itself was crowned with a massive pair of stucco horns. When all the evidence is marshalled, the sequence of events becomes reasonably plain. A team of young men and girls, all dressed alike in boys' clothes, left the palace and captured *Ill. 142* a bull in the nearby fields, either peacefully by means of a decoy *Ill. 143* cow or the hard way by snaring it in a net. Bringing in the bull may have been a spectacle in itself, and perhaps a scene of this nature once provided the missing focus of the 'Sacred Grove' fresco from Knossos, which shows a large crowd of people gathering among the trees and in the open space with its diagonal paths outside the west side of the palace. Meanwhile, crowds of courtiers were assembling to see the spectacle which seems, not unreasonably, to have formed one of the chief social and ritualistic occasions of palace life.

The purpose of the exhibition was basically religious, for the bulls are nearly always shown in an unmistakably ceremonial context of shrines and cult symbols, but by the time of the last palaces, to which most of the frescoes illustrating the performance belong, the social character of the occasion seems to have predominated. Curiously enough in so matriarchal a society as that of Minoan

Ill. 126. An acrobat in flight over a bull's back and his unsuccessful colleague trampled under its hoofs are carved on a seal stone. The illustration shows an impression taken from the seal, with the figures in relief.

Crete, the sexes appear to have been segregated in the audience. The women wore their best clothes, the men their finest jewels, and gossip and mutual emulation, along with the excitement of the spectacle itself, occupied their minds to the exclusion of solemn religious thoughts. Fragmentary though the frescoes are, they catch the spirit of the occasion with vivid immediacy. The painter, with a sound grasp of decorative values, has concentrated on the women, merely indicating the russet mass of sun-bronzed men by a few telling touches of black to sketch in dark hair, and white to highlight eyes and ornaments. The women, who are seated in a row across the centre of the picture, are drawn in more detail. Monotony of composition has cunningly been avoided by the variety of the attitudes in which they sit among their outspread multi-coloured flounces, bejewelled heads inclined together, white hands fluttering in gesture, black curls artfully arranged. Clearly the festival on which so much preparation had been expended was no mean show.

Ill. 132

Ill. 130

To the audience it was the most thrilling exhibition of their social calendar, but to the performers it was a matter of life and death. The usual interpretation is that the bull, probably infuriated by his unceremonious removal from the peaceful delights of the royal pastures, was loosed into the arena where the acrobats in their gilded loin-guards and impractically abundant curls and jewels, awaited his charge poised on the tips of their pointed boots. As he attacked, they threw themselves forward, between the long sweeping horns, and thrust upwards with all their might as he flung his head up to toss. The combined momentum sent the lucky ones flying over his head to alight on his back and jump off safely behind, steadied by a catcher close to the bull's retreating heels. The fate of the less fortunate, who were probably the great majority of the performers, requires little imagination to picture.

So fantastic a feat has been rejected out of hand as impossible by many people, including the rodeo experts whom Sir Arthur Evans consulted, with his usual admirable thoroughness, on the matter. It was pointed out that a bull charges forward, but tosses in a sideways movement, varying in extent from a slight flip to a massive sweep, so as to bring the horns (or at least one horn) into play with the weight of the body directly behind it. Indeed, common sense militates so strongly against the performance of this feat that only the testimony of Minoan art speaks in its favour:

Ill. 133 but the voice of the frescoes is too clear to be ignored. Their evidence should not be taken too literally, for the originals are pitifully mutilated and fragmentary in the extreme, and the faintly *fin-de-siècle* works reproduced in so many books on ancient art owe as much to enthusiastic modern restorers as to the Cretan fresco masters. However, it is not difficult to see where modern work ends and ancient begins, and there are works of art to vouch for

Ill. 127 almost every stage of this astonishing feat. An ivory figurine stands waiting for take-off, the young face grave with concentration and every line tensely expectant; a girl's white hand and arm are shown gripping the curve of a horn; a seal stone shows a tiny figure poised upside-down above a bull's head; and a magnificent bronze group

Ill. 131 consists of a charging bull, his head flung upwards after tossing the acrobat, who has completed the leap and has been caught by the artist at the moment of alighting, his feet on the bull's broad back and his hair still streaming over the animal's head. Other fresco fragments show boys and girls, arms outflung in a gesture of triumph as they spring away from the bull after the leap, or the anxious hovering figure of the catcher behind.

Some way must be found, then, of reconciling truth and probability. In the first place, there are the bulls themselves. The long-legged rangy Spanish fighting bulls of today, quick-witted and quicker-footed, with their sideways-spreading horns and sidelong goring movement, should be forgotten from the start. The frescoes show an animal of an entirely different breed, with little stumpy legs and an immensely heavy barrel body. The neck is so short and thick that much agility in the movement of the head would be out of the question, and the sweep of the long horns is upwards and forwards, like those of a brahma bull. In a confined space such an animal would not be able to get up much speed nor to stop and turn with any rapidity, and would be compelled by the growth of its horns to gore and toss frontally. There is another, grimmer, element to be considered. The frescoes mainly show us the successful acrobats, but they were obviously pathetically few in comparison with the numbers who must have been killed in so hazardous an attempt. Other representations show crumpled figures trampled under the bull's hoofs, and acrobats as limp as rag dolls tumbling helplessly over the animal's head in poignant contrast to the controlled curving flight of the successful leaper. The legend is very sure of the fate of the tribute youths and maidens. No one expected to encounter the bull-monster and return alive, and in this detail the myth is almost certainly correct. There was no need to endow the Minotaur with super-taurine characteristics in order to heighten the horrors of the encounter. Nevertheless, with a confined space and a slow, clumsy bull, it is just conceivable that once in a while an exceptionally skilled acrobat might succeed in performing perhaps the most dangerous circus turn of all time.

Academic controversy about the possibility of the bull-leap ebbs and flows, but there is one, and only one unanswerable way to settle such questions as, 'Could it be done?', and that is to go out and try it. The most exigent partisan of scholastic integrity could hardly expect dignified elderly academics—or undignified younger ones, for that matter—to go and expose themselves to a charging

Ill. 127. The tense figure of a slender bull-leaper, poised to await the life-or-death encounter with the bull, is portrayed in a Cretan ivory figurine picked out with gold. The sympathetic treatment of the theme and the richness of the detail indicate that the acrobats were much admired.

bull in a detached spirit of scientific enquiry; but there are places where the spirit of Theseus still lives, and the definitive answer can be found here. In the district of south-west France known as Les Landes a form of the bull game is still played, not with bulls, it is true, but with lively and aggressive cows specially bred for the purpose. The game here consists chiefly of provoking the animal and then dodging its charges by agile swaying movements of the body, the aim being never to move more than one foot in the process. Vaults from one side to another are also performed, but the crown of the spectacle is the 'Great Leap' in which the star acrobat throws a mighty double somersault over the charging animal from the front. This differs from the Cretan version in that nobody actually touches the bull, and that the animal's head movements are inhibited by a rope manipulated by an assistant, but the similarities are obvious, and this modified version of the ancient sport is conclusive proof that it could unquestionably be performed.

Ills. 128, 129

Although so many representations of the Cretan sport have survived, none of them clearly shows the details of the moment of take-off, and this is largely responsible for the amount of argument that has raged over the exact procedure. For the most part only

Ills. 128, 129. Cretan bull-leaping is kept alive in a modern French version of this dangerous sport. The animal's movements are impeded by a rope and cows instead of bulls are used, but the basic elements of the feat are the same, and the modern French Theseus meets his adversary with all the flourish and skill of his Cretan counterpart.

the bull and the acrobat are shown, but it has been suggested that the two girl assistants in the Knossos fresco performed the same function as the rope in the modern French sport by holding down the bull's head and distracting its attention from the chief acrobat. Their secondary duty was to loose their hold once the acrobat had cleared the dangerous head and stand by to help him escape. This reasonable interpretation is supported by a puzzling terracotta from Koumasá showing two tiny figures clinging to the bull's horns from behind while another swarms up its head from the front, and by the fresco fragment on which a horn clasped tightly under a girl's armpit can be seen. Such assistance as this would make the leap very much easier and safer, but there is ample evidence that it was not always forthcoming, and the acrobat sometimes had to take his chance unaided. On these occasions the encounter between the tribute youths and maidens and the Minotaur probably followed its legendary course in every detail.

Having identified the Labyrinth and the Minotaur, it remains only to be seen if one can conveniently be placed inside the other, for the legend is uncompromising on this point. The bull-monster and his victims must meet in the heart of the Labyrinth: that is,

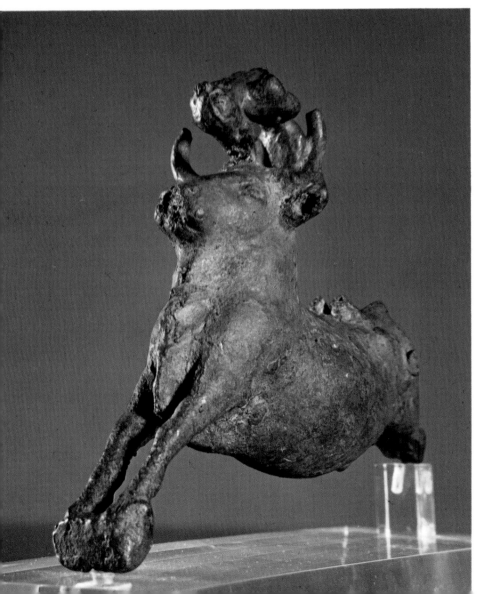

Ills. 130—133. The bull sports seem to have been one of the chief occasions of the Minoan social calendar. The whole court turned out to watch the spectacle (above), the ladies in their bright dresses and jewels (above right) taking pride of place in the audience. A magnificent bronze group (left) and a fresco, rather questionably restored (right), show the climax of the event as a leaper somersaults over a bull.

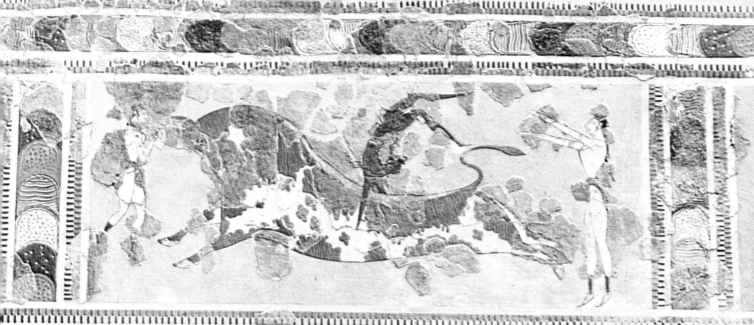

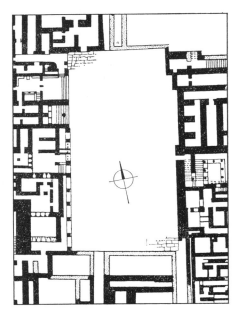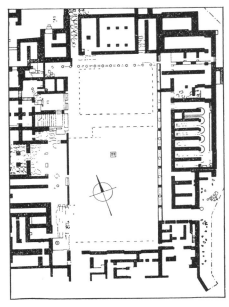

the acrobats must attempt the bull-leap in the middle of the palace. Two of the greatest Minoan scholars of all time, Sir Arthur Evans and J. D. S. Pendlebury, were convinced that the bull sports took place in a wooden enclosure outside the palace, on the level ground to the east of Knossos. Indeed, the idea of manhandling an angry bull into the elegant interior of the Labyrinth might seem to have too much in common with the proverbial bull in a china shop to be feasible. Even if the animal, suitably netted and hobbled, could be carried or dragged into the palace central court, the spectators' troubles would not be over because many of the buildings round the court had wide shallow stairs or open colonnades leading into ceremonial apartments. The bull might easily see such openings as a welcome refuge from his tormentors and make a disastrous incursion into the high priest's shrine or my lady's chamber. However, a temporary wooden palisade large enough to seat the enormous crowds shown on the 'Grandstand' and 'Miniature' frescoes (it looks as if the entire population of Knossos and the surrounding countryside turned out for the spectacle) is almost a contradiction in terms. Uprights of huge size and immensely deep foundations would be needed to support such a structure, and what of the massive painted and carved shrine shown in the middle of the 'Grandstand' fresco? It is hardly likely that this complex arrangement,

Ills. 134—136. The three main palaces differed considerably in over-all size, but the central courts and the areas immediately surrounding them show several striking similarities. The courts of Knossos (left), Phaistos (centre) and Mallia (right) vary by only two or three metres in size.

with terrace upon terrace of steps, seats and shrines and a roof over all (those white-skinned, bare-headed, overdressed beauties could never have consented to expose themselves to the sun), was assembled and dismantled for each performance, or that such a structure could have existed without leaving the slightest discernible trace.

It would indeed be a pity if the legend, having triumphantly dealt with such mountains as the Labyrinth and the Minotaur, should come to grief over a molehill like the location of the encounter, so it is worth devoting some attention to a detailed examination of the problem. The three main palaces of Knossos, Phaistos and Mallia vary in almost every detail of size, shape and disposition except for one constant element: the central court and its immediate surroundings. Whatever the over-all dimensions of the palace or the lie of the land where it stood, the court was always oriented north/south and roughly the same size, Knossos measuring 52 × 24 m., Phaistos 51 × 23 and Mallia 48 × 22. In the case of the two latter this is disproportionately large for the architectural requirements of the building, and it is difficult to avoid the suspicion that these dimensions were adopted to meet some specific need. If we take the optimistic view of the Theseus legend's veracity and

Ills. 134—136

Ills. 137, 138. The problem of confining the bull to the court may have been solved by temporary hurdles installed in the openings. A woman behind such a hurdle is shown on a fresco fragment (left), and the sockets for the uprights are preserved at Mallia (right).

assume that, practical considerations notwithstanding, the bull sports did actually take place within the palaces, we have the beginning of an explanation for this curious similarity.

The loggias, windows, balconies, steps and colonnades round the court would supply a shady vantage point from which even the most pampered palace dwellers could watch the sport without giving up the least of their accustomed comforts, always providing that the bull could be confined to the open space. There are indications that steps were taken to make sure that for the onlookers the bull game ran no risk of becoming anything more than a spectator sport. Sockets and postholes for doors and palisades appear in many places where they have no architectural right to be. At Phaistos, for instance, a large ceremonial hall is separated from the central court only by a pier on either side of a column. This attractively airy arrangement, however, was oddly disrupted by the addition of low walls from the sides to the piers and the installation of a gate or door on each side of the column. The court at Mallia was bounded on the east by a long colonnade of alternate square piers and round columns standing at least two metres apart, which would allow ample room for the bull to escape. The row of stone blocks on which these supports were based is still preserved, and between each of the uprights three small holes, about 3 cm. in *Ill. 138* diameter, have been sunk. They are too far apart to be a deterrent to a human being, particularly one as small as the average Minoan, but a large bull is another matter. If wooden hurdles were set up in these sockets to fill the gaps between the pillars, the colonnade would become a pleasant grandstand from which to watch the show in the court. Mallia has several other structural peculiarities of the same nature, such as gates to close off the steps to the upper storey on the west of the court and cross-walls built halfway across the opening of a passage leading into the south side of the court. In fact, none of the palaces has nearly so open a façade looking on to the court as appears at first. Corridors are few and narrow, sometimes deliberately made so by the addition of a buttress, and many of the surviving open spaces are provided with sockets for hurdles. A fresco fragment from Knossos shows a woman standing behind the *Ill. 137* shelter of just such a hurdle and gesturing excitedly at some unspecified sight.

Ill. 139. The so-called 'Priest-King' from the Knossos fresco looks too young to have held a high place in the civic or religious hierarchy. His loin-cloth, jewels and flowing hair are reminiscent of the appearance of the acrobats, and it may be that the plumed lily crown he wears so proudly was the reward of the successful bull-leaper.

Ills. 140, 141. Representations of the bull sports supply very little information on the site of the encounter. One of the rare clues is furnished by a seal from Priene (above left) which shows an object patterned with crossing bands of diamond shapes, exactly reproduced in a niche on the north side of the central court at Phaistos (left).

Ill. 140 The gem stone mentioned above showing the bull and the acrobat provides another clue. It is one of the rare illustrations of the bull sports representing anything beyond the chief performers. Most works of art show no background at all, or at best a few wavy lines under the animal's feet to indicate the ground, but this gem is distinguished by a curious detail. The bull's forefeet are apparently planted on or in a square object, possibly lower in the middle than at the sides like the 'horns of consecration', or shaped like a letter H when seen from the front. The side of the object is decorated with an edging of diamond-shaped lozenges, and two more lines of diamonds cross diagonally in the middle. Only one other example of this particular design is known in the whole of Cretan art. It is painted in red on the backs of two niches on the

Ill. 141 north side of the central court at Phaistos. The object on the gem is obviously not a niche of any kind, but the design helps to connect it with the general context of the central courts in the middle of the Cretan palaces.

None of this evidence is conclusive, but taken altogether it suggests quite convincingly that the bull sports did, in fact, take place in the very heart of the palace.

The aftermath of the spectacle is more obscure than any other part. The fate of the ritually-conquered bull and the reward of a successful acrobat are not known, but there were probably too few in either category to exercise the artists' imagination very

Ill. 139 thoroughly. Perhaps the proud-stepping young 'Priest-King' in his peacock-plumed lily crown represents one result, and the helpless

Ill. 144 bull lying trussed up to await the sacrificial axe on the offering table of the Hagia Triada sarcophagus is the other. But this, like so many other aspects of Cretan life, can only be speculation. Nevertheless, the basic facts are clear. There was once a Labyrinth at Knossos, in the heart of which a monstrous bull encountered chosen groups of youths and maidens, few of whom can ever have survived to tell the story.

When Theseus left Crete, his biographers found themselves faced with a considerable quandary: they were at a loss for a way to explain his desertion of Ariadne as anything less than a disgraceful and unmanly dereliction of duty, with the result that their stories dealing with this part of his life become very vague and frequently

Ills. 142, 143. The heavy short-legged Cretan bulls could sometimes be hobbled peacefully with the aid of a decoy cow (above), but on other occasions they were trapped in a hunting net, with explosively violent results (left). A pair of exquisite gold cups from a tomb at Vapheio shows both methods of catching bulls.

Ill. 146

Ill. 145

Ill. 147

Ill. 144. If honours and rewards awaited the successful bull-leaper, his conquered adversary may have been reserved for a grimmer fate. A painted sarcophagus from Hagia Triada shows a trussed bull awaiting sacrifice in a shrine.

contradictory. All the islands mentioned in the different variations have yielded signs of Bronze Age occupation, but archaeology cannot offer any evidence either to acquit or to convict Theseus of the charge of heartless opportunism brought against him. The most ingenious of his partisans have only been able to provide him with the traditional *deus ex machina* as an alibi, but this, being beyond the reach of archaeological verification, is unassailable.

Once Ariadne was disposed of, the hero's progress through the islands back to Attica could be described more specifically. Even if he did not actually build a shrine at Delos he could well have stopped there to make offerings, for important votive deposits of ivory have been found under the Artemision. One of these was a plaque bearing the relief figure of a Bronze Age warrior with a huge ox-hide shield shaped like a figure-of-eight and a conical leather helmet plated with boar's tusks. It is not difficult to believe that Theseus danced the Crane Dance to celebrate his escape; the Greeks have always expressed rejoicing this way, and to this day a line of dancers can be seen at any festival, commemorating Ariadne's thread by following each other through the maze of the dance with their hands joined.

Greek literature, both early and late, suggests that Delos was the centre of an important religious cult involving dances and an unusual "horn altar" from a very early date, but no trace has, as yet, been definitely identified as the remains of this monument, which Pausanias regarded as one of the wonders of the ancient world. A curious discovery at Dreros in Crete, however, certainly has some relationship to the cult and may supply a clue as to the construction of the altar. An altar found there in the form of a hollow stone chest had a wooden top (now lost) with a hole in the middle through which the horns of sacrificed animals were dropped. This arrangement (nothing but horns inside and a wall of stones round them) exactly matches the descriptions of Apollo's altar on Delos, although these imply that the altar was actually built of interlaced horns rather than simply being filled with them. The accompanying

Ill. 145. A votive deposit of ivories, including a warrior with a plated helmet and massive shield, shows that religious offerings were made on Delos in the Mycenaean period.

Ill. 146. Remains of a substantial Mycenaean building on Delos show that the island was already an important habitation centre in the Bronze Age.

Ill. 147. Theseus and his companions commemorated their safe arrival in Delos by joining hands to mimic the windings of the Labyrinth and dancing, and their present-day descendants still celebrate joyful occasions such as the annual wine festival at Daphni in the same way.

pottery of the Dreros shrine, with three bronze statuettes and two iron sacrificial knives, indicated a date in the Geometric period, but many elements suggest that the cult was a survival of much earlier beliefs and practices.

The Later Years   7

Anne G. Ward

THE THESEUS STORY after his return to Athens is marked by an inevitable flavour of anticlimax. The most enthusiastic Classical biographers were unable even to agree on the order in which his later escapades took place, and consequently the tale tends to be episodic and scrappy. The hero turns up in association with many other stories where he seems to have no mythological business to be; he is found, for instance, giving burial to the Argive dead, offering sanctuary to the blinded and exiled King Oedipus, and taking part in the voyage of the Argonauts. There are only two possible explanations for this: either he was an intolerable busybody, or the Athenians could not bear to be left out of any good story that happened to be circulating. The evidence to date suggests that there is a modicum of truth in both these hypotheses.

The historians claim that after he mounted the throne on the death of his father, Theseus made several long expeditions, including a campaign against the Amazons. Most of these excursions abroad, like the Trojan War, were probably nothing more heroic in historical fact than commercial rivalries. This may be less romantic than the mythological explanation, but it is considerably more practical, for trade was the lifeline of the Mycenaean communities, and *Ill. 149* without it they could not hope to achieve either the civic prestige or the military power on which their survival depended. Their *Ill. 151* trade was almost exclusively maritime, for all the reliable evidence of contacts and settlements has been found on coastal and river sites, never far from the sea. The backbone of their export trade was provided by their handsome pottery and metal work, but there were also trading colonies all along the Levant where Mycenaean *Ill. 150*

136

Ill. 148. Mycenaean trading exchanges carried their goods far and wide. A gold cup of distinctive Mycenaean design was found at Rillaton in Cornwall, but it should not be assumed that the Greeks themselves ever penetrated as far as Britain.

Ill. 148

craftsmen worked these fragile luxury goods on the spot. Imports included horses, silver and woven fabrics from Anatolia via Troy and the Dardanelles, purple murex dye, ivory and spices from the coast of Palestine, bronze from Cyprus and Canaan, gold, alabaster and faience from Egypt, and amber and liparite from the western Mediterranean. Journeys as far afield as Cornwall have been suggested on the scanty evidence of a gold cup and a dagger, but there is no other proof on which to base so far-reaching an assertion. If I own a piece of Chinese jade, it does not necessarily mean that I have been to China, or that a Chinese has been here to sell it; it could just as well have reached me via innumerable middle-men anywhere along the route from here to China, and the same principle probably applies to the Pelynt dagger and the Rillaton cup. It is true that there were highly productive tin mines in Cornwall and the Mycenaeans needed to import large amounts of tin for their bronze foundries, but there is no evidence that the Cornish mines were worked at such an early date, and the Mycenaeans had several other sources much nearer home. There were tin mines in Etruria and others, very much larger, in the Iberian peninsula. Though there is little evidence of direct contact with Spain (only a few spacer beads and arrowheads), a flourishing trade with the entrepots of Magna Graecia is well attested, and with these resources available it is unlikely that the Mycenaeans would have tackled the unknown seas beyond the Pillars of Hercules.

If Theseus' expedition against the Amazons was really a trading skirmish, there is no need to expend very much thought on the possible historical identity of these bellicose ladies. An ingenious theory has been put forward suggesting that they were actually the Hittites, since this warlike, horse-breeding people lived in the area traditionally attributed to the Amazons, and were in the habit of wearing skirts. This theory, however, does not explain why the story-tellers remembered the skirts which were, in any case, a common form of dress in the eastern Mediterranean, but managed to forget the dense woolly black beards affected by many of the Hittites. We are told that the Amazons were masculine in their behaviour, but surely not to this extent!

The disturbed times towards the end of the Mycenaean age, with their shifting alliances and sudden attacks and betrayals, are probably reflected in the story of Theseus' later years. The last king of Athens was killed in the last quarter of the twelfth century, not by a foreign invader but by raiders from south of the Isthmus, and all the legends are full of traditional wars and rivalries. Calydonia fought against Aetolia, Thebes against Orchomenos, Messenia against Elis, and Athens at various times against Eleusis, the Peloponnese and (with Boeotia) Elis. There is no evidence that there were any foreign attackers on Greek soil during the twenty years on either side of 1200. This is most clearly illustrated at Mycenae, where the rich merchants' houses outside the citadel were burned with their luxurious contents still in them, and some of the buildings inside the fortifications destroyed at the same time. The precipitate abandonment of so many valuable goods indicates a surprise attack, but it is very unlikely that a foreign enemy could have approached Mycenae unseen. There was a look-out post on the mountain behind the citadel. Linear B tablets from Pylos de-

Ill. 149. Although the Athenians attributed the beginning of their monetary economy to Theseus, coinage was unknown in the Bronze Age. Copper ingots may have been used as an exchange unit. This example from a shipwreck off Gelydonia was once thought to be Mycenaean, but its finder now believes that it is Phoenician.

scribe troops guarding the main approach roads to the palace (and we may assume contemporary Mycenae had similar defences). Their numbers and commanders are specified, and even their rations are known—a rather forbidding diet of porridge and figs, with a measure of wine to add savour. No major force could possibly have slipped past all these watchful eyes. A small raiding party might have approached Mycenae at night, and even succeeded in sacking the exposed houses outside the citadel, but the storming of the battlements to get at the buildings inside would require something infinitely more formidable. Add to this the fact that, if these were foreigners, they did not break a single pot or drop a single arrowhead or bury a single dead man, and the inference is obvious: Mycenae was assaulted by its own citizens.

The situation in Greece at this time does not sound very much like the orderly synoecism of the legend, nor do the massive ramparts of the Athenian Acropolis suggest domestic harmony in Attica, so it is perhaps as well that modern research into the constitutional history of Athens indicates that the political measures attributed to Theseus probably did not take place until long after the Dark Ages. If anything like the synoecism ever existed at all, it can possibly be identified as the brief period of peace immediately after the eclipse of Crete, when an alliance of some kind, whether voluntary or forcibly imposed, probably united most of Attica under the leadership of Athens. The frankly piratical enterprises involving Pirithous are much more at home than the benevolent synoecism in this troubled period. Border raids and unexpected alliances were common, and the uproar at the Lapith king's wedding feast no doubt represents another of these reversals (though to do their convivial spirits justice, there were probably few Bronze Age festivities which did not end in an uproar of some sort). As to the centaurs, the mythological existence of these creatures, half horse and half human, may be a measure of the shock sustained by the first inhabitants of the peninsula ever to see men on horseback. The wide grasslands of Thessaly have always been better suited to horse-breeding and cavalry exercise than any other part of Greece, and the home of the centaurs was naturally located in this district.

Among these piratical activities were attempts on various famous beauties of the ancient world; the capture of Helen was briefly successful, but the disastrous pursuit of Persephone ended in the long imprisonment in the underworld which cost Theseus his throne in Athens and, in a later version of the legend, half his posterior. It was told that the ruler of the underworld invited the two heroes to be seated on special thrones to which their flesh instantly adhered so that they could not rise again. When Heracles visited Hades in the performance of his twelve labours he took pity on the imprisoned Athenian, seized him and dragged him by main force from the throne. Theseus was freed, but only at the expense of leaving part of his flesh sticking to the seat. This painful and ludicrous incident the later Athenians, with truly wonderful ingenuity, turned to their own advantage by claiming it as the origin of their young men's slender hips. It has been suggested that the sojourn in Hades was a period of captivity during the course of the wars, but this cannot be reconciled with the Mycenaean rules of war as transmitted by the Homeric poems. The Bronze Age warrior subscribed to no ethical code demanding such unmanly weaknesses as justice or mercy where other people's lives and property were concerned. He had a perfect right to anything he could seize and keep. Hector was in no doubt whatever about his own ultimate fate in the event of a defeat, nor that of his wife and child. Fighting men, present or future, were always killed and women, even the highest born, were enslaved, to be used however their masters saw fit. Theseus as a sort of Bronze Age Richard Coeur de Lion languishing in captivity until ransom or rescue set him free is an idea which would never have entered an ancient Greek head; there were no prisoners of war in Bronze Age Greece.

Ill. 150. Not only raw materials but manufactured articles were brought to Greece from the Levant in large quantities. A bronze figurine found at Tiryns represents a native Syrian god.

The abduction of Helen is one of the few episodes of Theseus' later career for which any concrete evidence can be found, and which has some connections with the earlier setting of the legend, in the period immediately before the eclipse of Crete. A flat-topped hill covered with oak trees in north Attica, now called Kotroni, has been identified as the site of the ancient city of Aphidna, where Theseus hid the young Helen under the care of his mother. The hill-top, which stands 120 m. above sea level and measures roughly 120×100 m., dominates the north-west end of Marathon Lake and one of the routes to Boeotia. When the hill was first

Ill. 151. Contacts with Egypt added an important cultural element to the Bronze Age Aegean, and supply vital evidence for absolute dating. The cartouche of the Seventeenth-Dynasty Hyksos King Khian was found at Knossos.

investigated by a Swedish scholar named Wide in 1894, remains of walls were found associated with a great many fragments of Mycenaean pottery. Two years later the same archaeologist made an even more remarkable discovery some twenty-five minutes' walk from the hill, just south of the river Charadra. This was a large tumulus encircled by rounded stones, some of which were still in position, in which were thirteen Middle Helladic burials. The graves varied in depth and in style, some being plain unlined shafts, some cists lined with stone slabs, and some pithoi laid on their sides. The dead, who had not been cremated, were placed on a layer of pebbles and the pits or jars closed with a flat stone. The grave goods included an obsidian knife and arrowhead and a terracotta sling-bullet, which imparted a somewhat martial air to the burials, as well as gold and silver rings, crystal beads and a large quantity of pottery, all Middle Helladic monochrome and matt-painted ware with simple rectilinear decorations and some incised designs. Oddly enough, there were no bronzes.

This group of contemporary burials may be the aftermath of a battle, and the hill of Aphidna is the only place in the neighbourhood worth attacking. It is impossible to guess at the reason for the raid, but obviously the acropolis must have contained something or someone who supplied a very powerful incentive.

When Theseus turned his back on his home in Athens and retired to Scyros in misanthropic disillusionment, he was not by any means condemning himself to exile in a deserted wilderness, like his Shakespearian counterpart Timon. Scyros is the largest island of the northern Sporades, and the part it plays in a number of legends hints at a distinguished past. Theseus was not the only hero to find temporary sanctuary at the court of King Lycomedes. It was there that Achilles passed that humiliating part of his career when his anxious mother disguised him as a girl to keep him away from the Trojan War. The island is almost entirely occupied by two ranges of inhospitable mountains with a sandy isthmus between them, and is of little use for anything but goat pasturage. The present-day town of Scyros occupies the only really fertile and habitable lowland, which lies on the north-east coast of the island. A rocky acropolis there stands 400 m. above sea level, and it was from this height that Theseus traditionally fell, or was pushed.

All around the foot of the rock spreads a fair extent of good farming land, well watered by the river Kephisos. The inhabitants of the island have never had much choice of living quarters, and it is not really surprising that as long as there have been people on Scyros, this was the site they preferred. There has been little scientific excavation, and early correspondence hints tantalizingly at finds of gold, jewels, pottery, weapons and armour lost or destroyed soon after discovery, which will never now be identified. Recorded excavations have produced a rich harvest, not only of Mycenaean wares but of a wide range of pottery from the neolithic period onwards as well as beads, buckles, fibulae, bracelets, necklaces, swords and some curious gold discs rather like those from Shaft Grave III at Mycenae, but associated with much later pottery (sub-Mycenaean/proto-Geometric). The Bronze Age tradition obviously survived in this obscure Aegean outpost long after the mainland civilizations had disintegrated into decadence and chaos.

No one will ever know the exact historical identity of the warrior whose bones and equipment Cimon brought home to Athens. Even the location of the Classical shrine built to receive these venerated relics is lost apart from a vague reference in Pausanias to a sanctuary near the gymnasium associated with the later Ptolemies.

Cimon's pious pilgrimage was probably motivated more by shrewd calculations of political effect than by genuine veneration for the long-dead lord of Athens, but there are plenty of well-equipped Bronze Age tombs on the island of Scyros, and there is no reason why the relics should not have been at least contemporary with Theseus. The Muse of History has an odd sense of humour, however, and it would be typical of her more unnervingly whimsical aspects if the bones laid to rest with such carefully publicized reverence in the Athenian *heroon* really were those of Theseus. It is by no means beyond the bounds of possibility.

Ill. 152. The name of Theseus was not unknown in the contemporary records of Mycenaean Greece. On a clay tablet from Pylos listing land holdings, the first three signs of the fifth line represent the syllables *te-se-eu*, the Linear B form of Theseus.

8   Theseus in Classical Athens

W. R. Connor

BY THE TIME OF THE ATHENS OF THE PARTHENON, of Aeschylus, Sophocles and Euripides, of Cimon and Pericles, the legend of Theseus had become a part of the daily life of every Athenian. The most admired sculpture and painting of the day commemorated his exploits; the common utensils of the dining room and kitchen bore images of his great deeds. The politicians expounded his virtues and drew upon his life as an example. His festivals provided holidays and recreation. The tragedians found in his legends one of the most abundant sources for Greek drama. Theseus, more than any other man or demi-god, had become the hero of Classical Athens.

And yet this pre-eminence had not always been his. At the beginning of the sixth century BC, a century before the start of the extraordinary age of genius which we call Classical Athens, Theseus was a hero with little honour, even in his own country. To be sure his adventures in the Cretan Labyrinth were widely known and sometimes depicted with great beauty, as for example on the François *Ill. 29* Vase. But even on this extraordinary piece, Theseus has but a small part in the over-all composition of the work and it is mainly his exploits on the Cretan voyage which are portrayed, though he is also shown fighting the centaurs. Apart from this adventure he had as yet little place in poetry or art and was largely neglected and forgotten even in the city in which he was said to have been king, except perhaps by those Athenians whose family, cult or neighbourhood happened to make much of his saga. Veneration of him was particularly strongly rooted in Marathon and the hills that *Ill. 12* surrounded that plain; perhaps there his renown was always secure. But elsewhere his celebrity had not yet grown to its full stature.

The best indication of Theseus' relatively minor role in early Greek legend is provided by the Homeric poems. In the *Iliad* it is not Theseus' descendants who command the Athenian contingent at Troy, but Menestheus, the man who displaced him from his throne. Theseus is mentioned indeed only three times in the *Iliad* and the *Odyssey* and some of these references have been suspected in ancient as well as in modern times as late additions by the ruler Pisistratus or by other Athenians. These suspicions may be groundless, but the comparative rarity of allusions to Theseus is itself striking and paralleled by the subordination of his position in early Greek art. Moreover, no one in Athens boasted that they were descendants of Theseus, though many of the most prominent citizens claimed Ajax or Nestor, Homeric heroes from other states, as their ancestors. Nor was his name ever adopted by any tribe or village of Attica, though lesser heroes were often so honoured.

Yet, gradually, as the sixth century progresses, Theseus' fame and honour grow. He becomes more frequently represented in Athenian art. Festivals become associated with his deeds and he takes on an added splendour in Attic cults. Before the century ends, a whole epic, the *Theseis*, has been composed about him and he has become the most famous of Attic heroes. To what can we attribute this change in Theseus' standing in a little over a century? To answer this question we will have to take a wide view of the role of myth and legend in Greek life and try to understand the tendency to incorporate them not just into art and entertainment but into religion and politics as well. To Greeks of this period what we would call the 'myths' of their past were not fictions but living realities. They could be sources of great pleasure, of laughter and merriment, but they were still profoundly serious, and often highly practical. Thus Pisistratus, driven out of the city after he had seized power, could conceive a plan for his restoration which included a carefully contrived spectacle in which a handsome tall girl named Phye pretended to be Athena escorting him back into Athens. Pisistratus' plan worked, though not solely because of the pageant, for he had already accumulated the power needed to overcome his opponents. Yet Phye's part was still important; she represented Athena and seemed to be a visible indication of the divine favour which Pisistratus enjoyed. Thus the spectacle helped to account for and legitimize Pisistratus' control of Athens. Athena was backing Pisistratus. Who would wish to challenge a leader who had divine support? If we were to speculate about the attitude of many Athenians of this remote period, we would perhaps conclude that as they watched Phye and Pisistratus ride by, the girl was in some sense *identified* with Athena.

When we notice, then, that it is precisely during the rule of Pisistratus and his sons that the Theseus myth begins to grow in popularity and prominence in Athens, we naturally ask whether these rulers did not benefit from and perhaps encourage or even direct this development. Is this another case of Pisistratus' exploitation of the widespread belief in myth? This suspicion can be confirmed by some small but telling details. For example, we are told that Pisistratus had the line: 'The love of Panopeus' daughter, Aegle, tormented Theseus terribly' (fr. 298 Merkelbach and West) excised from one of Hesiod's poems, because it presented Theseus in a bad light. Further it is during the rule of the Pisistratids that we first hear of a special temple dedicated to Theseus. And Simonides, who was the guest of Hipparchus, the son of Pisistratus, was one of the first Greek poets we know to treat Theseus. His poem has perished except for the line, which describes the sail which Aegeus gave Theseus as he went off to Crete, 'Blood red sail dyed with elixir of blossoming ever-green' (Simonides fr. 45 Page), a description so rich in symbolism, so vivid in imagery, that it could not easily be forgotten. Finally, it seems likely that it was in the last years of the rule of the Pisistratids that the epic of Theseus was composed.

These indications of Pisistratid interest in the legends of Theseus are individually slight. But cumulatively they help to confirm our suspicion that Theseus' growth in popularity was encouraged by Pisistratus and the sons who followed him.

The reasons for such encouragement are easy to discern. Theseus was a hero who appealed to all citizens of Attica, had fought for Athens against an overseas despot, and was not tied to one region or one faction. Indeed his exploits were said to have included the creation of a unified Attic state:

When Theseus became King he showed himself as intelligent as he was powerful. In his reorganization of the country one of the most important things he did was to abolish the separate councils and governments of the small cities and to bring them all together into the present city of Athens, making one deliberative assembly and one seat of government for all. Individuals could look after their own property just as before, but Theseus compelled them to have only one centre for their political life—namely, Athens—and, as they all became Athenian citizens, it was a great city that Theseus handed down to those who came after him.

Thucydides II 15

Hence Theseus was a symbol of the unification of Attica into a single political unit. And therein lay his significance for the Pisistratids. Pisistratus himself had first risen to prominence by distinguishing himself in the cause of Attic nationalism—fighting to capture Salamis—and if he had exploited the regional rivalries of Attica in his climb to power, he had maintained himself in control partly by his ability to reconcile widely scattered and divergent segments of the Attic citizenry. He sent judges into the scattered villages and he himself made tours of the outlying districts to inspect everything and settle disputes (Aristotle *Constitution of Athens* 16. 5). He was, in short, like Theseus, a pan-Athenian leader.

As part of this policy of emphasizing and encouraging the unity of Attica, Pisistratus used, as any ancient leader would, myths, cults and festivals. It was under him that the Panathenaia, the annual festival of the union of Attica, was given a splendour which it had hitherto never attained. Every four years it was celebrated with special brilliance. Foreigners came from abroad to witness it and to compete in its contests. A special series of amphorae was produced as prizes, and as publicity for the flourishing Athenian pottery industry. And if in a quiet moment between processions, the all-night vigil, the athletic contests and the barbecue of sacrificial animals, some visitor asked what the origin of this splendid festival was, he would be told that Theseus founded it or at least improved and expanded it, just as Pisistratus had done quite recently.

The perceptive visitor to Athens in this period might hear other stories about the city that implicitly linked the Pisistratids to Theseus. Some he might dismiss as pure coincidence—Theseus' victory over the bull of Marathon had been won in the same area

Ill. 153. Coinage in Pisistratid times bore the ox-head symbol traditionally ascribed to the mythical coins of Theseus. The legend that Theseus introduced coinage has no historical basis, but may have been developed to supply a 'historical' precedent for the beginning of coinage.

Ill. 154. Women with offerings surround a youthful, garlanded Theseus, to whom Athena is holding out her hand. Pisistratus exploited the myths of both Theseus and Athena.

Ill. 153

Ill. 154

that Pisistratus had chosen for his return from exile, around 545 BC. Shortly after that date, Theseus' struggle with the bull of Marathon begins to appear on Attic vases. The victory that Pisistratus and the supporters who had flocked to him at Marathon won over his opponents at Pallene had its ancient exemplar in Theseus' triumph over the mythic heroes of that village, the Pallantids. One wonders, too, whether our hypothetical visitor to Athens would have heard the story about Theseus' coinage which Plutarch later recorded: that Theseus struck coins which bore the image of an ox (Plutarch *Theseus* 25). If so, it would appear that the introduction of coinage which came about in Pisistratus' day was represented as a revival of a practice of Theseus' day rather than as one of the most radical departures in the economic life of the city. The convergence of these stories about Theseus and the practices of Pisistratus was striking, for Theseus seemed to emerge as a mythic model for Pisistratus' rule: a strong, bold and successful ruler of a vigorous Athens, acting with the approval and support of Athens' patron goddess, Athena.

Theseus' exploits abroad were no less congenial to the rulers of sixth-century Athens. A vigorous Athenian foreign policy, aimed at maintaining Athens' power in the Saronic Gulf without excessively

147

antagonizing the other states which bordered on it and at encouraging trade and diplomatic influence throughout Ionia and even beyond, welcomed the precedent of a hero who had destroyed Knossos and Minos' oppressive thalassocracy. Since Theseus was a figure widely admired for this and other exploits, especially among the Greeks of Ionia, his glorification as an Athenian hero could not help but reflect favourably on Athens and its energetic leaders. His exploits, moreover, could provide a mythic tie between Athens and strategic spots in which the city was anxious to increase its influence. The island of Delos is a good example. It was an important religious centre for the Ionian Greeks and the worship of Apollo, and located strategically in the centre of the islands that lay between mainland Greece and the settlements on the coast of what is now Turkey. It was greatly to Athens' advantage to emphasize that Theseus had stopped there on his way back from Crete and had originated a ritual dance called the 'Crane' and instituted games there. A great deal was made of this connection and it was said in the Athens of Socrates' day that when Theseus and his fourteen companions went off to Crete:

Ill. 106
Ills. 16, 146

Ill. 155

Ill. 155. A Geometric hydria from Analatos shows an early version of the 'Crane Dance', a theme which was frequently used to stress the connections between Athens and Delos.

> The Athenians vowed to Apollo then that if the lives of these were saved, they would send a sacred mission every year to Delos; and they do it still, every year ever since that, to honour

148

Ill. 156. An early red-figure kylix shows the Chachrylion Potter's interpretation of the exploits of Theseus. Left to right: Sciron, Cercyon and the Marathon bull.

the god. As soon as the mission has begun, then, it is their law to keep the city pure during that time and to put no one to death before the ship arrives in Delos and comes back again.

Plato *Phaedo* 58 a and b

Indeed this was the embassy which delayed Socrates' execution so long after he was condemned to death. And even after Socrates' time the Athenians showed a thirty-oared galley which was said to have been the boat which Theseus sailed to and from Crete. Scholars have long suspected that the origin of these practices goes back not to the Bronze Age but to a much closer past, for many of them the days of the Pisistratids. In any event, there is an indisputable sign of the influence which Pisistratus exerted in Delos in the reliably attested story that he conducted an elaborate ritual purification of the island by exhuming all bodies buried within sight of the main shrine and reburying them elsewhere.

Likewise Athens' long struggle for security in and around the Saronic Gulf continued during the sixth century, and myth, as we might expect, reflected it. The operations against piracy, for example, of which Hippias, one of Pisistratus' sons, was in charge (Polyaenus V 14), have a mythological counterpart in Theseus' journey from Troezen to Athens during which he destroyed the monsters and

Ills. 5—9, 111, 156

149

robbers along the way—Sinis, Sciron, the Crommyonian sow, Cercyon and Procrustes. The correspondence is not likely to be entirely accidental for the stories of Theseus' exploits during this journey appear in Greek art and literature late in the sixth century, perhaps just at the time of Hippias' operations. Once again we have reasons to suspect that myth was being exploited—even fabricated—for the glorification of the ruling dynasty, and for propaganda among Athens' neighbours.

In the time of the Pisistratids we find some of the earliest examples of the Greek technique of using myth and religion for political purposes. The legends of the past, true or false, ancient or newly invented, performed for the Greeks many of the functions which spectacular feats of technology—Aswan dams and moon flights— fulfil in modern politics: assertions of national pride, and impressive demonstrations of power without excessively blatant intimidation.

But if it is correct that the Pisistratids deliberately utilized the Theseus myth, how did the legends of Theseus retain their influence after their rule had collapsed? The family's hold on power was never quite secure after Pisistratus' death in 528. Unrest became increasingly obvious as the rule of his sons turned gradually from benevolent paternalism to undisguised despotism. And when at the Panathenaic festival of 514 one brother, Hipparchus, was slain by two young nobles, Harmodius and Aristogiton, the rule of the other brother, Hippias, became a hated tyranny. A few years later the Athenian opposition and Spartan intervention brought the dynasty to an end and Hippias fled ignominiously to Persia. The decline in Pisistratid fortunes was rapid and decisive; could we not expect a similar deflation of the Theseus legend?

At first glance it seems there are some signs of just such a process. Theseus' name is not among the heroes after whom the new tribes were named in the reorganization that followed the tyranny. A surprising omission. But the fact that one tribe was named after his son Acamas shows that his exclusion from the list was not due *Ill. 157* to any feeling against Theseus. On the contrary, it may have been because Theseus' reputation as a pan-Athenian figure was too firmly established and too useful to allow him to be tied to any one tribe or section. Whatever the explanation the fact is clear: Theseus' hold on the imagination of the Athenians continued unabated.

Ill. 157. The two sons of Theseus, Demophon and Acamas, are shown escorting their aged grandmother Aethra on a red-figure crater.

Indeed it is only in the very late sixth and early fifth century that the full cycle of Theseus' stories becomes truly popular in Athens. Now (as has been pointed out in Chapter 2), his image constantly appears on Athenian vases and the range of exploits depicted widens. In addition, it was probably in this period that honours to Theseus were introduced into a far earlier fertility cult which invoked the help of the goddess Athena. This festival, the Oschophoria, originally an agricultural rite, now became a national festival commemorating Theseus' departure for and return from Crete. In it two youths carrying branches (a survival of the old fertility rite) headed a procession and played the parts of companions of Theseus, while women brought bread and meat to the port of Phalerum and acted as the parents of the children sent off on the gruesome expedition.

Shortly after the fall of the Pisistratids, then, Theseus is made the centre of a dramatic and popular festival, a role which he could only have attained if the previous exploitation of his legend had not tarnished his appeal. A further indication points to the same conclusion, or rather helps explain Theseus' sustained popularity. He becomes a democratic hero. The figure who a few years before had been a prototype of the dynamic autocracy of Pisistratus and his sons now emerges as the mythic founder of the democratic institutions of Athens. The orator, Isocrates, and other writers of the fourth century BC, believed that Theseus established a democratic form of government which lasted down to the time of Pisistratus. As historical fact such a story has little to commend it—Athens was no democracy before Pisistratus. But the tradition is a revealing one, for it is likely to contain a clue to the attitudes of the Athenians at the time when they were first developing a democracy; that is, in the years following the overthrow of the Pisistratid tyranny. Surely the practice of representing Theseus as a democratic leader goes back to the fifth century, for Euripides in his *Suppliant Women* had made him a constitutional monarch in a city with a strong assembly. In that play Theseus rebukes a Theban herald who has made the mistake of asking, 'Who's the ruler of this land?' as his first question. Theseus explains to him:

> This city is not ruled by a single man, but is quite free. The people are in power taking turns in holding annual offices, and I might add the rich are not given preferential treatment and even the poor man has a fair and equal chance.

These are the clichés of the Athenian fifth-century democracy, of which Theseus by Euripides' day had become the symbol and the representative. Moreover, nothing in the play suggests that presenting Theseus as a democratic politician was a particularly radical innovation by Euripides; rather he seems to be working within an already established tradition that held that Theseus' actions were a precedent for the democratic changes of the fifth century. Thus Theseus, probably quite soon after the end of the tyranny, came to be represented as a democratic leader and institutions were ascribed to him which were in fact sharp departures from preceding Athenian practice.

We can now begin to see more clearly a pattern of political and mythic thinking among the Greeks. Innovations, especially important or radical ones, are frequently represented as reversions to past procedures. Someone 'discovers' that Theseus had instituted coinage or that he had renounced absolute power to become leader of a democracy. The effect of these discoveries is to make acceptable and legitimize new practices and to invest them with the venerable dignity of the past. Later in the century we find a reform movement

Ill. 158

Ill. 158. To emphasize the concept of popular support, the personifications of the people (*Demos*) and democracy (*Democratia*) were sculpted on the top of a stele publishing a decree. The sculptor Euphranor, in his version of this scene, added Theseus, perhaps thereby attesting Theseus' legendary role as the founder of Athenian democracy.

that sought changes in the constitution arguing about what was the ancestral form of government, as if its discovery would solve the problems of contemporary democracy.

Not only Classical literature but also Classical art attests the democratization of Theseus. The fourth-century sculptor Euphranor portrayed him beside a man, Demos (the people) and a woman, Democracy, a sort of father of the bride at the wedding of the people of Athens to their cherished constitution. Even more interesting in their iconography are the earlier sculptures which adorned the temple of Hephaestus overlooking the Agora in Athens. This temple was for long misidentified as the Theseum, Theseus' shrine, but although that label was quite incorrect Theseus does figure prominently on the friezes of this attractive temple of the second half of the fifth century. On the west side Theseus is shown combatting the centaurs, a favourite theme in Athenian art. The east frieze is more difficult to interpret but it probably shows Theseus struggling against the Pallantids, the chief opponents of his rule. But these friezes contain an added iconographical nicety, which reminds the spectator of Theseus' democratic disposition and his opposition to tyranny. The figure that must be identified as Theseus on the east frieze bears a striking remseblance to the tyrannicide Aristogiton

Ill. 158

Ill. 159

Ill. 160

Ill. 161

Ills. 159—161. The temple of Hephaestus on the east of the Athenian Agora is still popularly (though erroneously) known as the Theseum because of the frieze showing the exploits of Theseus, who is tacitly identified with the overthrow of tyranny. The west frieze (below) shows the battle with the centaurs (Theseus is the figure at the extreme left) and on the east frieze (opposite) Theseus, on the left, is fighting the fifty sons of Pallas for the crown of Athens.

and that on the west to Aristogiton's companion, Harmodius, as the two were depicted in a famous group that stood in the Agora of Athens. Thus Theseus, as C. H. Morgan who first noted this similarity remarked, 'appropriates the guise of the historic foes of tyranny' (*Hesperia* 31 [1962] 226). He becomes in posture and in deed the archetypal enemy of despotic rule.

The process by which Theseus came to be a hero of the Athenian democracy was accelerated by a story told about the Battle of Marathon (490 BC). Disagreement with Persia, and then war, followed soon after the overthrow of the Pisistratid tyranny. The invading armies of Darius were eventually forced back, but only after a badly outnumbered Athenian army commanded by Callimachus and Miltiades had stood up against what seemed overwhelming odds. The Greeks fought with passionate frenzy—the brother of the poet Aeschylus had his hand chopped off by a Persian axe when he refused to let go of the prow of a Persian ship that was attempting to escape—and when the battle was over the Greek victory seemed as miraculous as it was joyous. Stories of divine assistance began to circulate and were believed and regarded as signs of the greatness of the Athenian success—for the Greeks never felt that the assistance of a hero or god belittled human accomplishment. The excitement and confusion of a hard-fought battle, moreover, were perfect for the growth of conjecture and legend. Pan was said to have appeared, and a strange rustic figure was said to have slaughtered many of the

invaders with a plough. The Athenians concluded he must have been a divinity and accorded him appropriate worship. And 'many of those who fought at Marathon against the Medes thought they saw a vision of Theseus in arms rushing on in front of them against the barbarians' (Plutarch *Theseus* 35). The story that Theseus had once again appeared on the plain where long before he had fought the Marathonian bull and where he had for long been venerated very quickly spread and with it Theseus' reputation as a protector of his city.

The story of his appearance at Marathon, his appeal as a pan-Athenian figure, his utility as a mythic precedent for the innovations of an emerging democracy combined in the first decades of the fifth century to ensure for Theseus a continued prominence in the legends of his city.

Once again Classical Athenian art responded to political and historical events in the world around it. Old legends were remodelled and given new significance. In the aftermath of the Persian invasion this happens to the tale of Theseus' battle with the Amazons. His exploits with these barbarian women warriors had long been sung — a fine story of exciting adventures with a dash of romance, especially in the episode in which Theseus carried off one of the Amazons,

Ill. 162. To the Classical Greeks, the Amazons represented barbarian invaders from the east, and Theseus' victory recalled their own defeat of the Persians.

Ills. 18, 47

Antiope, with whom he had fallen in love. But now, after the Persian attacks, the Amazon myth was seen in a new light. It appeared as a prototype of the more recent barbarian attack which the Athenians had just warded off. The legend metamorphoses. No longer is the stress on Theseus' invasion of the Amazons' country, but on the Amazons' incursion into Attica. And Theseus is no longer a swashbuckling adventurer but the defender of his beleaguered city. Tourist guides in ancient Athens pointed out in the centre of the city spots where he was alleged to have driven back the invaders:

> the left wing of the Amazons extended to what is now called the Amazoneum and . . . with their right they touched the Pnyx . . . with this left wing the Athenians fought, engaging the Amazons from the Museum . . . the graves of those who fell are on either side of the street which leads to . . . the Peiraic gate . . .
>
> Cleidemus in Plutarch *Theseus* 27

Ills. 162, 173   In art Theseus is frequently the protector of the city battling off barbarian Amazons.

One of the principal contributors to the Athenian victory over the Persians was Miltiades; his son, Cimon, came to be one of the chief architects of the Theseus myth for subsequent generations of Athenians. Like his father, Cimon was a brilliant general and a clever politician. He rose rapidly to prominence in the first years of the operation of the league which many Greek cities set up after the Persian Wars to harass the Persians and ward off the threat of further invasions. Since many of the members of the league were Ionians, it was natural that it should have its headquarters in the religious centre of Ionia, the island of Delos. Since Athens was the principal military power in the league, it was equally natural that it should take on a great role in its affairs. Its generals, among them Cimon, helped shape this Delian league and soon won for it a spectacular series of successes—the enemy was driven back, subject cities were freed, and as useful by-products of its expeditions captives for slaves and booty for the treasury were won. No less important, the league encouraged trade by suppressing piracy in the Aegean and by ensuring fair treatment of commercial disputes among its members.

It was after an outbreak of piracy in the northern Aegean that Cimon moved to eliminate the pirates on the island of Scyros. Once this was accomplished he remembered a legend that Theseus had ended his days on that island. It was said that he was driven out of Athens by the usurper Menestheus and later murdered by the king of Scyros. The Athenians, moreover, had received an oracular response from Delphi bidding them to bring home the bones of Theseus and to honour him with splendour befitting a hero. To Cimon it must have seemed that nothing could be more appropriate than for the son of the victor of Marathon to bring back the relics of the hero who had helped Athens win that victory. Always sure of his cleverness, Cimon began the search for the bones.

He had good luck, or perhaps he would have said he had the cleverness to recognize and take advantage of divine assistance. When one day he saw an eagle clawing at a mound of earth he moved quickly to excavate. The mound turned out to be a tomb—perhaps *Ill. 163* a Mycenaean tholos tomb—which contained a skeleton of extraordinary size with bronze spear and sword. Under such circumstances *Ill. 164* who would wish to be sceptical? Clearly Theseus' bones had been found and the oracle could now be obeyed.

The sequel to Cimon's archaeological foray on Scyros is highly revealing about both Greek religious practice and ancient politics. When the remains were brought back to Athens, the citizens were, predictably, enthusiastic and received them 'with splendid processions and sacrifices, as though Theseus himself were returning to his city' (Plutarch *Theseus* 36). But the enthusiasm of the Athenians did not stop there. The celebration was institutionalized and an annual feast, the Theseia, added to the state festival calendar. The feast was to be celebrated immediately after the Oschophoria, a rite into which as we have seen honours for Theseus had already been introduced. A great series of Theseus celebrations thus filled the calendar in the early autumn of every Athenian year.

Several inscriptions that once were set up around the ancient temple of Theseus and, although broken, have survived to modern times tell us a good deal about the form this festival ultimately took. We know, for example, that in the second century BC it included a tattoo in which Athenian soldiers, trumpeters and heralds demonstrated their expertise, as well as wrestling and boxing

Ills. 163, 164. Cimon's expedition to Scyros may well have found one of the many surviving Bronze Age tombs, perhaps a tholos (left). These tombs often contained skeletons, with weapons and armour by them (right).

matches, horse races, torch races, long-distance races, shorter races, races in heavy armour, and a special race for the commanders of the various divisions of the army.

We also have on these stones records of the expenses that the wealthy citizens assigned to finance the festival had to pay out. These expenses often totalled two or three thousand drachmae, a very considerable sum.* To be sure the fifth-century festival may have been less elaborate than these later extravaganzas, but it was surely a splendid and popular affair: a holiday, a chance to eat free meat from public sacrifices, a fiesta, and, not least, an annual reminder of Cimon's great success and good service to the city.

It was only appropriate, of course, that the relics which Cimon brought back should be preserved in a shrine of appropriate beauty and dignity. Hence shortly after his triumphal return a new Theseum rose near the centre of Athens to house the bones and serve as a public building for a multitude of purposes—a council chamber, a meeting place for boards and casual gossipers, an armoury for troops mustering for expedition, and a refuge for slaves and the poor. It

* The exact monetary equivalent of the drachma in Classical Athens is difficult to determine but an idea of its value can be deduced from the fact that in the fifth century BC the standard pay for jury duty was a third of a drachma a day. This was probably a subsistence allowance.

was decorated with three paintings by Micon commemorating three
great deeds of Theseus: first his battle with the Amazons, then the
fight between the Lapiths and centaurs in which Theseus assisted   *Ill. 165*
the Lapiths and finally Theseus' dive into the palace of his father
Poseidon to recover a ring which Minos threw into the sea.   *Ill. 166*

The building and decorating of the Theseum, his fame in poetry
and the plastic arts, and the annual festival in his honour all brought
Theseus to a pre-eminence among Athenian heroes. And much of the
splendour which surrounded him reflected back on Cimon. For just
as Edward I found, in 1278, that the bones discovered in Glastonbury
Abbey in 1190 could, when identified as King Arthur's, be used to
support his claims to Scottish and Welsh overlordship, so Cimon
found that the Theseus myth could contribute to his political success.
'This was the chief reason the people took kindly to him' says
Plutarch (*Cimon* 8).

The next few years bear testimony to the measure of Cimon's
success. He was frequently returned to the generalship, an elective

Ill. 165. The central medallion
of a kylix by the Foundry Painter
from Vulci shows a heavily-armed
Theseus killing a centaur during
the battle at Pirithous' wedding
feast. This subject was illustrated
by Micon in one of the three
paintings which decorated the
Theseum.

160

Ill. 166. Theseus' connection with the gods helped to enhance his popular prestige and that of the statesmen who hoped to be associated with him. A red-figure kylix shows him visiting the undersea palace of his divine father Poseidon (with the trident). This was another of the scenes depicted by Micon on the Theseum.

office in Athens, and justified his elections with steady and sometimes spectacular victories. Moreover a rivalry with Themistocles, his most prominent competitor, was resolved by another success for him—the ostracism of his rival for ten years. One clue exists which suggests that even in this contest the Theseus myth played some part. Admittedly, the chronology is disputed and the evidence is not as full as one might hope, but there is a highly suggestive detail. In one version of the story of the last years of his life, Theseus is made a victim of the democratic institutions which he founded. He is said to have been attacked by a demagogic politician named Lycus who was largely responsible for his expulsion and Menestheus' usurpation. This version cannot be traced with certainty back before the fourth century BC but one detail points to an earlier date and to an association with this ostracism of Themistocles. That is the name Lycus. The mythical Lycus was presumably a member of the royal family which was displaced when Aegeus came to the throne. He was therefore someone who had strong reasons for wishing Theseus out of Athens. An Attic drinking bowl painted in the red-figure style and datable not far from the ostracism of Themistocles shows on one side Theseus slaying the Minotaur and on the other Lycus and some of his brothers complacently chatting. As so often on Greek vases the two sides are closely related; in this case the one side, Theseus' victory over the Minotaur, is an ironic comment on the other, the insouciance of Lycus and his brothers. Like the suitors in the *Odyssey* they misjudge their young opponent and find out too late what sort of a man he is. But the most interesting point about the name Lycus is not its appearance on this vase, but its occurrence as the name of the founder of one of Athens' most prestigious and powerful clans, the Lycomidae. And the best known member of that clan in the fifth century was Themistocles. It is difficult to know the extent to which mythological propaganda affected the political decisions of Athenian citizens, but it is clear that it often played a role in their thinking. A mythological reminder that Themistocles belonged to a group whose founder was a self-seeking opponent to a benign and devoted leader may have had a place in anti-Themistoclean propaganda.

A decade after this ostracism Cimon himself was to find his policies becoming unpopular and then watch the potsherds with his name inscribed on them accumulate against him in another ostracism. But Cimon was recalled from exile after only a few years and reassumed a respectable place in the city. Shortly after his return two major artistic projects were undertaken which reflect a continued interest in Theseus and perhaps also a sustained effort to use his myth for political purposes. Both works—the decoration of the Stoa Poikile in Athens and a group of statues sent by the Athenians to Delphi—depict the Battle of Marathon and Cimon's father, Miltiades. In each Miltiades is given full, perhaps even excessive, credit for his role in the battle. Further, both depict Theseus and in both iconographical clues suggest that Cimon's hand was behind them.

Let us consider each work separately. The Stoa Poikile received its name from the four paintings within it: (1) the Battle of Marathon, including Miltiades and Theseus; (2) Polygnotus' portrayal of the Greeks after the capture of Troy; (3) the Athenians led by Theseus fighting the Amazons; and finally (4) a battle between Athenians and Spartan troops at Oinoe near Argos. The back wall of the stoa held the two mythological scenes, Troy and the Amazons, and the two fifth-century battles, Marathon and Oinoe. The prominence given to Miltiades in the former battle was surely congenial to Cimon and his supporters. In addition one detail hints that Cimon's

Ill. 167

Ill. 167. A potsherd (*ostrakon*) bearing the name of Cimon, son of Miltiades, as a candidate for ten years political exile: ostracism.

Ill. 168. An amphora by Exekias shows Acamas and Demophon, the sons of Theseus, with the names of popular favourites inscribed about them.

Ill. 168

interest in this stoa was far more specific. When Polygnotus painted the Greek leaders after the victory at Troy he worked into his picture the likeness of Cimon's sister Elpinice. The Hellenic princes were surrounded by captive Trojan women, one of whom, Laodice, resembled Elpinice (Plutarch *Cimon* 4). Thus like, Benozzo Gozzoli painting the likenesses of the Medici into the *Procession of the Magi* for the Palazzo Medici in Florence, Polygnotus paid a compliment and acknowledged the connection between his work and the house of Cimon, a powerful and generous patron. Nor was his choice of Laodice as the woman who should be made to resemble Elpinice entirely random. For Laodice, a daughter of King Priam and Queen Hecuba of Troy, had had a love affair during the long siege of the city with one of the Greeks, a son of Theseus. She had indeed borne him a son, named Mounitos. Considering the frequent allusions to the Theseus legend by the house of Cimon such a selection was clever and appropriate.

The second project in which Cimonid utilization of the Theseus myth can be detected is a dedication of statues which the Athenians sent to Delphi. The date is uncertain but it was perhaps not long after the completion of the paintings of the Stoa Poikile, that is, in the 450s BC. The statues, which commemorated the victory at Marathon, were by a relatively young man who was to become the most famous sculptor of his day, Phidias. The tendency we have seen in earlier treatments of the battle, to laud and exalt Miltiades, is now complete. He stands apart from all other mortals with only gods and heroes for company. He was grouped with Athena and Apollo at one side of the monument. The middle section consisted of statues of the heroes after whom the Athenian tribes were named, and at the far end another group of three figures balanced Miltiades and his divine friends. This triumvirate consisted of Theseus, and a later king, Codrus, whose descendants were the legendary founders of many of the Ionian cities that belonged to the Delian league. In our only description of the monument (Pausanias X, 10), the name of the third figure in this group is corrupt, but an easy and convincing emendation is almost surely correct, Philaios. This name, too, ties this project to Cimon, for Cimon was connected to a clan which was named after and allegedly founded by Philaios, some fifteen generations before. At almost the same time that Phidias was working on these statues, Pherecydes of Athens was publishing a work that traced Cimon's family connections back to Philaios, and then ultimately to Zeus, for Philaios was a son of the Homeric hero Ajax, hence a great-grandson of Zeus. The inclusion of Philaios in the monument, like Polygnotus' introduction of Elpinice's features into the mural in the Stoa Poikile, tells us much about the origin and intention of the work. The statues are in honour not just of a great Athenian triumph, but more specifically in praise of the clan to whom that victory was largely due. The earliest and the most recent leaders of that clan, the Philaids, were represented at opposite sides of the monument, Miltiades and Philaios. Cimon himself is missing, as good taste would dictate, but the monument is no less eloquent an advertisement of his claims to leadership for being discreet.

When we read today of these transparent efforts to use myth and religion for the purposes of individual, group or national aggrandizement we are often surprised, incredulous and sometimes mildly shocked. The deliberate exploitation of myths and religion seems deplorable even to us who are not committed to belief in them. Is this really the way the Golden Age of Greece treated its legends? Was cynicism so rampant?

Cicero's famous comment that he was always surprised that two Roman soothsayers did not burst out laughing when they passed each other on the street reminds us that some ancients were well aware that popular belief and piety could be crassly manipulated. And no doubt deliberate falsifications and flagrant distortions did take place. But we must also remember that the Greeks (and Romans) did not draw the sharp distinctions between the sacred and the secular which we do and that many of them had rather less rigorous conceptions than we about the criteria for determining the truth or falsity of legends. As Thomas Mann pointed out in his essay 'Freud and the Future':

> The ego of antiquity and its consciousness of itself was different from our own, less exclusive, less sharply defined . . . The Spanish scholar Ortega y Gasset puts it that the man of antiquity, before he did anything, took a step backward, like the bull-fighter who leaps back to deliver his mortal thrust. He searched the past for a diving bell, and being thus at once disguised and protected might rush upon his present problem . . . Alexander walked in the footsteps of Miltiades; the ancient biographers of Caesar were convinced, rightly or wrongly, that he took Alexander for his prototype. But such 'imitation' meant far more than we mean by the word today. It was a mythical identification, peculiarly familiar to antiquity, but in operation far into modern times . . .
>
> Thomas Mann

Cimon, like Pisistratus before him, understood mythic identification in a way that is often hard for us to comprehend. Theseus, to use Mann's metaphor, was his diving bell, his step back before the thrust. In this respect he was not so much cynic as man of his age, for in Greece, especially down to the time of Socrates, myth was the language of domestic and international politics and a living reality which affected all aspects of life. The past, however remote, was not dusty remnants of value and interest only to antiquarians; rather, as Pindar's poetry shows, it was a storehouse of patterns, individual and national, desirable and undesirable. And it would appear that in the formation of individual character the exploration and selection of a model, real or mythic, contemporary or historic, played at least as important a role as the characteristically Hellenic gnomic injunctions of didactic poetry or any more abstractly intellectual activity. When we find a figure in ancient history emphasizing one myth, then, it is likely that he is affirming thereby something fundamental about the patterns of behaviour and even the policies which he intends to follow. Cimon's frequent utilization of the Theseus myth is, I believe, of this sort. The legends of Theseus symbolized his policy—Athenian prowess on the sea, opposition to marauders and robbers, and obstinate hostility to the barbarian invaders. And Cimon, whatever vanity or silliness we may find in him, lived this policy and died following it, in 451 on a naval expedition against the Persians.

In the years following his death, Persia moved gradually to the periphery of Athens' concerns in foreign policy and Sparta came increasingly closer to the centre. This Dorian city in the southern Peloponnese felt itself threatened by Athens' growing power, especially by the ever-tightening grip which was moulding the Delian league into an Athenian empire. Rivalry between the two cities intensified until eventually in 431 the long, exhausting Peloponnesian War broke out. One might contend that this rivalry between Athens and Sparta found its mythological reflection in the tendency to assimilate the myths of Theseus and the Dorian Heracles or indeed to assert, as Isocrates does, that the Athenian hero was no inferior of the Dorian:

The fairest praise that I can award to Theseus is this—that he, a contemporary of Heracles, won a fame which rivalled his. For they . . . followed the same pursuits, . . . they cherished also kindred ambitions; for they alone of all who have lived before our time made themselves champions of human life. It came to pass that Heracles undertook perilous labours more celebrated and more severe, Theseus those more useful, and to the Greeks of more vital importance.

Isocrates *Helen* (X) 23—24

It was a very old tendency in Greek art and thought to juxtapose the two heroes. On a Corinthian bowl, for example, dated early in the seventh century BC, Theseus and Heracles are set together, *Ill. 169*

166

Ill. 169. Theseus slaying the Minotaur appears alongside Heracles wrestling with Achelous on a faded seventh-century Corinthian bowl. (The Athenians were anxious to use Theseus to displace Heracles as a popular hero.)

Ills. 170—173

Heracles struggling with the river deity Achelous, Theseus with the Minotaur. The parallelism between their legends continues as time goes on; both heroes fight the Amazons, both capture rampaging bulls. And as might be expected in Athenian art during the fifth century there is a tendency for the exploits of Theseus to displace those of Heracles, as Athenian national pride asserted itself.

Yet Theseus' growth, sometimes at Heracles' expense, is not the most interesting development in the years near the start of the Peloponnesian War. Rather it is his apparent absence in a work where he might be very much expected. Not long after Cimon's death, Athens, at Pericles' instigation, began a huge building programme, financed largely with funds drawn from the treasury of the Delian league. Much of what we see on the Acropolis of Athens today was part of that programme: the monumental gateway, some of the smaller temples, and the Parthenon itself. For the interior of the Parthenon Phidias was commissioned to build a gold and ivory statue of Athena. The result must have been one of his greatest masterpieces, an awesome, overpowering figure according to the ancient writers who describe it. The gilded silver shield which leaned beside the great goddess Athena had embossed on it the representation of the battle with the Amazons which Plutarch describes in this fashion:

When he [Phidias] wrought the battle of the Amazons on the shield of the goddess, he carved out a figure that suggested

167

Ills. 170—173. As time progressed, the feats of Theseus which paralleled those of Heracles were increasingly stressed. Heracles is said to have fought the Cretan bull (above left) which fathered the Minotaur, and in some versions this was the very same beast that Theseus mastered at Marathon (above right). In the black-figure portrayal of Heracles' battle with the Amazons (below left) the barbarian aspect of the invaders is not so strongly emphasized as it is in the Theseus encounter (below right).

himself as a bald old man lifting on high a stone with both hands, and also inserted a very fine likeness of Pericles fighting with an Amazon. And the attitude of the hand, which holds out a spear in front of the face of Pericles, is cunningly contrived as it were with a desire to conceal the resemblance, which is, however, plain to be seen from either side.

Plutarch Pericles 31,

The statue and all its accoutrements have long since disappeared, but enough copies and adaptations of the shield were made in late antiquity to allow us to see what Plutarch meant. On one of the clearest of these adaptations, the Strangford Shield in the British Museum, we can see a highly individualized bald-headed man slaying an Amazon, albeit with an axe rather than with a stone; next to him stands another boldly impressive figure whose pose coincides with Plutarch's description of Pericles. *Ill. 174*

Figures corresponding to Phidias and Pericles are thus plainly visible upon the shield, but if Plutarch is right, where is Theseus? Surely he would be conspicuous in any Athenian representation of one of his greatest exploits. Admittedly the copies and adaptations of the shield vary a good deal and scholars continue to disagree about the exact arrangement of the original. But almost all assign to the figure which we have identified as Pericles a dominant place in the composition. We expect this figure, if any, to be Theseus. Is it he, or is it Pericles? Or is it both, Theseus appearing as, and identified with, Pericles?

What we have already seen about the Athenian use of mythic identification makes it very likely, I believe, that the last of these is the correct answer. The use of myth as a prototype and justification for innovation, its function as a repertory of character types and models gave it an extraordinary role in the formation of personality in the age of Classical Athens. But its significance did not stop there. For the artist it provided a means of transcending the usual conventionalizations of reality, of breaking down the barrier between present and past, and of revealing the present as the renewal of the past. Thus Phidias could conceive of Pericles as a new Theseus and himself as his ally. The shield of Athena is then a great compliment by the artist to the man who made his work possible, almost as

Ills. 174, 175. The crowning glory of Classical Athens, Phidias' gold and ivory statue of Athena was subtly used to associate Pericles with Theseus and both with the city's greatest achievements. A copy of the goddess' shield (right) shows Theseus-Pericles battling with the Amazons accompanied by an incongruous bald-headed man sometimes identified as Phidias, and the hero also appeared on the throne of the great Zeus statue at Olympia, reproduced on a fifth-century gem (below).

extravagant praise as he had paid to Miltiades when he surrounded his statue with the gods and heroes of Athens. Yet simultaneously it is a challenge to be as Theseus was: the bold protector of a unified Attica and a hero not only for Athens but for all Greece.

Once more, late in his life, Phidias returned to the Theseus myth. He had left Athens: suspected of peculation and disliked in some quarters for his close association with Pericles, he had chosen to go to the Peloponnese where a commission for another major statue awaited him. There, in Olympia, where Zeus was honoured with cults and games, he spent the early years of the Peloponnesian War at work on a statue of that divinity, seven times the size of a man, made of the most expensive material—gold, ivory, ebony—and decorated with jewels. Zeus was seated on his throne with his eagle by him, gleaming among the shadows, filling the whole temple with a sense of his presence. Again the materials were too valuable and too easily plundered for this statue to survive to modern times, but there is a possibility that we will be able to form some adequate impression of it not only from ancient descriptions and copies but also from some extraordinary finds made by the excavators of Olympia. A sculptor's workshop of the last third of the fifth century has turned up, and with it a goldsmith's hammer, bits of bone and ivory, a smelting furnace and a cup bearing the inscription, 'I am Phidias's'. Recent reports indicate that within this workshop moulds have been found that look as if they might have been used for pounding and shaping sheets of gold. Thus, though the statue has disappeared, the workshop and some of the tools may have survived and may yet tell us more about this extraordinary statue.

Ill. 177

Ill. 178

Ill. 176

Since Phidias was in the employment of the enemies of Athens it could not be expected that an Athenian hero would have a very prominent place in his work. Yet Theseus *is* present, much in the same way he was present in the work on the Acropolis at Athens. He is not, to be sure, the central figure, but he has an important role in the work none the less. On one of the wide panels that ran between the legs of the huge throne of Zeus, Phidias contrived an elaborate Battle of the Amazons in which Theseus and Heracles fought as allies (Pausanias V, xi, 4). Although some precedent for this juxtaposition could be found in early Greek epic, it was a bold choice for an Athenian artist at work in Peloponnesian territory during wartime, and a highly expressive one as well. It symbolized the hope for reconciliation between the divided factions of Greece and expressed a message not unlike that which the sophist Gorgias is said to have articulated in a speech at Olympia given at approximately this time, that Greek cities should turn their weapons not against one another but against the barbarians in Persia.

This portion of the throne can be seen then as a call for unity and concord among all Greeks. The statue of itself conveyed the same feeling, it would seem, for the divinity was not the thunderbolt wielding warrior but a lofty and reconciling father. This aspect of the statue still impressed the preacher and rhetorician of the early second century AD, Dio Chrysostom. In his 'Olympian Oration' he conjectured what Phidias would have said about his own work and concluded that it would be this eagerness for reconciliation which Phidias would emphasize:

But our Zeus is a god of peace and universal compassion, *guardian of a Greece that is united in concord.* The intelligent and noble city of Elis and my own skill have depicted the god, gentle and yet awesome, whose presence is blessedness, the giver of all good things, father, saviour and protector of all men.

Dio Chrysostom XII 74f.

Dio has perhaps universalized Zeus' compassion beyond the limits that men of the fifth century might have imposed when he makes him the protector of *all* men, not just of Greeks. But his conception of the statue accords fundamentally with Phidias' decision to bring together the two great heroes, Theseus and Heracles, in a work that implicitly appealed for peace and reconciliation between the opponents in a brutal and senseless conflict.

That same theme is made explicit in a work of Euripides which was also approximately contemporary with Phidias' statue. The *Heracles Driven Mad* is a play of violence and of revenge gone wrong, and ultimately of reconciliation and humanity. Heracles at the opening of the play is off on his labours, having left his wife, father and children in Thebes where, in his absence, a usurper named Lycus has seized the throne. The opening scenes are pure melodrama, as a villainous Lycus threatens to kill the innocent children of Heracles. Just in the nick of time Heracles appears, learns of Lycus' plan and goes off stage to kill the villain. But here the action takes a strange turn. Iris and Madness appear on stage and announce Hera's intention to drive Heracles insane and force

Ills. 176—178. The great gold and ivory statue of Zeus at Olympia, one of the seven wonders of the ancient world, was made by Phidias in Olympia after his banishment from Athens. Striking evidence of his presence has been found during the excavation of a workshop of the period (below centre). A cup bearing the name of Phidias (below left) identifies the complex, where tools, a furnace (below right), moulds and left-over scraps of ivory shed light on the sculptor's working methods and on the appearance of the vanished statue.

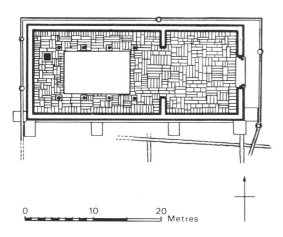

him to kill his own sons. The killing he has begun with Lycus cannot be stopped until he has slain his own children. Then a dazed Heracles slowly learns from his father what he has done, turns from exultation to despair and contemplates his own destruction. This is the second moment of desperation in the play, and once again it is followed by the arrival of a new character, this time Theseus. The two heroes are presented as friends and allies, as they were on the Olympia throne, and Theseus predictably tries to console the mighty hero who has fallen so low. But the means which he adopts are surprising and unconventional, for he violates some of the strongest religious scruples of the Greeks as he uncovers Heracles to the bright rays of the sun and, despising all the taboos of ritual purity, takes him by the hand:

> Heracles: Why have you exposed me to the sun?
> Theseus: Why? You're human; you can't pollute the gods.
> Heracles: Leave me, you fool, I am a blasphemous contagion.
> Theseus: No harm can come to friends from friends.
> *Heracles Driven Mad* 1231—1234

At last Theseus persuades Heracles to come and be honoured in Athens and to live there as his friend, and the two men quietly, sadly, walk off stage. There is no apotheosis of Heracles or of Theseus, no ranting against the gods or the violent folly of men, no trite resolution of the conflicts of the dramatic action. But there is in this simple act of friendship between two fallible men something profoundly human, and hence profoundly Greek. Heracles, who knows what sort of man he has met, says all that can be said as he turns to leave the scene of his sufferings:

> Oh father, choose a man like this for friend.
> *Heracles Driven Mad* 1404

9　The Roman and Medieval Theseus

Simon Tidworth

THE DEGREE OF BELIEF which the Classical Greeks accorded to their gods and the myths in which they figured varied, as we have seen, and is practically impossible for a modern reader to assess. Aristophanes could use the myths as subjects for burlesque, and their humour must have depended upon a certain degree of serious belief; and although Plato wished to discredit them for moral reasons he refrained from dismissing them wholesale. With the Romans we are on slightly firmer ground and we can be certain that by the first century BC, when Latin literature was assuming the mantle of Greece, sophisticated Romans regarded the story of Theseus as an amusing old folktale, useful as a framework for poems and plays and capable of arousing pity and terror if properly handled, but not much more than that.

In the realm of the imagination it has continued to exert its fascination, every age dwelling upon those aspects that seem to answer its own particular preoccupations. It is in order to follow these changing interpretations as clearly as possible that I have concentrated on the central episodes of the myth—Theseus' journey to Crete, the birth and death of the Minotaur, the abandonment of Ariadne and the story of Phaedra and Hippolytus—and ignored almost all the rest. Theseus' other adventures—the Amazons, Daedalus and Icarus, Bacchus (Dionysus) . . . all these are relevant to the theme, but would lead us too far afield. They do not have the unity that belongs to the Cretan episodes, and their interest for later ages has been comparatively superficial.

Of the Roman writers who were drawn to the Theseus story, the three most important are Catullus, Ovid and Seneca. Catullus comes first in time; his longest surviving poem (LXIV) is a lyrical description of the wedding of Peleus and Thetis, and a great part of it is devoted to a coverlet upon which is embroidered a picture of Ariadne abandoned on Naxos. In a sort of flashback the poet tells the story of Theseus' visit to Crete, how Ariadne fell in love with him, how he killed the Minotaur ('tossing his horns to the idle wind'—*vanis iactantem cornua ventis*) and how they fled together to the place where she now—in the picture—cries after him. Catullus then gives her a long lament, the gist of which is that no man is to be trusted. Then, in a flash-forward, as it were, comes the end of Theseus' voyage, his neglect of the sails, and the death of Aegeus. In another part of the embroidery are Bacchus and his train approaching, beating timbrels, clashing cymbals, blowing horns—the signal of the imminent joy that will soon console Ariadne for the loss of Theseus.

Ovid relied heavily on the whole body of Greek mythology to create his dream-world of prettiness and magic, a conception that characterized the whole subject for centuries. He uses most of the Theseus adventures, often several times. In *Metamorphoses* Book VIII he tells the story of Minos and Pasiphaë, and of how Daedalus built the Labyrinth to conceal the Minotaur, 'deceiving the eye by a conflicting maze of divers winding paths', so that he himself was baffled to find a way out again. Theseus and Ariadne are here described very summarily, and Ovid passes to a vivid description of the death of Hippolytus, as described by himself after his miraculous recovery.

The *Heroides* are a series of poetic epistles from unhappy women to their (mostly) unfaithful lovers. The tenth is that of Ariadne to Theseus. She describes with pathetic feeling how she awoke and looked vainly for him, running along the shore, shouting his name. She can do nothing: *Quid faciam? Quo sola ferar?* She reproaches him by recalling her services to him at Knossos: 'Are my bones to lie unburied, the prey of hovering birds of the shore?'

Heroides IV is a letter from Phaedra to Hippolytus. She has tried to speak to him, but her courage has failed; she now resolves to write. She cannot master her passion: Theseus and Theseus' son have been the undoing of her sister and herself—*Thesides Theseusque duos rapuere sorores*. She describes how she first saw Hippolytus,

Ills. 179, 180. Right, Ovid's poems turn the myths, including the Theseus cycle, into charming and pathetic human stories, and as such they were enjoyed throughout late Classical and Medieval times. These two illustrations are from sixteenth-century manuscripts of his *Heroides*: right, Ariadne abandoned by Theseus and, far right, Phaedra giving Hippolytus the letter in which she declares her love. The gaunt nude figure is still completely Gothic in convention, reminding us of Eve, Vanitas or the resurrected souls in a Last Judgement, but the cap, necklace and shoes give her a touch of eroticism.

Ill. 179

Ill. 180

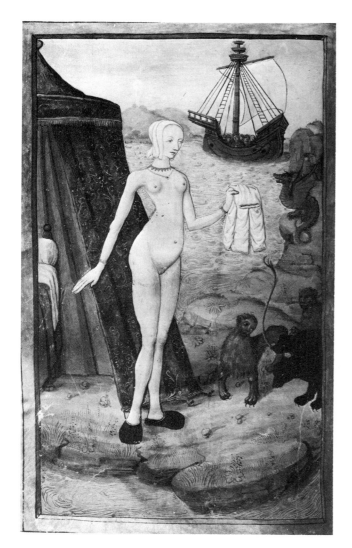

how she admired his prowess in the chase and his devotion to
Diana. She pleads with him to love her: 'Bend, proud one, your
spirit! My mother could pervert the bull; will you be fiercer than
a bull?'

Flecte, feros, animos! Potuit corrumpere taurum
Mater. eris tauro saevior ipse truci?

Ovid is a brilliant rhetorician, playing with his stories and with
his readers' emotions like a skilful musician, but not, one feels,
taking them altogether seriously himself. There are many further
allusions to Theseus. In *Fasti* III, for instance, Ariadne, having
been deserted by Theseus, is again deserted by Bacchus. Ovid gives

her another even more bitter lament, wittily comparing the horns worn by Bacchus to those of Pasiphaë's bull: 'The horns of a handsome bull won my mother's heart; thine won mine.'

> *Ceperunt matrem formosi cornua tauri,*
> *Me tua.*

Bacchus in the end takes pity on her and makes her a goddess, her golden crown set with gems becoming stars in the sky—the 'Knossian Crown'.

Again, in *Ars Amatoria* I, Ovid describes in even lusher imagery how Bacchus appeared on Naxos to comfort Ariadne, in a chariot drawn by tigers, the god leaping down to her lest she should swoon from fear. It was a picture that was to haunt the imagination of Renaissance artists.

Seneca, the implacable moralist and the author of some of the most harrowing plays in any language (if the two Senecas of whom we know are the same man) strikes a very different note. His *Phaedra* is a development of Euripides' *Hippolytus*; but the emphasis has shifted, the passions are darker, the quality of life more cruel. Seneca dispenses with the gods, so that the supernatural element (Hippolytus' scorning of Aphrodite) counts for nothing. Phaedra is a woman in the grip of irresistible infatuation. Love masters her—*Amoris in me maximum regnum fero*—and love, as she observes,

> . . . lies not lightly
> On any daughter of the house of Minos;
> We know no love that is not bound to sin.

Seneca brings Phaedra and Hippolytus together, where Euripides had kept them apart. She confronts him, pleads with him, humiliates herself and is rejected with contempt. The nurse, seeing that all is lost, immediately raises the cry that Hippolytus has tried to rape her mistress. When Theseus returns Phaedra confirms the story. There follows a long description of Hippolytus' death, far more gruesome than in Euripides, sparing none of the details of his hideous injuries. Phaedra confesses the truth and stabs herself. Theseus has the mangled remains of his son brought to him and tries to put them together, in a scene so horrible that one is inclined self-defensively to find it ludicrous:

Here is a piece,
Misshapen, horrible, each side of it
Injured and torn. What part of you it is
I cannot tell, but it is part of you.
So . . . put it there, not where it ought to be
But where there is a place for it.

Seneca's plays were probably never acted, though the reason can hardly have been public squeamishness. Suetonius relates that Nero staged a ballet called *The Minotaur* in which 'an actor disguised as a bull actually mounted another who played Pasiphaë and occupied the hindquarters of a hollow wooden heifer—or that, at least, was the audience's impression'. And if we are to believe one of Martial's epigrams a similar spectacle was still being performed at the time of Domitian.

These three poets, especially Ovid, gave the various episodes of the Theseus story the forms that they were to have for the next two thousand years. Other Roman writers, however, also made use of the legend in varying and powerful ways. Virgil, in Book VI of the *Aeneid*, has Aeneas see Phaedra and her mother Pasiphaë, along with Dido, among the spirits of unhappy lovers. In Book VII he again alludes to the story of Phaedra, and tells how Hippolytus was rescued from the shades by Trivia, was spirited to Italy and lived unknown under the name of Vibius. As always, Virgil leaves whatever he touches fixed in some consummate phrase: the Minotaur 'mongrel breed, double offspring, record of monstrous love'— *mixtum genus, prolesque biformis, Veneris monumenta nefandae.*

The *Fabulae* of Hyginus record a few details from Greek sources that have otherwise not survived; Statius' *Thebais* presents Theseus in his capacity of duke of Athens, but is mainly the story of Eteocles and Polynices, 'the seven against Thebes'; Servius, in his fourth-century commentary on Virgil, supplies a few further scraps of legend. The story, indeed, was the common property of Latin poets and came readily to their minds to point a moral or adorn a tale.

Much the same can be said if we look at the visual arts. Well-to-do Roman houses were decorated with mural scenes mostly taken from mythology and obviously regarded as simply ornamental. It cannot have mattered a great deal to most Roman householders

Ills. 181—184. Four Roman frescoes of the first century AD, from Pompeii and Herculaneum. Daedalus (left) presents the hollow cow, which moves on a platform fitted with wheels, to Pasiphaë. Ariadne abandoned (above left) was one of the most popular subjects. Ariadne surprised by Bacchus (above right) is in a pose similar to that of one of the most famous Roman frescoes, the female initiate in the 'Villa of the Mysteries'. Both this and the Pasiphaë scene on the left come from the house of the Vettii, a family with a particular fondness for sexual scenes. Theseus (right), having killed the Minotaur, is greeted by the Athenian youths and maidens.

exactly which myths the painter chose, though occasionally some graceful compliment to the owner's family or profession can be recognized. The greater part of such art has of course vanished, but from what remains at Pompeii, Herculaneum and Rome, we can tell with certainty that the Theseus legends were as popular as any other. There are paintings of Theseus lifting the rock to find his father's tokens; of Pasiphaë, Daedalus and the bronze cow; of Theseus killing the Minotaur and receiving the homage of the Athenian youths; of Theseus leaving Ariadne; of Dionysus (*i.e.* Bacchus) finding her; and of Hippolytus and Phaedra.

Ills. 181—185

The same themes recur, rather surprisingly, on sarcophagi, and here they may well have had a more serious purpose. Many of the subjects chosen for sarcophagi had an allegorical meaning, alluding to the hope of a happy after-life, and this is probably the significance of the motif of Bacchus and Ariadne—the awakening to new birth after apparent death. It is more difficult to see the symbolism of the Phaedra-Hippolytus story, though the legend that Hippolytus was restored to life by Aesculapius may be the answer. At any rate,

Ills. 186, 187

such scenes are comparatively plentiful; a few of the best are to be seen at Rome, Agrigento, Arles, Pisa, and at Woburn Abbey in England. An unusual example in New York, besides showing Theseus killing the Minotaur and abandoning Ariadne, shows the two of them at the door of the Labyrinth, thread in hand—an image irresistibly suggestive of the mystery of death.

Larger scale sculpture on the Theseus theme has not survived, but certainly existed. In two Roman museums are fragmentary busts of the Minotaur, probably copies of a lost Greek original; and one

Ill. 188

of the most famous statues of antiquity is the *Sleeping Ariadne* in the Vatican, perhaps part of a group belonging to a sanctuary of Bacchus. It was discovered in 1512 and with its sensuous pose—head thrown back, arms raised, body langorously relaxed—became the prototype of dozens of Renaissance and Baroque nymphs.

One more important aspect of the legend remains to be noted: the Labyrinth. Pliny, in his *Natural History* (Book XXXVI) concluded that Daedalus adapted his design from the famous ancient Egyptian labyrinth but made it a hundred times smaller. 'It contains passages that wind, advance and retreat in a bewilderingly intricate manner. It is not just a narrow strip of ground comprising many miles of "walks" such as we see in our tessellated floors, or in the ceremonial games played by our boys on the Campus Martius; but doors are let into the walls at frequent intervals to suggest deceptively the way ahead and to force the visitor to go back upon the very same

Ills. 186, 187. Scenes from Roman sarcophagi now in the Campo Santo at Pisa. The end (below left) shows Bacchus finding Ariadne. The long side tells the story of Phaedra and Hippolytus; on the right he rides away to be confronted by the sea-monster.

tracks that he has already followed in his wanderings.' Although Pliny uses the present tense, he admits later that 'no traces of it survive'; but he does mention another, at Lemnos, which did exist in his day, and an Etruscan 'labyrinth', doubtless a series of tombs, made by King Porsena.

Labyrinths were firmly linked in the Roman mind with thoughts of Knossos and the Minotaur. Knossian coins with labyrinths began to be issued in Classical Greek times and they continued into the Roman period. The pattern on them is fairly consistent, and became the standard pattern of Roman mosaic mazes. The 'path' runs inward a short way, then turns right and goes almost a full circuit, then back in the opposite direction and so by a series of full circuits to a dead end in the middle. They can be either circular or rectangular, but there are no alternative paths, no choices, no problems about finding one's way out again; in the technical language of labyrinthology, they are 'unicursal' as distinct from 'multicursal'.

As we have just seen, Pliny spoke of labyrinth mosaic floors as commonplace, and one good example from his time has come to light at Pompeii, in the so-called *Casa del Labirinto*: it shows in its centre Theseus and the Minotaur struggling on the ground, watched by frightened girls. Another house in Pompeii has a labyrinth scratched on the wall with an inscription reading *Labyrinthus. Hic habitat Minotaurus*—evidently a joke at the expense of the owner.

Ill. 189. A Roman joke—'The Labyrinth. Here lives the Minotaur'—scratched on the wall of a house in Pompeii. The labyrinth follows the same pattern as that in the coin opposite.

184

There are many other labyrinth floors all over the Roman Empire, some featuring the Minotaur, some not. One of the best is at Salzburg. It has a square labyrinth (divided into four quarters, but again unicursal), and Theseus killing the Minotaur in the centre. Around the sides are other mosaic panels showing Theseus and Ariadne joining hands over an altar, Theseus putting Ariadne ashore, and Ariadne on Naxos. Other mosaic floors with the Minotaur can (or could) be seen at Aix-en-Provence in France, at Susa in Tunisia, Cormerod in Switzerland and Brindisi in Italy. The last two have birds around the edge, perhaps alluding to the mechanical birds made by Daedalus to escape from his own labyrinth. Examples without the Minotaur were found at Verdes in France, Caerleon in Wales, and Harpham in England.

It was natural that Roman labyrinthine patterns should find a place in the mosaic decoration of early Christian churches, but highly surprising that the Minotaur should follow them. Not that this is always the case. The earliest of all Christian labyrinths, that at St Reparatus, Orleansville, Algeria (probably fourth century) is purely decorative, having no entrance. It is divided into four, with

Ills. 190, 191. Above, in the third century BC, Knossos, then a minor provincial town, looked back to its legendary past and issued a series of coins bearing labyrinths. The earliest had Minotaur figures on them (*Ill. 13*), but these were soon replaced by Demeter, Persephone, or, as in this case, the owl of Athena.

Ill. 192. A well-preserved Roman mosaic floor at Salzburg. The central panel contains the Labyrinth, with Theseus killing the Minotaur in the centre. The three smaller panels show him swearing faith to Ariadne, abandoning her on Naxos, and Ariadne alone.

four separate centres, so there is no real point to it. In the centre of the whole floor is a *jeu-de-lettres* on the words SANCTA ECCLESIA, which can be read in any direction starting from the middle.

In Lucca Cathedral, set into the wall, is a mosaic labyrinth only 49.5 cm. across, which may go back to the tenth century. It is said formerly to have had Theseus and the Minotaur in the centre, though they are now unrecognizable. Opposite the 'entrance' is the following inscription:

> *Hic quem Creticus edit*
> *Daedalus est labyrinthus,*
> *De quo nullus vadere,*
> *Quivit qui fuit intus,*
> *Ni Theseus gratis Ariadne*
> *Stamine intus.*

Ill. 193. This strange labyrinth now set into the wall of Lucca Cathedral perhaps formed part of the floor of an earlier church. The inscription—'This is the Labyrinth which Daedalus the Cretan built, from which nobody escaped who had gone inside, nor Theseus without the help of Ariadne'—is one of the earliest attempts to give the labyrinth a symbolic meaning.

At San Michele in Pavia there is another labyrinth, also on the wall and also thought to be about tenth century in date, which does clearly shows Theseus killing the Minotaur. The latter has the form commonly used in the Middle Ages to represent the Minotaur: a bull's body and human torso and head—i.e. a centaur. The Pavia labyrinth bears the inscription: *Teseus intravit monstrumque biforme necavit* ('Theseus entered and killed the hybrid monster').

At Cremona is another fragment of a labyrinth, which may be even earlier than that at Pavia. It showed a man fighting a centaur, with the inscription *Centaurus*.

How could such blatantly pagan imagery be justified in Christian churches? A labyrinth formerly to be seen in San Savino at Piacenza may provide the answer. This had no Minotaur, but did have an inscription allegorizing the labyrinth as a type of the world, broad at the entrance, narrow at the exit, so that the man who is ensnared can regain life only with difficulty.

Numerous other variants might be mentioned. One in polychrome marble at Santa Maria in Trastevere, Rome, is 3.5 m. in diameter, probably dating from 1190. The centre is simply a series of concentric rings, which may be an adaptation of the labyrinth idea to the Circles of Beatitude, or may simply be the result of bad restoration. Another at San Vitale, Ravenna, is just as big, and has the way to the centre obligingly marked by arrows inset in the marble.

The largest medieval mosaic labyrinths were those made in the thirteenth-century cathedrals of northern France. The one at Chartres (still to be seen, though usually hidden under rows of chairs) is 13 m. in diameter, and was included by Villard de Honnecourt in his thirteenth-century sketchbook. It used to be known as *La Lieue*, i.e. 'the league', although its total length is only 137 m. Other labyrinths were called *Chemin de Jérusalem*, *dédale*, and *meandre*. The centre was called *le ciel*, or *Jérusalem*.

Two other very large labyrinths used to exist at Amiens and Reims, and were used to record the names of the architects of the two cathedrals. The central stone of the one at Amiens survives in the local museum. That of Reims was destroyed in 1779 by a certain Canon Jaquemart, who disliked the noise made by children following it round during the service. Records survive of at least nine others in France and Germany and doubtless there were more.

What meaning was attached to these labyrinths in the Middle Ages is a mystery. The allegorical interpretation quoted from Piacenza is obviously one explanation. Suggestions have been made that they were penitential (people going round them on their knees as a sort of substitute pilgrimage) or that they were a Masonic symbol, alluding to Daedalus as the first builder. Both are possible, but there seems to be no evidence either way. Mazes went on being made—in turf, topiary or other material—from the Middle Ages until today, and continued to be called *dédales* or *maisons de Dédale*. In the seventeenth and eighteenth centuries they were endowed with elaborate allegorical programmes, and the literature includes illustrations of fascinating complexity.

But we have been led further than we intended, and like Theseus must retrace our steps. Whatever the significance of the mosaic labyrinths, the early Christian fathers set themselves firmly against pagan mythology in any of its forms. Here is Lactantius (in the chapter 'Of the False Worship of the Gods' from the *Divine Institutes*) on the subject of Bacchus and Ariadne:

He was most shamefully overpowered by love and lust. For being conveyed to Crete with his effeminate retinue, he met with an unchaste woman on the shore; and in the confidence inspired by his Indian victory, he wished to give proof of his manliness, lest he should appear too effeminate. And so he took to himself in marriage that woman, the betrayer of her father, and the murderer of her brother, after she had been deserted and repudiated by another lover.

Even during the disintegration of the Roman Empire, however, Ovid, Virgil and Seneca were read and enjoyed, not least in those strongholds of the new orthodoxy, the monasteries; and inevitably the old myths made their insidious way into the new Christian imagination (one of the most curious instances is the story, recorded by Prudentius in his *Hymns*, of a certain St Hippolytus, who was martyred by being torn to pieces by horses). As a symbol of the new order one might take a Roman sardonyx jug carved with the story of Phaedra and Hippolytus. Some time during the Dark Ages it found its way to the church of Saint-Maurice-d'Agaune in Switzerland. Given a setting of barbaric Frankish gold, enamel and paste, it took its place in the church treasury, where it may still be found.

The admission of pagan stories into Christian scholarship entailed a radical reinterpretation. But the medieval mind turned naturally to allegory, and it required no undue ingenuity to fit the exploits of Hercules, Jason and Theseus into a scheme of moral *exempla* in the same way as history, zoology, astronomy and every other science had been fitted. The Roman world had even given a start in that direction. A late Latin text, *Graphia Aurea Urbis Romae*, preserved in Florence, advises: 'Let there be represented [on the emperor's robe] a labyrinth of gold and pearls, in which is the Minotaur, made of emerald, holding his finger to his mouth, thus signifying that, just as none may know the secret of the labyrinth, so none may reveal the Emperor's counsels.' The fifteenth-century painter Bartolommeo Veneto must have known the passage, for he included just such an emblem in a picture now in the Fitzwilliam Museum, Cambridge.

Theseus' appearance in the literature of the early Middle Ages is sporadic and seems to reflect no consistent or particularly significant attitude. Collections of historical stories mention him, sometimes with illustrations. The *Liber Floridus*, written about 1120 by Lambert, canon of Saint-Omer, and now in the University of Ghent, contains

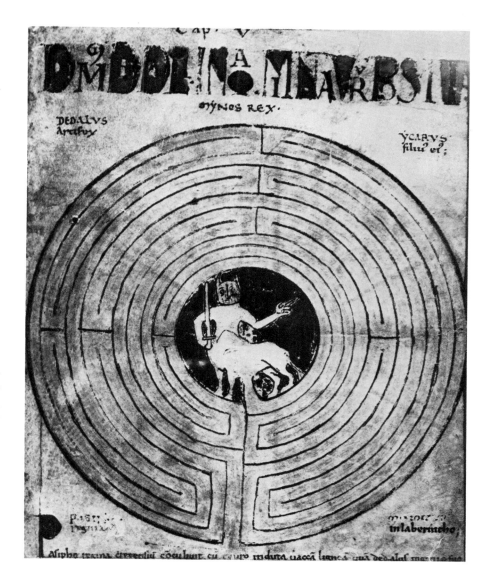

Ill. 194. The twelfth-century labyrinth page in Lambert's *Liber Floridus* must surely be derived from a Classical scene, either mosaic or manuscript. It is an ingenious variation of the Roman 'unicursal' maze, in which the centre is reached by traversing every path—a tedious and exhausting procedure but one in which it is actually impossible to get lost. The Middle Ages almost always portrayed the Minotaur as a centaur.

Ill. 194

a large full-page illumination of the Labyrinth and the Minotaur in the middle, with the caption: *Domus Dedali in quia Minotaurum posuit Mynos rex. Phasiphe, regina Cretensium, concibuit cum tauro.* ('The house of Daedalus in which King Minos placed the Minotaur. Pasiphaë, queen of the Cretans, lay with the bull.') The *De VII Miraculis Mundi* (Regensburg, *c.* 1175—1200) has a similar picture, with a Minotaur whose face resembles a pig rather than a bull. Geoffroi de Vinsauf, in his *Documentum de modo et arte distandi et versificandi* of about 1200 uses the incident of Androgeos' death as an excuse for a flowery rhetorical exercise in lamentation. He makes the young prince a student of philosophy, a point that recurs in later medieval retellings of the legend.

By the thirteenth century scholasticism had already succeeded in incorporating the myths into its complex framework of abstraction and symbol. According to a certain Albricus, *De Deorum imaginibus libellis*, Venus revenged herself on the five daughters of the Sun because Apollo had revealed her guilty amour with Mars; and these five daughters were to be interpreted as the five senses: Pasiphaë, sight; Medea, hearing; Circe, touch; Phaedra, smell; Dirce, taste.

Dante, writing in the early years of the fourteenth century, assumes a familiarity with the Theseus story, and incorporates it in his narrative at both the literal and allegorical levels. During their descent into the Seventh Circle of Hell (*Inferno* XII) Dante and Virgil are confronted by the Minotaur guarding the road, the symbol of bestiality and perverted appetite—*l'infamia di Creti*. Virgil taunts it with having been outwitted and killed by Theseus, and when the Minotaur rushes at them like a mad bull they manage to slip past him and continue their journey.

Pasiphaë is used as the type of lust in the Seventh Terrace of Purgatory, and in *Paradiso* XVII Dante's great-great-grandfather, Cacciaguida, tells him of his imminent exile from Florence and compares the false accusations of embezzlement that will be made against him to the false accusations of Phaedra against Hippolytus.

The generation after Dante saw the first humanist enquiries into Classical civilization, and a new interest in myth. The effect upon literature and art was twofold: the ancient heroes become at the same time more human and more intellectualized. They are seen as real men and women experiencing real emotions, and also as symbols of complex intellectual ideas.

In Petrarch's *Triumph of Love*, Theseus appears between Ariadne and Phaedra, justly punished for his desertion of the one by the attempted adultery of the other. Phaedra herself, *amante terribile e maligna*, is condemned for her threefold betrayal—of Ariadne, Theseus and Hippolytus.

Petrarch's greatest follower in Classical studies, Giovanni Boccaccio, plunged deep into the problems of mythology, trying, in true Renaissance style, to combine the wisdom of the ancient world

Ill. 195. Right, Phaedra killing herself, after confessing that she had slandered Hippolytus, from Boccaccio's *De Casibus virorum illustrium*. Neither Boccaccio nor his fifteenth-century illustrator could think of classical stories in any but contemporary terms.

with the certainties of medieval Christianity. His most sustained philosophical treatment of the Theseus cycle is in his Latin work *De genealogia deorum*, written between 1350 and 1364. Pasiphaë, the daughter of the Sun, is the soul, the child of God; her husband Minos is human reason, which rules over the soul and guides it along the right path; Venus, his enemy, is concupiscence, and

Ill. 196. Theseus capturing the bull of Marathon, from a French translation of Boccaccio's *De Casibus*. The age of chivalry has by now endowed Theseus with all the attributes of knighthood.

from the union of the soul with pleasure is born the Minotaur, the vice of bestiality.

In a later book of the *Genealogia deorum* Boccaccio tells the story of Ariadne, and how she was abandoned by Theseus on Naxos. Naxos, he notes, was famous for its wine, and he offers the theory that Ariadne was in fact the worse for drink when Theseus left her. It gives him the chance for a lengthy dissertation upon the degradation of drunkenness, especially in women.

In another Latin prose work, the *De Casibus virorum illustrium*, written at about the same time, Boccaccio assembles a collection of stories from every source (Classical and northern mythology, the Bible, history) revolving round the misfortunes suffered by famous men and women. Book I contains the whole story of Theseus' visit to Crete—the death of Androgeos, Minos' victory over the

Athenians, the tribute, Pasiphaë and the bull (Boccaccio mentions the story, already noted in the Greek sources, that the bull was really a Cretan general called Taurus, see page 46), the flight of Theseus with Ariadne and Phaedra, his desertion of Ariadne and his marriage with Phaedra. Fortune, Boccaccio has to admit, has been particularly unkind to Minos, though he had done nothing in particular to deserve it. The Phaedra and Hippolytus episode follows, with its share of moralizing asides. Phaedra is censured for slandering Hippolytus, Theseus for drawing hasty conclusions. Thus every tale teaches a useful lesson.

De Casibus was immensely popular all over Europe, and con-

Ill. 195 siderable artistry was often lavished on its illustration. A fine manuscript of 1470 exists in the British Museum. It was soon translated into Italian, French, German and English. The French translation, by Laurence de Premierfait (*c.* 1400) survives in several illustrated manuscripts, a particularly good one being in the

Ill. 196 Bibliothèque de l'Arsenal in Paris. It was this version that Lydgate used for his English poem, *The Fall of Princes*. Lydgate was not a great poet, but he manages to endow his sources with a certain naïve charm that makes him worthy of consideration in his own right:

> [The place] callid Laboryntus, dyvers and unkouth,
> Ful off wrynkles and off straungenesse,
> Ougli to knowe which is north or south,
> Or to what part a man sholde hym dresse;
> Folk were ther brent with furious derknesse;
> Who that entred, his retourn was in veyn,
> Without a clue for to resorte a-geyn.

Of this too there is an exquisite manuscript in the British Museum with illustrations of the Minotaur, 'Aryane', Hippolytus and Phaedra.

Of the Latin poets discussed at the beginning of this chapter Catullus was unknown between the fall of Rome and the Renaissance, when a single manuscript came into the hands of the humanist scholar Salutati. But Seneca, Ovid and Virgil were known and read all through the Middle Ages, and some of the most beautiful late medieval manuscripts are of their works. Theseus and Hippolytus

Ill. 180 are portrayed as knights of chivalry, and Phaedra might be a

Within the illustration (manuscript text columns):

ii les avoit tenir · pour ce
diable en ferrer comanda
li rois mynos dedalus q
li sist fere une maison a
tant tenuceastres que ele
monte na ature sil sust
retens q iames peust ue
nir a lentree · car · c · huis
i auoit puis compassoit li
pmiers qui desnioit ceus
qui retens estoient · En cele
maison su as minotaur°
enclos · En cel temps estoi
ent si al dathenes si subg
et a trou ymnos de acte q

creanci a tenir cele couue
nenche · Et tantost a la se
damoy selle a dedalus q en
quist coment elle le pourroit
celiurer · q dedalus li dist
qnl meslast pois q soi en
semble · si le pourralt auec lui
q quit il uendroit tenant
le monstre si ligetast · te
nant q il tantost · le uodro
it mengier · mes il tant ne
pourroit maistier qnl le pr
ust au aler · q entrementie
rs qul a ce entendroit
le pourroit tixesens occure · et

Ill. 197. Before the Renaissance no distinction was drawn between myth and history, and the Theseus stories were retold in many encyclopaedic compilations that began with Adam and continued to the writer's own day. This illustration from a French *Livre des estoires* was made by an artist who seems to have understood the tale rather imperfectly. The Minotaur, shown as a bull, tramples on the body of a dead man, but the Labyrinth is represented only by an elaborate cage.

lady from the court of France. There is space here merely to mention illuminated manuscripts of Seneca in the Fitzwilliam Museum, Cambridge, in the Bodleian Library, Oxford, and in Vienna; and of Ovid in the British Museum (several examples), Balliol College, Oxford, and the Bibliothèque Nationale in Paris. All these contain miniatures of the Theseus legend; the last is of special interest since it includes a nude representation of Ariadne—a pathetic skinny figure wearing a cap and shoes, waving a scarf to her disappearing lover and being watched with sympathy by an assortment of fabulous animals.

In addition to the Classical texts themselves, there are universal histories based partly upon them and often incorporating the same stories. A French manuscript at Naples, for instance, of 1350, has several pictures relating to the Theseus story, including Theseus killing the Minotaur in a labyrinth, watched by Ariadne. The Minotaur even turns up in a fourteenth-century Flemish manuscript containing a Latin translation of an Arabic astrological work on the signs of the zodiac and the seven planets.

Ill. 198. Another history of the world, written by a Venetian friar at about the same time, shows a complex labyrinth and the familiar centaur-Minotaur. Limbs of its victims strew the ground.

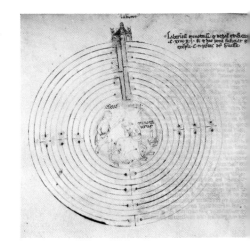

10 From the Renaissance to Romanticism

Simon Tidworth

WITH THE DAWN OF THE RENAISSANCE the classics were not only recopied (and eventually printed) but translated into most of the European vernaculars. The *Aeneid* was translated into Spanish, Italian and French during the fifteenth century, and English in the sixteenth. Ovid's *Metamorphoses* was accorded a German version as early as the thirteenth century. Italian and French translations followed in the fourteenth and English (translated by Caxton from the French) in 1480. The British Museum possesses a superb manuscript of the French translation by Octavien de Saint-Gelais, bishop of Angoulême. One of its illustrations again shows Ariadne, this time in bed on her island with four wild animals round her—heralds, presumably, of Bacchus' arrival. Seneca was being imitated in fourteenth-century Italy and was the dominant influence on Renaissance tragedy everywhere. As usual, Spanish and Italian translations appeared long before any English ones.

This is to anticipate, but it serves to make the point of the universal popularity of the old stories and their universal accessibility. They were told not only for their own sakes but for the sake of practically any message than an author wished to impart. During the fourteenth century, the *Metamorphoses* was subjected to an exhaustive and exhausting process of allegorization in a French work of over 70,000 lines known as *Ovid moralisé*. The Theseus stories are typical of the poet's methods, a mixture of translation, invention and interpretation. He 'moralizes' on Pasiphaë's passion for the bull, analyses her mental conflicts and writes 'complaints' in the traditional style and at the traditional length. Bacchus, curiously, is introduced as the king of Naxos—*le roys de la contree*—not a god.

195

There was a similar work in Italian of *c.* 1370 by a certain Giovanni dei Bonsignori, and the Theseus story crops up in a host of other literary contexts—in Machault's *Le Jugement du Roy de Navarre* and in the works of Christine de Pisan, who leaned heavily on Boccaccio in much of what she wrote; a manuscript in Brussels has a charming illustration showing Pasiphaë dressed like a Burgundian fashion-plate giving the bull an affectionate kiss on the nose. Next to them stands the young Minotaur, in the form of a centaur, looking distinctly puzzled.

Ill. 199

Most of these medieval glosses attempt to explain and expand Ovid, adding details that were supposed to clarify the stories: for instance that Phaedra accompanied Theseus and Ariadne on the understanding that she was to marry Hippolytus (this occurs first in Boccaccio); that Ariadne gave Theseus a lump of pitch to stuff down the Minotaur's throat; or that they were aided in their escape by Daedalus. All these details make for slight differences between the various versions, so that scholars can occupy almost any amount of time in discussing who copied from whom—e.g. whether the tribute was to be paid every year or every third year; whether there were seven youths or only one; whether Theseus was chosen by lot or volunteered, etc. These are of little interest for our present purpose, but they do serve to fill in the background for the most accomplished retelling of the story in the 1400 years since Ovid: that of Chaucer.

The Legend of Good Women, which Chaucer never finished, consists of eight and a half narrative poems of some 300 lines each, telling the stories of the heroines of antiquity. Chaucer's genius is of so deceptively simple a kind that it is not easy to give an idea of it in a few words. Part of its attraction is its unforced naturalness: his men and women, in spite of his source stories, are the opposite of heroic. Whatever deeds they may perform, and whatever sufferings they may endure, they never lose those qualities of ordinary human frailty which Chaucer relished so keenly and expressed so directly. So in his hands Theseus becomes an impulsive young man in a tight corner, and Ariadne a girl not too smitten with infatuation to try and think about the future.

Chaucer does not explain the origin of the Minotaur, but simply sets the situation before us:

Ill. 199. Right, Pasiphaë, the bull and their offspring the Minotaur in a fifteenth-century illustration from the poems of Christine de Pisan. The palace of Minos, in the background, has something of the magic of the castles in the *Très Riches Heures*, but the artist cannot be said to have succeeded in making a convincing Minotaur. Christine de Pisan, one of the first Renaissance bluestockings, had a wide knowledge of Latin, Italian and French literatures.

Pour tant se pasiple fu fole
Ne vueilles sire a ton escole

This Minos hath a monstre, a wikked beste,
That was so cruel that without areste,
Whan that a man was broght in his presence,
He wolde him ete, ther helpeth no defence.

Theseus, he relates, was put into a dungeon, where Ariadne and Phaedra hear him lamenting his fate. They take pity on him. Phaedra proposes that they give him lumps of wax,

> . . . that, when he gapeth faste,
> Into the bestes throte he shal hem caste,
> To slake his hunger and encombre his teeth.

And that they should also give Theseus a ball of thread:

> . . . for the hous is crinkled to and fro,
> And hath so queinte weyes for to go—
> For hit is shapen as the mase is wroght.

Before he fights, Theseus swears fealty and service to Ariadne, and promises to take both the girls home to his father Aegeus in Athens.

> A seemly knight was Theseus for to see,
> And yong, but of a twenty yeer and three;
> But who-so hadde y-seyn his countenaunce,
> He wolde have wept, for routhe of his penaunce.

Ariadne, however, still has some scruples about her own and her sister's reputation:

> Yit were hit better that I were your wyf.

Theseus agrees, as also to the suggestion that Phaedra should marry his son Hippolytus (Chaucer forgetting that he has just made Theseus only twenty-three years old). This small but very significant touch, that the proposal comes from Ariadne rather than Theseus, is apparently Chaucer's own invention. The plan succeeds. The Minotaur is killed. They flee, and sail to the country of 'Ennopye', where

> . . . he had a frend of his knowinge.
> Ther festen they, ther dauncen they and singe,
> And in his armes hath this Adriane.

Then they set sail again until they come to an uninhabited island, where Theseus leaves Ariadne asleep and goes off with Phaedra— with only one line of explanation from Chaucer:

> For that her suster fairer was than she.

The poem ends with Ariadne's awakening; at first she is afraid that Theseus has been killed by wild beasts, but soon she sees his ship disappearing across the sea. Vainly she tries to signal to him:

Her kerchief on a pole up stikked she.

Chaucer reproaches Theseus as a traitor to love, but forbears to repeat everything that Ariadne said upon the subject:

Hit is so long, hit were an hevy thing.
In her epistle Naso telleth al.

Chaucer uses the story again, briefly, in *The House of Fame*, and it is retold at greater length by his friend Gower in the *Confessio Amantis*. Gower gives a full account of Pasiphaë's affair with the bull, which took place, according to him, while Minos was away at the siege of Troy! His vigorous three-foot lines have a good deal of narrative energy, but they lack both Chaucer's poetry and his understanding of motivation:

Fedra her yonge suster eke,
A lusty maid, a sobre, a meke,
Fulfilled of all courtesie,
For love which was hem betwene,
To sen her suster made a quene,
Her father left and forth she went.

The point of the tale is again Theseus' bad behaviour toward Ariadne,

Whereof the wrong shall evermo
Stand in cronique of remembraunce.

Neither Chaucer nor Gower pursues the legend as far as the Hippolytus episode.

There is in these fifteenth-century versions of the myth an unmistakable feeling of novelty and adventure. This comes through even more strongly in the art of the period, and most of all in the art of Italy. One can see Theseus emerging from the wintry stylization of the Middle Ages into a new springtime of naturalism.

An illuminated chronicle of 1435—42 by Leonardo da Bosozzo, formerly in Berlin, still relies on full-length portraits of historical personages, elegantly dressed, standing against a verdant landscape and holding attributes suitable to their age and fame. Theseus, like a character in a masque, holds a large circular labyrinth resembling a dish. A few years later, another Italian artist, certainly a Florentine and perhaps Maso Finiguerra, made a picture chronicle in the form of large folio-size drawings, representing the history of the world from the creation onwards, and combining, as usual, sacred and pagan mythology indiscriminately. His Theseus page is a masterpiece of Renaissance draughtsmanship. Theseus, dressed much as in the earlier picture, stands gracefully on the left, holding a ball of thread. The Labyrinth, a circular walled structure, is on the right. In the background Ariadne waves distractedly from a cliff top, falls down and is rescued and carried up to heaven by Jupiter. Theseus sails away with his black sail, and in the distance Aegeus throws himself from a tower. (The book is now in the British Museum. It was formerly owned by Ruskin, who describes this particular picture in loving detail in *Fors Clavigera*, No. 28. He thought it was by Botticelli.)

The story is told even more fully in an attractive pair of *cassone* panels now in the Campana Collection in the Louvre. One side shows Theseus arriving in Crete, being given the thread by Ariadne and her nurse, negotiating the Labyrinth, killing the Minotaur, and departing in a boat with Ariadne. On the other side he leaves her sleeping in the nuptial bed, in spite of the nurse who tries to hold him back. Ariadne runs up and down the sea shore distraught with grief; Bacchus arrives in a chariot drawn by griffins. In the distance, once again, Theseus is seen coming back to Athens without

Ill. 201. Right, a *Triumph of Bacchus and Ariadne* drawing attributed to Botticelli. The Bacchantes on the left, especially, are Botticellian in the flowing lines of their drapery and the poetry of their movements. ▶

Ills. 205, 207

Ill. 206

remembering to change the sail, and his father is throwing himself from a tower.

A popular detail (destined to become far more popular in later centuries) was the 'triumph' or wedding procession of Bacchus and Ariadne. Two examples are of the highest quality, and both convey to perfection the freshness and innocence that the early Renaissance found in rediscovering the world of the myths. One *Ill. 200* is a *cassone* panel by Cima da Conegliano that is now in Milan. A fantastic antique cart is pulled by leopards, led by *putti*. Bacchus, sitting in the chariot, crowns the kneeling Ariadne with flowers. Behind them walks a satyr-like figure carrying a basket of grapes. *Ill. 201* The other scene is a drawing attributed to Botticelli of which engravings survive, though the original is lost, in which Bacchus and Ariadne sit in a chariot pulled by music-making centaurs; the chariot is made of living vines, and the whole composition is enmeshed in a tangle of branches and leaves.

The exhilaration that breathes through these works, and which finds its most perfect image in Botticelli's big mythological paintings of the *Birth of Venus* and *Primavera*, is epitomized in a famous quatrain by Lorenzo de' Medici, which happily for our purpose is the beginning of his poem *Il Trionfo di Bacco ed Arianna*:

Ill. 200. Left, Renaissance enthusiasm for the classics included the staging of elaborate *trionfi*, allegorical processions with specially designed costumes and sets. It is no doubt one of these that is reflected in Cima de Conegliano's *Triumph of Bacchus and Ariadne*, which might almost be an illustration to Lorenzo de' Medici's poem (opposite).

Quant' è bella giovinezza   (How beautiful is youth, which is
Che si fugge tuttavia!   ever fleeting. Whoever wants to
Che vuol' esser lieto, sia,   be happy, be happy now! There
Di doman non c'è certezza!   is no certainty about tomorrow.)

The last two lines recur as a refrain, reiterating the happiness which Bacchus and Ariadne find in each other, and that of Silenus, the nymphs and the satyrs in making the most of the pleasures of life while it lasts—*Viva Baccho e viva Amore!*

In the High Renaissance this quality is retained and enriched, and the theme of Bacchus and Ariadne was to remain one of the most powerful of all its expressions. To trace the various transformations through which it went during the next hundred and fifty years is to see in miniature the whole history of Italian painting from Renaissance to Rococo.

Titian, in the famous picture in the National Gallery in London, *Ill. 202* chooses the moment when Ariadne, gazing after Theseus' vanishing ship, is suddenly surprised by the riotous arrival of Bacchus and his companions. She turns in dismay, while the procession comes to a sudden stop and Bacchus leaps from the chariot—a dynamic movement which until that time had not been attempted in art. The painting seems poised on the brink of some enormous fulfilment, making us experience it on the same spiritual level as those Roman sarcophagi in which Bacchus was the very promise of eternal happiness. Above Ariadne's head, unseen by her, shines the pale circle of stars which she is destined to become.

It is instructive to compare this painting with that of Tintoretto *Ill. 203* in the Palazzo Ducale at Venice. The same moment is represented, but Tintoretto views it from a new and disconcerting angle. The space, instead of being clear and rational as in Titian, is strangely undefined. Bacchus, a lonely supplicating figure, rises from below towards a naked Ariadne, who gazes at him without fear, while Venus hovers over her with the crown of stars. The promise is still there, but its content is now equivocal. We are on the threshold of Mannerism. In whatever sense one chooses to use that dangerous word, there is no denying the increasing self-awareness, sophistication and complexity of the painters who follow those of the High Renaissance.

The same discovery could not be made twice. The men of the mid-sixteenth century looked again at the myth of Theseus and searched for something new. What they found was eroticism.

With Giulio Romano—in both painting and architecture, in technique as well as in subject matter—innocence has finally and

Ill. 202. Titian's *Bacchus and Ariadne* was commissioned by Duke Alfonso d'Este in 1518, as part of the decoration for a small room in the castle of Ferrara. Titian based his picture very closely on Ovid and Catullus, producing unprecedented effects of realism in a subject still fairly rare in Renaissance art. The figure towards the right, enmeshed in snakes, is based on the *Laocoön*.

unmistakably yielded to experience. Fittingly enough, it is in his work that the theme of Pasiphaë and the bull returns to major art. He tackled it at least twice. A large fresco in the Palazzo del Tè in Mantua shows Pasiphaë stepping (fully clothed) into the wooden cow made for her by Daedalus, who stands next to it helping her. The bull is below on the right, gazing up at the cow yearningly. In another fresco, in the Villa Madama in Rome (of which a drawing survives in the Uffizi) Giulio showed Daedalus at work on the cow with mallet and chisel. It is a charming scene of busy activity, with a crowd of cupids lending their assistance by sawing and carrying wood.

Ill. 204

The painters of the school of Fontainebleau took up the theme as well as the style. An engraving by Antoine Caron might almost be based on the Giulio Romano drawing. The cow stands on a wooden platform and Daedalus is putting on the finishing touches; again helpful cupids cluster round him. (As a final postcript to this subject, we might look forward to Jean le Maire in the seventeenth century. His scene is heavily Classical, with Daedalus working in a colonnaded,

Ill. 203. Tintoretto's *Bacchus and Ariadne*, painted for a room in the Palazzo Ducale in Venice in 1578, sixty years after Titian's. Tintoretto takes the incident away from considerations of a particular time or place and gives it a generalized, cosmic setting. The flying figure of Venus, bringing Bacchus and Ariadne together, and holding the crown of stars over Ariadne's head, looks ahead to Baroque art.

Ill. 204. Daedalus, Pasiphaë and the Bull, by Giulio Romano, Raphael's chief assistant and most brilliant follower. In these frescoes that he did in the Palazzo del Tè at Mantua his love of the bizarre, the violent and the novel was given free play.

tunnel-vaulted arcade. Pasiphaë stands nearby, leaning gracefully on the bull's shoulder, waiting for Daedalus to finish.)

Eroticism was not confined to this bizarre episode, which must surely have been blatantly abnormal in any age. Other artists could convey sophisticated sensuality in more acceptable ways, and two types of Bacchus and Ariadne pictures became especially popular. One was that showing the lovers alone in poses of playful intimacy — as in an oval panel by Jacob Soens, with the thin, serpentine, elongated figures typical of northern Mannerism. The other was the scene of Bacchus finding Ariadne asleep, a scene rich in suggestive possibilities. Frans Floris, in a delicate drawing, shows Ariadne asleep, Bacchus bending over her and touching her lips to wake her. Louis Le Nain, in a strange picture now in a private collection in Paris, placed the sleeping Ariadne in the foreground, Bacchus — his face full of concern — stepping out of a boat on to the shore, and the whole centre of the canvas filled with burly realistic sailors. *Ill. 208* The Bacchus of Jacob Jordaens (in Boston) is a podgy boy holding up the crown of stars like a trophy; Ariadne lies naked and asleep, while at the back a row of satyrs leers at her over a hedge. In a

205

Ills. 205—207. These two panels from a fifteenth-century Italian decorated chest (*cassone*) make up the most detailed of all pictorial versions of the Theseus story. In the first (above), Theseus arrives by boat at Knossos; Ariadne and her nurse give him the thread; he enters the Labyrinth, kills the Minotaur and departs for Naxos. In the second he leaves Ariadne sleeping in a canopied bed, in spite of the nurse's remonstrations; Ariadne is seen running up and down the shore; Bacchus arrives in a chariot drawn by griffins. In the distance Theseus reaches Athens but has forgotten to change the sail and Aegeus throws himself from a tower. Right: a detail from the first panel. Behind the Labyrinth are episodes from the Minotaur's early life; it kills people and is captured by men with ropes (see *Ill. 143*).

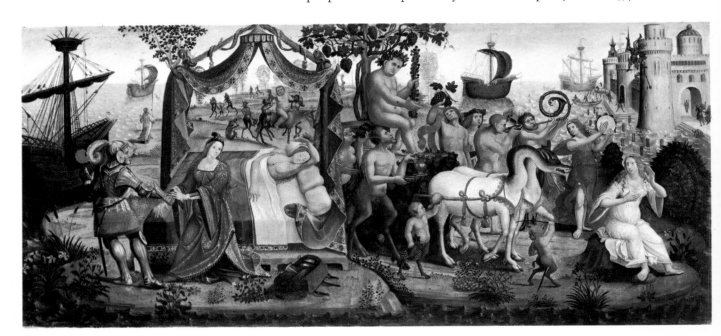

Ill. 208. The theme of Bacchus finding Ariadne became immensely popular in the seventeenth century. This example by Jacob Jordaens owes much to Rubens, the Ariadne herself being descended via Titian from the Roman statue shown in *Ill. 188.*

Ill. 209. Right, the same episode by Guido Reni. The painting's merits—dignity, chastity, repose— are strangely at odds with the subject matter.

large canvas by Luca Giordano in Dresden Bacchus descends from the clouds, like an angel annunciant, towards a swooning and ecstatic Ariadne.

Guido Reni painted the same subject but gave it an insipid sentimentality that rather drains it of much meaning. His Ariadne leans weakly against a rock while Bacchus approaches with a questioning look, almost as if interviewing her for a job. The painting, in the Galleria San Luca in Rome, is curiously static and un-Baroque, which must have endeared it to the neo-Classical Anton Raphael Mengs, for he made a copy of it.

Any student of the arts of the seventeenth century is bound to meet Bacchus and Ariadne at every turn. Their appearance in the mainstream of Baroque painting must wait for a later section of this chapter. But they were almost equally popular on engraved rings, on bronze plaques and on Flemish tapestries. A Flemish

Ill. 209

Ill. 211

printed textile in the Victoria and Albert Museum in London shows them like masque characters posed against a single Ionic column and surrounded by exotic plants and birds; there is a distinctly Indian look to the design, which is of course not an impossible influence.

Ill. 210   Two majolica plates, also in the Victoria and Albert Museum, depict the story of Hippolytus and Phaedra, while the motif of the Labyrinth occurs more than once in emblem books and on signets. The emblem of Gonzalo Perez, secretary to Charles V and Philip II of Spain, translator of the *Odyssey*, was the Labyrinth seen in perspective with the Minotaur in the attitude of a pugilist in the centre. His motto, *In silentio et spe*, comes from Isaiah XXX, 15 ('In quietness and in confidence [shall be your strength]'). Another similar emblem has the motto, *Fata viam invenient* ('The fates will find the way').

By the mid-sixteenth century, the Italian poetic imagination had turned from the ancient world to the Middle Ages. Ariosto and Francesco Bello, known as Il Cieco da Ferrara, both make passing allusions to the Theseus story in their long romantic epics (*Orlando Furioso* and *Il Mambriano*) but add nothing in the way of insight and interpretation. The same can be said of the pastoralists and writers of idylls such as G. B. Marino whose *Sampagna* (1620) includes Ariadne along with Orpheus, Actaeon, Europa and Proserpina in a series of lyrical pieces in a highly-wrought, artificial style, calculated to intrigue the fancy rather than to stimulate mind or heart.

It was through this pastoral convention that the Ariadne story entered music, an art in which it was to find itself at once perfectly at home and in which it was to inspire at least two outstanding masterpieces.

One of the earliest of all operas was Monteverdi's *Arianna a Nasso*, with libretto by the Florentine poet Ottavio Rinuccini, performed at Mantua in 1608 to celebrate the wedding of Francesco Gonzaga and Marguerite of Savoy. It began with an aria by Venus prophesying Theseus' abandonment of Ariadne and invoking Amore to protect her. Theseus appears and after a sad scene with Ariadne leaves her alone and inconsolable. This was the moment for Ariadne's great aria, *Lasciatemi morire*, which moved the audience to tears and was long remembered as a model of what lyrical drama could achieve. The chorus, however, tells Ariadne that Bacchus has seen her and offers her his love. Venus returns and the wedding is celebrated.

It would be gratifying to describe the music, for it was surely a work of genius. But only the lament of Ariadne survives, and that in an altered form—a madrigal arrangement made by Monteverdi after the opera's success and given a religious interpretation, which one can only regret.

The subject must have been a fairly common one in 1608. In *The Two Gentlemen of Verona*, dating from about fifteen years earlier, the disguised Julia tells Silvia how she took part in 'a pageant of delight' at Pentecost, and played a woman's part:

> Madam, 'twas Ariadne passioning
> For Theseus' perjury and unjust flight;

Ill. 210. Right, a sixteenth-century Italian majolica plate tells the story of Hippolytus. On the right he escapes from Phaedra's advances and rushes from the palace. On the left, pursued by Theseus, he drives his four-horse chariot towards the sea. The coat-of-arms is that of Isabella d'Este, for whom the plate was made.

Which I so lively acted with my tears
That my poor mistress, moved therewithal,
Wept bitterly.

For the next three hundred years, hardly any subject was to be more constantly resorted to by librettists in search of an affecting story. There are dozens of *Ariannas* and *Teseos*, scores of *Arianna e Baccos*, almost as many *Arianna a Nassos* (I have found only one *Incostanzo trionfante*). Composers who set them to music included Benedetto Ferrari (called 'della Tiorba'—Tuba—from his expertise in that instrument), the Englishman Henry Lawes (who used a libretto by William Cartwright), Handel, Adolfati (a pupil of Galuppi, famous for the fact that he was the first to use 5/4 time) and Haydn. When Hofmannsthal (see page 236) came to choose a subject that would be typical of eighteenth-century opera he could not have chosen more accurately.

The operas, cantatas and ballets used the ancient story as a convenient vehicle for melody and sentimental interest but had nothing serious to say about its meaning. For that we must turn back to literature.

The Renaissance, as we have seen, had made the original sources more accessible and more comprehensible. For those who lacked the time or stamina to master these, there were dictionaries or handbooks of mythology. Probably the most widely read was the *Mythologia* of the Venetian Natalis Comes, published in 1554. Natalis tells all the important myths, dividing his book systematically into Books and Chapters, adding interpretations very much in the medieval manner. The Labyrinth, for instance, represents the entanglements of the world, from which only virtue and skill can extricate us; the story of Pasiphaë teaches us that when the soul deserts reason and gives way to excessive passion (of any kind) the result will be monstrous.

Similar works were not slow to appear in England. The modest title of one of the earliest, that of Charles Stephanus (1555), is too good not to quote: *Dictionarium historium ac poeticum omnia gentium, hominum, locorum, fluminum, ac montium antiqua recentioraque*. A later one, known as Cooper's *Thesaurus* (1565), has all the Theseus stories under convenient headings, and an interesting study has been made

Ill. 211. Bacchus' wedding with Ariadne became in the seventeenth century one of the most common symbols of the good life, offering a magnificent opportunity for the display of beautiful nude bodies, exotic food, precious objects, flowers and foliage. It appears on innumerable tapestries, reaching its peak in those made at Beauvais in the eighteenth century. This example, from a set showing the loves of the gods, was woven from designs made by François Boucher about 1754.

to show how the Elizabethan poets depended upon it and similar compilations.

The English public, in fact, only became fully aware of the Classical heritage in the sixteenth century. Two of the most famous translations from Classical authors, Golding's *Ovid* and North's *Plutarch*, appeared in 1567 and 1579.

In 1566 a minor literary figure, Thomas Underdowne, published *The Excellente Historye of Theseus and Ariadne*. Elizabethan poets were not so prone as medieval ones to interpret all stories in strictly moral terms, but they did all feel obliged to take sides in the matter of Theseus and Ariadne. Underdowne is definitely pro-Theseus, chiefly because he is anti-women. His book, he tells us, is written 'in commendacion of all good women; and to the infamie of suche lyght huswyves as Phaedra the sister of Ariadne was, which fled away wt Theseus her sisters husbande'. Ariadne, however, is not allowed to be much better: 'Assuredly, he that desireth a fair woman armeth himself to a right great and dangerous adventure: and why? a fair woman is nothing but a gazing stock of idel folkes. Thus much I have said', he concludes (realizing perhaps that it has had no great relevance to the story he is going to tell) 'because Ariadne's idleness caused all her grief; for if she had not been idle, she would not have gone out of her chamber, and if she had not gone out of her chamber, she had not come to the labyrinth where Theseus was. . . . Idleness is therefore the ground of all vice.' The poem itself, written in ballad stanzas, goes through the story of Pasiphaë, the birth of the Minotaur, Theseus and Ariadne; and the author has the grace to pay a conventional tribute to Ariadne's unhappy fate:

> Thus said, the gods did her translate
>   Into the starry sky;
> And gave her place among the stars
>   Where she shall never die.

Another treatment of some interest, though admittedly again not for all tastes, is that of George Pettie, the founder-father of Euphuism before *Euphues*, in his *A Petite Pallace of Pettie his Pleasure*, published in 1576. It is written in the elaborate convoluted prose that Lyly was to bring to an even more unreadable pitch of artifice, and tells a number of stories from Ovid, including that of Pasiphaë. He (and Cooper too) mentions the story that the bull was really a man called Taurus, but he retains tradition in his own version. It has indeed touches of tender invention, as when he describes how Pasiphaë used to bring specially succulent boughs for the bull to feed on, and how jealous she was of the cows that he seemed to fancy.

Spenser's *Faerie Queene* belongs to the category of the Italianate romantic epic, and of him too one can say that generally speaking he has no particular interest in ancient myths. He does, however, give three stanzas to Hippolytus and Phaedra, of which the first may be quoted as a fair sample of his quality:

Hippolytus a jolly huntsman was
That wont in charret chase the foaming bore;
He all his Peeres in beauty did surpass,
But Ladies love, as loss of time, forbore:
His wanton stepdame loved him the more,
But when she saw her offered love refus'd,
Her love she turn'd to hate, and him before
His father fierce of treason false accus'd,
And with her gealous termes his open eares abus'd.

John Shepery, in 1586, repaired an omission in the ancient poets, and wrote a Latin reply of Hippolytus to Phaedra—*Hippolytus Ovidianae Phaedrae respondens*. It served as the model for a version in English verse by Richard Brathwait, who lingers it out into a poem of nearly fifty stanzas, which is more than the subject will bear. It is prefixed by an 'Argument' telling us that Hippolytus 'seeks by all means to repress her inordinate lust' by reminding her of Theseus' virtues, of the scandal that the affair will provoke, of the unnaturalness of her desires, of the gods' prohibition, of the inevitability of punishment, and finally of his resolution that

... if these motives cannot caution you,
Not to adulterize your *Nuptiall bed*,
Be you assured to Theseus I will show
These undigested humours which are bred
By your unsettled thoughts.

Feeble though Brathwait's effort may be, it is at least an example of an Elizabethan poet taking a Classical story and using it as the medium for his own moral feelings and his own thoughts on human conduct.

Shakespeare did exactly that in *Venus and Adonis* and *The Rape of Lucrece*, but he wrote no *Theseus and Ariadne*. The story seems to have interested him very little. Theseus appears in his conventional role as duke of Athens in *A Midsummer Night's Dream*, but apart from that all we can gather are a few scraps of simile like

Thou mayst not wander in that labyrinth;
There Minotaurs and ugly treasons lurk

from *Henry VI Part I*.

In the seventeenth century a sort of medievalizing tendency seems to have returned to literature, and allegory came back into intellectual fashion. George Sandys first published his translation of Ovid in 1626; it was re-issued in 1632 with an elaborate commentary giving 'The Philosophical sense of the fables of Ovid'. His interpretation of the Minotaur story combines ideas from a wide variety of sources, most of which will now be familiar. The Labyrinth is 'the condition of man', only passable by 'the conduct of wisdom and exercise of unfainting fortitude'. Pasiphaë is 'the soul of man', Minos 'Justice and Integrity', the bull 'sensual delights' and Ariadne 'sincere affection'.

The most extreme example of allegorization comes in 1647 in *Mystogogus Poeticus* by a Scottish schoolmaster called Alexander Ross. Ross's cast of mind is completely medieval, but he goes further than any medieval commentator. For him Theseus is nothing less than the type of Christ. Here are three of his 'interpretations':

1. In Theseus' killing of the infestuous thieves and subduing of monsters is set down a fit example of valour and justice for princes to imitate.
2. Theseus was guided by Ariadne's thread to get out of the labyrinth; the word of God is the thread that will direct us through the winding and intricate labyrinth of this life . . .
9. Our blessed Saviour is the true Theseus, who was persecuted in his infancy, and in his lifetime overcame many monsters, but far more in his death; he went down to hell, and from thence delivered mankind, which had been there detained in everlasting chains of darkness if he had not ascended . . .

The last example of this medieval convention that I have found in relation to Theseus is not English but German. It is an edition of Ovid published at Salzburg in 1705, containing an engraving of Theseus and Ariadne, with the Labyrinth (looking like a piece of eighteenth-century topiary work) in the background in which Theseus is fighting the Minotaur. A *Morale* is appended, where the Labyrinth is interpreted as 'the confined life at court today, in which, if a person should get lost, he can rarely find his way out'. The Minotaur is the type of tyrant who 'sucks up the very sweat and blood of his hard-pressed subjects'. The only way to escape, the author concludes, quoting St John Chrysostom, is to keep silence. As Theseus escaped from the Labyrinth, so some men have succeeded in escaping from court:

Wie aus dem Labyrinth sich Theseus geschwungen,
So ists am menschem Hoff auch manchem offt gelungen.

In France, the second fatherland of Classicism, there was less tendency to treat the myths as excuses for the expression of private foibles. Respect for antique models was deeper than in any other country outside Italy, and this is true whether one looks at architecture, painting or drama. As early as 1573 Seneca's *Phaedra* had been adapted to the French stage by Robert Garnier. It is an academic exercise, but indicative of great things to come. In 1606 followed Alexandre Hardy's *Ariane ravie*, described as 'tragi-comédie'. It is interesting to see that the unity of place was not regarded as obligatory at this date. The first act takes place at Knossos after Theseus has fled with Ariadne and Phaedra; the last four take place on Naxos. The development can hardly be called dramatic: the whole of Act IV consists of a single monologue by Ariadne nearly 300 lines long. At the end of it she throws herself off a cliff, but is only stunned and wakes up to find herself in the arms of Bacchus. So all ends happily.

Plays on Classical themes dominated French drama during the middle and late seventeenth century. There were at least three other versions of *Phaedra* between Garnier's and 1677, when a work raised the theme once more to the level of genius: Racine's play *Phèdre*. Racine based himself mainly on Seneca, and although he is usually considered to have surpassed his original in the delineation of passion, it is not so certain that he was equally successful dramatically. To begin with his Hippolyte is not the chaste votary of Diana, but a more ordinary figure with a sweetheart of his own, Aricie. (Not Racine's own invention, incidentally: he says he took the idea from Virgil who relates that Hippolytus married her after Aesculapius had restored him to life—hardly a satisfactory excuse.) Phaedra, therefore, can no longer be consumed with a hopeless love for an impossible object, but merely becomes an unsuccessful rival, filled with jealousy. She is more human, but less sublime—or rather she would be if the tremendous power of Racine's verse did not give her a new sublimity:

Je le vis, je rougis, je pâlis à sa vue ;
Un trouble s'éleva dans mon âme éperdue ;
Mes yeux ne voyaient pas, je ne pouvais parler ;
Je sentis tout mon corps et transir et brûler ;
Je reconnus Vénus et ses feux redoutables,
D'un sang qu'elle poursuit tourments inévitables.

Another departure from tradition in Racine stems from Aricie: she belongs to a branch of the royal family, and when a false report of Theseus' death reaches Troezen there is a political crisis with Phèdre's son, Hippolyte and Aricie all contenders for the throne. This complicates the action and distracts attention from the main theme. Strong dramatic scenes, however, there certainly are: Phèdre at the beginning of the play is sick of a mysterious illness, which with reluctance she reveals to the nurse, Oenone: she loves Hippolyte. The report of Theseus' death gives her the courage to meet Hippolyte and confess her love. She does this slowly, painfully, with shame. He rejects her, and flees from the palace. Theseus unexpectedly returns and the nurse conceives the idea of slandering Hippolyte. Phèdre is about to admit the truth to Theseus when he tells her that Hippolyte loves Aricie. She remains silent. The end is the same as in Seneca, with a fine narration of Hippolyte's death.

What raises *Phèdre* to its eminence is its psychology and its poetry, neither of which can meaningfully be suggested here, since they depend upon the long build-up of sustained, precisely observed, perfectly expressed emotion. Suffice it to quote the two most famous lines: the superb image of a dominating and irresistible infatuation—

C'est Vénus, toute entière, à sa proie attachée

—and the ominous line with which Phèdre herself is first introduced at the beginning of the play in a speech by Hippolyte:

La fille de Minos et de Pasiphaë.

In the Preface to *Phèdre* Racine explains why he found the story so well suited to tragedy: 'Phèdre is neither completely guilty nor completely innocent. She is led by her destiny and by the anger of the gods into a forbidden passion, which at first horrifies her. She makes every effort to overcome it. She would rather die than

Ill. 212. Illustrations to Racine's *Phèdre* provide a record of changing styles devoted to a single theme. This drawing by Brunck was published in 1942.

reveal it to anyone. And when she is forced to reveal it, she speaks with a confusion which shows clearly that her crime is rather a punishment of the gods than an act of her own will.'

The first performance of *Phèdre* was the occasion for one of those literary feuds that made Racine's life a misery and finally persuaded him to give up writing altogether. A rival poet, Pradon, was put up to writing another play on exactly the same subject, to be performed two days after Racine's. The merits of this need not detain us. Racine's *Phèdre* is still performed regularly in France, though it seems to be untranslatable into any other language. Illustrated editions have included drawings by de Sève (1750) and Brunck (1942).

Of French Classical plays concerning Theseus the only other notable example is Thomas Corneille's *Ariane*, published in 1672. Thomas Corneille adopted a lyrical, rather sentimental verse style closer to Racine than to his brother Pierre. *Ariane* elaborates the Ovidian story into a typical drama of intrigue. Bacchus, of course, disappears. Naxos is given a king, Enarus, who loves Ariadne. Ariadne loves Theseus; Theseus loves Phaedra; Phaedra loves Theseus. They all try to do the correct thing. Enarus renounces Ariadne; Theseus recommends that she accept him. She agrees, but upon learning that it is her sister Phaedra who is her rival, she stabs herself.

The play was extremely successful and was famous for the acting of La Champmêlée in the title part. Madame de Sévigné describes how powerful the effect was—'Every heart was interested, every eye dissolved in tears.' Voltaire, who edited Thomas Corneille's plays, was more critical of *Ariane*, but he thought the subject ideal: 'A princess who has done everything for her lover; who has delivered him from a cruel death and sacrificed all considerations for his sake; who loves him generously; who thinks herself loved in return, and deserves to be so; who finds herself, at last, abandoned by the man whom she adores, and betrayed by a sister whom she also loved—a woman thus situated forms the happiest subject that has come down to us from antiquity.'

It is interesting to compare this cool aesthetic appraisal with the morally loaded judgements of critics a few generations earlier. The play continued to be popular for years to come. Madame Duclos was another famous actress, and a portrait by Nicolas de Largillière in the Comédie Française shows her in the part—a lady of mature charm wearing a rich velvet dress and registering some emotion that might equally well be grief or joy, while a cherub holds a crown of stars over her head.

Ariane was adapted into English as *The Rival Sisters* by Arthur Murphy (1793), in which Mrs Siddons played Ariadne; and two years later by the Rev. Thomas Stratford as *The Labyrinth, or Fatal Embarassment*, a work which deserves a place in any anthology of bad poetry.

The latter part of the seventeenth century and most of the eighteenth was not a period in which the Theseus myth acquired many interesting new interpretations. Greek mythology in general went through a certain devaluation. In Baroque and Rococo art it tended to be conventional and trivial; while the neo-Classical movement, which brought a new moral earnestness, turned to Roman history rather than to Greek legend. One exception to these generalizations comes at the outset. Nicolas Poussin, in a single picture, gives us back Theseus the hero, but it is characteristic that he avoids the whole Cretan episode and chooses the scene of Theseus recovering his father's weapons. The architecture that surrounds the figures is Roman, and the whole composition seems to breathe a discipline and a masculinity that is closer to Livy than to Plutarch.

Several paintings of Bacchus and Ariadne have been attributed to Poussin, but are not admitted into the canon by Sir Anthony Blunt. One of his few close followers was Jean le Maire, already mentioned, who was *peintre du roi* and a specialist in architectural and perspective drawing (it is reliably said, indeed, that the background of Poussin's painting is from the hand of le Maire). His version of the same theme is even more devotedly Classical; slabs of relief sculpture lie about, and through an arch in the background one sees the ruins of the Colosseum.

It was the Bacchus and Ariadne episode, however, which almost alone of the Theseus cycle appealed to the artists of the seventeenth and eighteenth centuries. It became one of the clichés of secular Baroque art, and there is no need here to multiply instances of the same thing. A few of the earlier examples have already been mentioned.

Ill. 213. Right, *Theseus Raising the Stone*, to find his father's sword, by Nicolas Poussin. Poussin stands out in the seventeenth century for the seriousness of his treatment of myth, which links him with his contemporaries in literature (Corneille, Racine), rather than those in art. Much of the grandeur of this scene is due to its architectural setting.

Ill. 213

Ill. 214

More influential than any other was probably Annibale Carracci's large fresco, the *Triumph of Bacchus and Ariadne* in the Palazzo Farnese in Rome, a rich, varied, sensuous painting that exactly typifies the taste of the age. The subject, one feels, does not matter a great deal. In the Bacchic throng, Ariadne is merely one among his votaries, his chief partner in pleasure. (Hogarth parodied this picture in one of his illustrations to *Hudibras* in 1726—the episode of the 'Stimmington', a rural custom in which shrews and henpecked husbands were tied together on a horse and escorted through the village.)

Ill. 215

Giambattista Tiepolo, in one of several paintings of the same theme, treated the subject as an Assumption, with Bacchus and

Ariadne seen from below and surrounded by flying cherubs. In the same style, Francesco de Mura used the whole Theseus cycle in his decoration of the ceiling of a room in the Palazzo Reale, Turin. Its energy and accomplished Baroque rhetoric make it an attractive work, but it is not by any means obvious exactly what is happening in any particular section, and one gets the impression that the artist did not very much care.

The episode of Bacchus finding Ariadne offered rather more scope for individual invention. In a fine painting by Cornelis Mebeecq, a Dutch artist who worked in Italy, Ariadne reclines langorously naked on a couch with Bacchus hovering over her as cherubs prepare to cover them both with a huge blanket; in the background the three Graces dance. Sebastiano Ricci treats the scene almost like a profane *Adoration of the Shepherds*. Bacchus and his followers enter reverently from the right; on the other side a male and a female figure might easily be Joseph and Mary; while on the ground, instead of the Christ Child, lies the sleeping Ariadne.

In a painting by Giovanni Battista Pittoni, cupids blindfold Ariadne, who sinks back on a bed while Bacchus arrives on a cloud bearing the crown of stars in his hand. Hendrick van Limboch

Ill. 216

Ill. 214. Annibale Carracci's *Triumph of Bacchus and Ariadne*, painted on the ceiling of a hall in the Palazzo Farnese, Rome, is one of the seminal paintings of Italian Baroque. Interest in the story is minimal; the scene becomes primarily an exercise in the rhetoric of ecstasy.

Ill. 215. Giambattista Tiepolo treated the theme of *Bacchus and Ariadne* several times, making it part of his peculiarly magical world of effortless happiness. Here Ariadne reclines lazily while Bacchus, astride a huge boulder, holds the crown of stars over her.

Ill. 216. Cornelis Mebeecq's *Bacchus and Ariadne*. The warm sensuality of Titian and Rubens has become a cool and almost calculated eroticism.

applies the same general treatment to an earlier part of Ariadne's career, when Theseus is preparing to set off for the Labyrinth. She lies nude on a bed; Theseus leaves her, holding the ball of thread, while two *amorini* flutter round, promising a happy ending. A little poem by John Gay, the author of *The Beggar's Opera*, exactly catches in words the quality of erotic prettiness that these painters obviously wanted. He describes a painted fan, on which were depicted a series of 'saints of Cupid', including Ariadne:

> Here let the wretched Ariadne stand,
> Seduced by Theseus to some desert land,
> Her locks dishevelled waving in the wind,
> The crystal tears confess her tortured mind;
> The perjured youth unfurls his treacherous sails
> And their white bosoms catch the swelling gales.

If Angelica Kauffmann had not, in fact, painted just such a scene, this would be enough for us to imagine it.

One reason, perhaps, why the myths no longer tended to be used to convey deeply felt truths about human nature was that the scholars had begun to look at them for the first time with critical attention. Throughout the eighteenth century, especially in France, works on ancient religion appeared which tried to find some rational explanation for what was, everyone agreed, nonsense. The author of the article 'Minotaure' in Diderot's *Encyclopédie* of 1765 agreed with Frenet's view that myths are always badly remembered history. The flight of Daedalus and Icarus, for example, referred to the fact that they escaped in sailing boats, Icarus being shipwrecked. The rest is the work of poets and 'whatever certain modern writers may say, fable, fiction, and everything that springs from the imagination, is the very soul of poetry'. Another writer, Dupuis, however, saw myths as reflections of religious practices (he believed that Christianity itself was a sun cult).

Parallel with these early efforts in comparative religion went the beginnings of archaeology. As the Classical sites of Greece and the Roman Empire became more frequently visited and publicized, a few travellers took the time and trouble to wander round Heraklion looking for remains of the Labyrinth. Of course they found nothing.

Most of them decided in favour of the theory that it had really been the caves of Gortyna. As early as 1632, Sandys, in his notes on Ovid already quoted, records that although Pliny says that no trace of the Labyrinth survived 'yet at this day the inhabitants undertake to show it unto strangers. For between the ruins of Gortina and Grossius, at the foot of Ida, are many Meanders, hewn out of the rock underground, in so much as not to be entered without a conductor. I have heard a merchant say, who had seen it, that it was so intricate and vast, that a guide who for twenty years together had shown it to others there lost himself and was never more heard of.' In 1700, G. P. de Tournefort visited the caves and concluded that they were an ancient quarry. At the end of the century another French traveller, C. E. Savary, believed that Gortyna was the site of the Minotaur legend but *not* the Labyrinth built by Daedalus at Knossos.

The most interesting fruit of this archaeological interest is the attempt by the great Austrian architect Fischer von Erlach to reconstruct the Labyrinth from a Roman coin and the description in Pliny. In his large volume of careful engravings published in 1721 and containing both contemporary buildings and reconstructed ancient ones, Fischer showed the Labyrinth as a vast prison, the lines formed by high barrack-like blocks with tiny windows and the spaces by the prison yards: a grim and extraordinary conception.

The revived interest in the ancient world had its effect, of course, on art, though only intermittently on themes connected with Theseus. Laurent Delvaux produced a sleeping Ariadne, based vaguely on the Vatican prototype but with the figure nude instead of draped. More original is a bronze by the German sculptor Johann Heinrich von Dannecker (sketched in 1803, finished 1810) showing Ariadne reclining rather precariously on a Bacchic leopard. Pierre-Narcisse Guerin's *Hippolytus Accused by Phaedra* (*c.* 1802) tries unsuccessfully to bring neo-Classical *Romanitas* to bear upon Racine: Hippolytus stands silent before Theseus' anger, while Phaedra, holding the naked sword, listens to the nurse's promptings. Best of all in this style is Canova's *Theseus Triumphant* of 1781—82. Canova made it during his early years in Rome; at first he intended to show Theseus and the Minotaur in combat, but Gavin Hamilton advised him to concentrate on the moment of calm after victory (the composition,

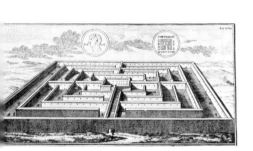

Ill. 217. The great Austrian architect, Fischer von Erlach, was among the first to attempt scholarly reproductions of ancient buildings, but it is hard to know how seriously he took the fantastic version of the labyrinth as a prison.

Ill. 218

in fact, owes something to one of Hamilton's own paintings). The image of the dead Minotaur goes back to a Pompeiian fresco.

Canova went back to Theseus for other large groups showing him fighting a centaur. Theseus the hero is here decidedly reborn, appropriately enough in the age of Napoleon and of the beginnings of nationalism. Hegel called for a 'new Theseus' to unite Germany, and the recollection that he was the founder of Athens begins for the first time to influence Theseus' image in art and literature. He becomes the athletic champion of civilization against barbarism, an interpretation implicit in the statue by Antoine-Louis Barye (1846) where the Minotaur, a slightly smaller figure than Theseus, clings to his enemy with both legs while Theseus holds his shoulder with one hand and is about to plunge a sword into his skull with the other. Imitated from Archaic Greek models, he personifies calm intelligence versus brute stupidity.

Ill. 219

The idea of Theseus the patriot enjoyed wide popularity all through the nineteenth century and is still current. The public exhibition of the Theseus (now thought to be Heracles) from the Parthenon among the Elgin Marbles strengthened the image ('a proud and mighty spirit', in the words of Barry Cornwall's poem, *On the Statue of Theseus*), and it was given rousing expression by the ever-fertile Mrs Felicia Hemans in a poem called *The Shade of Theseus* where his ghost fights with the Greeks at Marathon (see page 156).

The Romantic movement remoulded the old stories in its own image, characterized by two contrasting and rarely coexisting qualities—violence and sentiment. The violent side of Romanticism found a rewarding subject in the death of Hippolytus. Fuseli treated it in his best nightmare manner: Hippolytus is a panic-stricken naked figure surrounded by the wild heads and plunging bodies of his horses.

Sentiment may be represented by Romney's portrait of *Lady Hamilton as Ariadne*. Romney painted Emma Hamilton in a whole series of Classical roles, and her expression remains much the same whether as Circe or Ariadne or anybody else. As the nineteenth century progressed the emotion to be derived from the scene of Ariadne abandoned grew warmer. Théodore Chassériau made a fine ink study of a distraught girl clinging to a tree and gazing out

Ill. 218. Right, it is characteristic ▶ of Canova and of neo-Classicism that he should have chosen the moment of calm after victory rather than the fight with the Minotaur itself. His *Theseus Triumphant* was carved during his first period in Rome, in 1781—82.

Ill. 219. Antoine-Louis Barye's bronze *Theseus* may be compared with the Canova on the previous page— Romanticism versus neo-Classicism. Barye made a speciality of gruesome fights between men and animals or between two animals. The Tuileries gardens in Paris contain many of his works.

across the sea. Delacroix, in a calm and lyrical composition, imagined Bacchus raising Ariadne gently to life from the depths of despair—two intense figures against a background of rock and sky. With the end of the century in England comes the near-pornography of the Edwardian academic style, represented by John Lavery's *Ariadne*, a seductive young girl seen from behind and clad in transparent drapery which hides nothing.

Sentiment in literature found no sweeter exponent than Leigh Hunt. His *Bacchus and Ariadne* of 1819 is a fluent exercise inspired by *Endymion* and the description of Ariadne awakening in her leafy bower has genuine charm:

> . . . sweet, self-willed content conspired to keep
> Her senses lingering in the feel of sleep;
> And with a little smile she seemed to say—
> I know my love is near me and 'tis day.

The account of Bacchus and his train owes as much to Titian as to Keats, and the poem ends with a luxurious wedding.

We know what Byron thought of Leigh Hunt's verse. One would give much for a *Bacchus and Ariadne* in the *Don Juan* manner, but Byron only touches upon the Theseus stories briefly and in passing: the theory, for instance, that the whole Minotaur myth is an allegory for the increased production of beef on Crete in order to build up the troops:

> That Pasiphae promoted breeding cattle
> To make the Cretans bloodier in battle.

To follow the fortunes of Theseus, Ariadne, Phaedra and Hippolytus through the lush by-ways of Victorian lyric poetry we should have to invoke the shades of R. S. Ross, Professor J. S. Blackie, W. M. W. Call, Sir Lewis Morris . . . names which have earned their oblivion and whose rest we do not propose to disturb. Of real significance are only two short dramatic fragments—Swinburne's *Phaedra* and Browning's *Artemis Prologuizes*. The first, published in *Poems and Ballads* (1866), consists of a dialogue in blank verse between Phaedra and Hippolytus, with interjections from the chorus. Swinburne affects a stark style which reads like a translation from the Greek, but his conception of Phaedra is strikingly new. She is a woman without guilt, confronting her desire with joy rather than trying to suppress or hide it. It is Hippolytus, in her eyes, who should be ashamed, though she knows—and relishes—the fact that the world calls her passion sinful: 'I have strange blood in me'.

When Browning's *Artemis Prologuizes* begins, the tragedy is over. Aesculapius bends over the mangled remains of Hippolytus, trying to restore him to life. Hippolytus was doomed because he offended Artemis, but when he was finally brought back to Theseus, she says,

> I, in a flood of glory visible,
> Stood o'er my dying votary and, deed
> By deed, revealed, as all took place, the truth.

It is a slow-moving, austere poem, the names (a habit of Browning's) given their authentic Greek spellings: Hippolutos, Phaidra, Olumpos.

11 Theseus in the Modern World

Simon Tidworth

DURING THE SECOND HALF OF THE NINETEENTH CENTURY, views on the nature and meaning of myth were revolutionized by the new sciences of psychology and anthropology, now crucial to thought on the subject, as the earlier chapters of this book sufficiently show. John Ruskin was neither a psychologist nor an anthropologist in any scientific sense, but his approach to myth, and the insights towards which he was feeling his way, can only be called psychological. His views therefore represent an interesting transitional phase.

Ruskin's treatment of Theseus comes in Nos. 22 and 23 of *Fors Clavigera*, 'Letters to the Workmen and Labourers of Great Britain', of which eighty-seven were published monthly from 1871 to 1878. The tone of these pieces now seems unbearably condescending and the information dubious, but Ruskin certainly thought he was doing good. In *Fors Clavigera* 22 he takes Theseus as 'the founder of the first city whose history you are to know', and his fight with the Minotaur as 'the fable through which the Greeks taught what they knew of the more terrible and mysterious relations between the lower creatures and man'. Theseus never deserted Ariadne, says Ruskin, 'but she him—involuntarily, poor sweet maid—Death calling her in Diana's name' (this refers to the Homeric version of the story, noted in Chapter 2). No. 23 returns to the subject with a discourse entitled 'The Labyrinth'. After treating the workmen to a little sermon on how much better off they would be walking in the fields on Sunday rather than going to the British Museum, as they insisted upon doing, he traces the origin of the Greek key pattern to the meander or labyrinth, and plays with the idea that 'the House that Jack built' may originally have been the Labyrinth, 'the cow with the crumpled horn' the Minotaur, and 'the maiden all forlorn' Ariadne. Daedalus he interprets as 'distinctively the powers of finest human, as opposed to Divine, workmanship or craftsman-ship . . . labour of the hands separated from that of the soul', and Theseus himself as 'the Peace maker . . . the exterminator of every bestial and savage element, and the type of human, or humane, power, which power you will find in this, and all my other books on policy, summed in the words Gentleness and Justice'. What the workmen of Great Britain made of it all one would dearly like to know.

To Frazer, in *The Golden Bough*, Knossos was the seat of a great sun cult, the Minotaur an embodiment of the sun god, and 'Ariadne's dance' through the Labyrinth an imitation of the sun's dance through the sky. (The Dance of Delos, i.e. the Crane Dance, was supposed to have been begun by Theseus; its connection with other dances, the Roman 'Troy Game', etc., is a fascinating by-way of the Theseus story.)

A. B. Cook supported Frazer, considering the Labyrinth 'an *orchestra* of solar pattern presumably made for a mimetic dance'. The dancer who represented the sun, he thought, masqueraded in the Labyrinth as a bull; probably he was the Cretan crown prince. Others connected the story with human sacrifice, comparing it with Kronos devouring his children; with sacrifices to Moloch (whom Frazer conjectured to have been worshipped in Crete with the head of a bull); and with a Sardinian Bronze Age cult in which a bull god was worshipped in a subterranean temple.

G. R. Levey noted that 'both the winding path and the rope, or clew, appear in European tales of entry into an actual or subjective spiritual maze'. Parallels that have been drawn include the Sleeping Beauty's spindle and the ball of wool unwound by the kitten before Alice goes through the Looking Glass, while Mircea Eliade sees the whole Theseus story as 'dependent upon an initiatory scenario. Many episodes in the saga of Theseus are in fact initiatory rituals.'

The early psychologists give disappointingly scant treatment to the myth; but Jung, seeing Theseus as simply one manifestation of a common type, interpreted all the conflicts with monsters, especially those which the hero encounters in caves under the earth, as symbolic encounters with the mother-imago which must be overcome before we can advance to maturity. He also has this to say about Hippolytus and related stories:

> The young growing part of the personality, if prevented from living or kept in check, generates fear. The fear seems to come from the mother, but actually it is the deadly fear of the unconscious, inner man, who is cut off from life by the continual shrinking back from reality. If the mother is felt as the obstacle, she becomes the vengeful pursuer. Naturally, it is not the real mother, although she too may seriously injure the child by the morbid tenderness with which she pursues it into adult life, thus prolonging the infantile attitude beyond the proper time. It is rather the mother-imago, that has turned into a lamia.

Psychological and anthropological theories of this kind opened up a world of fresh possibilities to artists and poets. Not only could they now perceive unsuspected new depths in the old stories but they began to use them as parables for their own preoccupations in a way which earlier generations—for all their predilection for symbolism—had never attempted.

From the turn of the nineteenth century onwards, in fact, there ceases to be any general conventional attitude to the Theseus myths, and it is therefore pointless to continue a chronological treatment. I shall simply trace the various transformations of particular themes, grouping them under three headings: 1, the Phaedra-Hippolytus story, 2, Ariadne, and 3, Pasiphaë and the Minotaur.

First, Phaedra and Hippolytus. Passion and Chastity, Sensuality and Responsibility are personified as the two goddesses in T. Sturge Moore's poetic drama, *Aphrodite against Artemis* (1901). It is set in a rustic hut where Hippolytus, surrounded by girls but indifferent to them, is resting after the hunt. He worships Artemis alone. In an extraordinary scene which it is hard to take quite seriously, Phaedra dresses up as Artemis and comes to him while he is asleep. At first he believes in her and embraces her but soon he realizes his mistake. In a heady, sexy scene (which Moore considered out of the question to put on the stage) she tries to seduce him; is rejected; kills herself leaving a letter accusing Hippolytus . . . and so on, as in the traditional story. Hippolytus is brought back dying, and nobly forgives his father, but Artemis appears and delivers judgement on all the characters. Aphrodite, who has been present all through the play in disguise (unknown to the audience) ends with a speech on behalf of passion and she then proceeds to burn the hut down.

The feeling for human motivation that eluded Sturge Moore was possessed in full measure by the Italian poet and patriot Gabriele d'Annunzio, whose *Fedra* was published (in a highly aesthetic format and with an Art Nouveau title page) in 1909. D'Annunzio takes up Swinburne's conception of Phaedra as a rebel against conventional morality, and expands it into a vastly ambitious symbolic drama. His Fedra defies not only man but the gods; she becomes a sort of female Prometheus or Faust. Both Aphrodite and Artemis are her enemies, and she treats them not as divinely superior beings, but as equals, as rivals. She brings about Hippolytus' death, not out of revenge for his rejection of her, but in order to defeat Aphrodite and to 'overthrow the old law, setting up a mysterious law of her own'. Deliberately she calls down upon herself the wrath of Artemis, deriding her as a chaste and helpless protector of Hippolytus: *O dea, tu non hai piu potenza*. Artemis may kill her, but she wins after all, united with Hippolytus in death: *Ancora vinco! Ippolito, son teco*. She is a creation on the grand scale, a true product of Romanticism, *'indimenticabile Fedra'*.

By the 1920s Romanticism was played out, and all that was left was the vapid affectation of longing for the unattainable. The American poetess Hilda Doolittle's *Hippolytus Temporizes* (1927) lacks both dramatic energy and poetry, but it none the less has some interest for the ideas which it attempts to embody. Hippolytus is the type of the aesthete, the man devoted to the ideal, symbolized for him by the chaste Artemis. Doolittle's Phaedra resorts to a trick which would be beneath even Sturge Moore's, and causes a drug to be given to Hippolytus, under the influence of which he takes her for Artemis herself and makes love to her. In the morning he drives off in an intoxicated frenzy, and Phaedra kills herself—an oddly unmotivated act in these new circumstances. When Hippolytus is brought back dying from his fall by the sea shore, Helios and Artemis debate whether he should be allowed to die. Helios brings him back to life, but he realizes that he has been deceived and that true beauty is really eternally inaccessible. Artemis sadly agrees, gives him one kiss and returns him to death.

The most thoughtful of all twentieth-century treatments of the story is that of the Spanish philosopher, critic and poet Miguel de Unamuno. Unamuno's is a Christian *Fedra*. Written between 1911 and 1912, it is set in modern Spain: Fedra and Hipólito retain their classical names but Theseus becomes Pedro.

The play is Christian in two senses. First, in a fairly obvious way: Fedra has been brought up in a convent; her nurse is a conventionally devout Spanish woman; and part of her tragedy is that she cannot repent and confess in the required way. She calls upon the Virgin of Sorrows, but receives no comfort and feels herself rejected. Pedro too, in his crisis, cannot pray.

But the play is Christian at a deeper, more moral level, in that each character subjects his own conduct to the searching examination of conscience. All are basically good, all suffer because they bring suffering upon others; and all are in a sense redeemed by their suffering. Fedra, who is the same age as Hipólito, has loved him from the first and has struggled to control her love. The dénouement is brought about by Pedro (Theseus) asking Fedra to use her influence to persuade Hipólito to marry. Hipólito, a simple youth with an almost Wordsworthian feeling for nature, replies that he is not in love and will not marry until he is. Fedra brings herself gradually to her own confession: 'If you did marry, I should not be able to live, to see you belonging to another woman.' He realizes her meaning and leaves her. The nurse tries to offer the consolation of religion, but it is a situation full of tragic irony—that Fedra should pray to the Virgin to intercede *with her Son*.

In Unamuno's version Hipólito is accused and banished by his father but does not die. Fedra, overcome by remorse, takes poison, leaving a letter to explain the truth. She knows that she has sinned, but knows too that she was helpless to do anything else—the strength of her passion constituting a sort of predestined fate (this is one of several Romantic themes in Unamuno that puts him close to D'Annunzio; Fedra is a woman justified by passion: 'If it is love, it is not guilty', as she says herself. Hipólito tells her that healthy love grows 'little by little'; 'No—all at once', Fedra vehemently replies to him).

It is after her death, when in other versions of the story the drama is over, that Unamuno's real point is made. Pedro and Hipólito ask themselves in what ways they themselves have been to blame: Pedro for seeking another young wife instead of devoting himself only to Hipólito, for failing to understand her and for throwing them together; Hipólito, for not realizing the truth before, for insensitivity. Each comes to the conclusion that he has lived selfishly. But the Christian lesson, as Fedra has seen before she dies, is that sin and suffering are not wasted. On the contrary, only through sin is redemptive sacrifice possible. 'After all', says Pedro, 'she was a holy martyr. She knew how to die.' Hipólito: 'Let us know how to live, father.'

To turn now to the Ariadne episode. Since Monteverdi chose her in 1608 she had retained the favour of the operatic stage. *Ariane* by Massenet was performed in Paris in 1906 with a libretto by Catulle Mendès. Whatever the shortcomings of this work musically and dramatically, it certainly provided some fine opportunities for scenic effects. One of the acts is set in Hades: Phaedra, learning that Theseus loves her more than her sister, has killed herself and descended there. But Ariadne, like a female Orpheus, follows her and bribes Persephone (by a gift of rose petals) to let her return. They rise through the depths of the sea. Phaedra is restored to life and Ariadne—so it seems—to Theseus. But his inclination soon reverts to Phaedra, and Ariadne, with saintly resignation, descends again to the depths: *Elle descend dans la mer. On ne la voit plus.*

This was typical operatic silliness, but six years later came the most profound of all musical versions, that of Richard Strauss and Hugo von Hofmannsthal. Like several of the works produced by these two great collaborators, the finished *Ariadne auf Naxos* turned out to be very different from its original conception. It began by being part of Strauss' incidental music to an adaptation of Molière's *Le Bourgeois Gentilhomme*. Instead of Monsieur Jourdain's 'Ballet des Nations', a short opera on the subject of Ariadne was to be substituted. A company of Italian comedians led by the vivacious dancer Zerbinetta, however, is also due to appear before him, and Monsieur Jourdain, to save time, decides that both entertainments—the dance-burlesque and the tragic opera—shall be

Ills. 220, 221

Ill. 220. A scene from Richard Strauss' *Ariadne auf Naxos*, in which the gay Zerbinetta and her troupe of Italian comedians attempt to comfort the love-lorn Ariadne— the principle (as the librettist Hofmannsthal saw it) of expediency confronting that of fidelity.

performed simultaneously, with the Italians appearing on Ariadne's desert island to console her and cheer her up. Protesting and complaining, both troupes are obliged to agree.

From this rather unpromising situation, Hofmannsthal was able to create an interpretation of extraordinary originality and beauty. The two women, Ariadne and Zerbinetta, represent two contrasting values, attitudes to life, Ariadne standing for love and Zerbinetta for pleasure. The conflict in Ariadne's mind in transferring her affections from Theseus to Bacchus is thus set forth in explicit terms. When Bacchus does appear she takes him to be Death (an echo from Homer or from Wagner?). 'What it is about', wrote Hofmannsthal to Strauss, 'is one of the straightforward and stupendous problems of life: fidelity; whether to hold fast to that which is lost, to cling to it even unto death—or to live, to live on, to get over it, to transform oneself, to sacrifice the integrity of the soul and yet in this transformation to preserve one's essence, to remain a human being and not to sink to the level of the beast, which is without recollection. . . . Zerbinetta is in her element drifting out of the arms of one man into the arms of another; Ariadne could be the wife or mistress of *one* man only, just as she can be only *one* man's widow, can be forsaken by only *one* man. One thing, however, is still left, even for her: the miracle, the God. To him she gives herself, for she believes him to be Death: he is both Death and Life at once; he it is who reveals to her the immeasurable depths of her own nature. . . . But what to divine souls is a real miracle, is to the earthbound nature of Zerbinetta just an everyday love-affair. She sees in Ariadne's experience the only thing she *can* see: the exchange of an old lover for a new one. And so these two spiritual worlds are in the end ironically brought together in the only way in which they *can* be brought together: in non-comprehension.'

Strauss, a less complex character than his partner, had not understood the libretto until this letter, and was even then doubtful whether an operatic audience would grasp it: 'a superficial musician like myself would not, of course, have tumbled to it. But isn't this a little dangerous?' He begged Hofmannsthal to go through it again 'so as to make the symbolism clearer', and he did. The result inspired Strauss to his most brilliant *tour-de-force* of musical invention, perhaps the last great masterpiece of Romanticism, a miraculous combination of Classical myth and the *Liebestod*.

Postscript: in 1928 Darius Milhaud produced *L'Abandon d'Ariane*, a skit which stands to Ovid as *La Belle Hélène* stands to Homer. Ariane, on a desert island inhabited by gypsies and gay vagabonds, is trying vainly to escape Theseus' attentions, which she finds odious. Phèdre, on the other hands, longs for them. They both pray to Bacchus, who is present disguised as a beggar. He gives Theseus a cup of wine which has the effect of making him mistake the sisters for each other, so everyone is satisfied. The score is full of vigorous musical numbers, including a tango.

L'Abandon d'Ariane is one of three one-act operas to be performed on the same evening. The third is *La Délivrance de Thésée*, a skit on Racine's *Phèdre*. Hipolyte complains to his friend Théramène how pestered he is by Phèdre and how much he prefers Aricie. Phèdre accuses him of rape; Thésée sends him out to fight a monster and he is predictably killed. But now a new twist: Théramène kills Phèdre, Thésée hangs Théramène, and the evening ends with his happily paying court to the bewildered Aricie.

The theme of Theseus' early relationship with Ariadne, which curiously failed to appeal to earlier periods, is treated by two twentieth-century writers, F. L. Lucas and Nikos Kazantzakis. No two men could be more different—one an English aesthete of the 1930s trying to wring emotion from an essentially cerebral talent; the other a Greek poet for whom the only problem is how to make sense of the violent and the unconscious forces of which human life consists.

Lucas wrote *Ariadne* in 1932, before he wisely renounced poetry for criticism. In a prologue he defends escapist literature on the grounds of the general nastiness of modern life, but, apart from a certain frail sensibility, his own poem has little to offer in its stead. He invents another sweetheart for Theseus, called Aegle, one of the sacrificial maidens who accompany him to Crete, though it is Book III before we arrive there. Ariadne falls in love with him and the story pursues its expected course. The only real stroke of originality is to make the Minotaur Minos himself disguised in

Ill. 221. Bacchus finds Ariadne and brings her back to a new life: the climax of *Ariadne auf Naxos*.

a bull mask. On Naxos Ariadne learns of Theseus' earlier love for Aegle, and decides to leave him while the image of her own love is still fresh. Besides, an ordinary love affair is not what she wants; she has to seek the Ideal (Bacchus).

Kazantzakis' drama *Theseus* is also replete with symbolism, but at so much richer a level that it is practically impossible to summarize. Its main theme is development and maturity, the superseding of the old order by the new, both in terms of mankind as a whole, progressing from Minoan to Mycenaean and then to Archaic Greek civilization, and in terms of the individual, passing through the two crises of adolescence and middle age. At each stage the emphasis is upon the inevitability of change (summed up in the word 'destiny') and the achievement of maturity through the willing acceptance of change.

At the beginning of the play Theseus stands waiting to confront the Minotaur, whom he regards as a simple external enemy, and whose low moaning roar is heard echoing from the depths of the Labyrinth. Theseus is young, inexperienced but arrogant, totally convinced of his mission. The first half of the play consists of a long verbal duel between him and Ariadne, the virgin high priestess of Crete. She has been sent (we learn later) by her father Minos to seduce Theseus: the old gods have deserted Knossos; the death of the Minotaur will mean the end of the Minoan order.

Theseus refuses to listen to her, seeing her as a representative of the darkness (the moon) which he has come to dispel. He wants no distractions, only action, struggle. 'No, you want something else', says Ariadne. 'What?' 'To take me on board your ship and ravish me.' She challenges him to another struggle—with her: 'You will lose yourself in the inextricable labyrinth of my spirit and my body.' Theseus, the adolescent facing sexuality for the first time, hesitates. The balance now shifts, and it is Ariadne, the seductress, who is afraid: 'I do not know how women give themselves to men.'

Theseus' realization that his relationship with other people, and with himself, is a more difficult struggle than that against enemies may be compared to Wagner's portrayal of Siegfried's similar realization, his learning of the meaning of fear through his first meeting with woman.

Theseus for the moment accepts her, but not on her own terms. Seeming to have seduced him, she finds that it is he who has seduced her. His destiny is the stronger—she must now aid him in his struggle by guiding him through the Labyrinth: 'Help me to fulfil the first duty of man—to kill.' She protests that he is asking her to betray her father and her country. 'That is what love is', answers Theseus. (In the same way Brünnhilde, having brought Siegfried to manhood, becomes the servant of *his* heroic mission.)

The second half revolves round the conflict between Theseus and Minos. Theseus' destiny is simple: to kill the Minotaur and supplant Minos. Minos' is more complex: the choice between resistance and acceptance (in Jungian terminology, he has reached the point in middle age when the ego has to resign its ambitions to the claims of the self—again the parallel with Wagner, Wotan's voluntary abdication to Siegfried).

Minos is in fact Theseus seen at a later stage of development. As a youthful hero he too had conquered *his* Minotaur, by imposing a new order upon the earlier chaos. He knows that he in turn must be superseded 'so that the world may advance a little', but he knows also that in achieving this advance the hero himself must suffer because he destroys the order that gave him birth. Theseus recognizes Minos as a father-figure, asks his blessing and enters the Labyrinth with Ariadne.

Theseus' fight with the Minotaur is the most complex piece of symbolism in the play. He conquers it, but not simply by force. In the midst of the struggle, as both hear the flute of Ariadne (femininity), he becomes aware of an affinity between himself and the Minotaur. What began as a battle ends as an embrace—a synthesis instead of destruction. (The same had been true of Minos: the story of Pasiphaë had already been interpreted by Theseus as an allegory of Minos' creation of the new order—the mastering of passion by absorbing it, body united with brain.)

After Theseus will come another Theseus to overthrow him as he has overthrown Minos, and so on for ever. Ariadne, priestess of the old order, is no longer useful to him. He refuses to take her. Lacking her father's mature wisdom, she urges resistance. Although knowing it to be meaningless, Minos blows his horn. The door of the Labyrinth opens, and the Minotaur stands before them—a new

Minotaur 'resembling Theseus only bigger, more beautiful, calmer'. He is Kouros, Archaic Greece, the new age. The sun rises; the moon sets; Ariadne falls lifeless; Minos bows in resignation. Theseus and Kouros set off together to face new combats.

One cannot say that Kazantzakis always avoids obscurity. In particular, the ambiguities of the Minotaur (the Jungian 'shadow') become so complex that it can mean almost anything. But the play is certainly the most ambitious attempt so far to trace the myth back to its source in the unconscious levels of personality.

It is the Minotaur and its mother, in fact, who have provided the twentieth century with its most original insight into the whole Theseus story, both morally and psychologically. Not only has Pasiphaë engaged attention in a way that is completely new, but the Minotaur itself—man in the form of beast, beast in the form of man—emerges from darkness after twenty centuries of repression and fear to find acceptance and even a certain awed respect.

It was natural that the Pasiphaë story should have appealed to Swinburne (one only regrets that no one suggested it to Beardsley); he wrote a short verse dialogue in which Daedalus introduces the queen to the wooden cow he has made for her. Swinburne's language, as usual, is too imprecise to be obscene, but he represents Pasiphaë as driven forward by unconquerable appetite and eager for the moment when

> I may fare heifer-wise beneath a bull,
> Being clothed with cow and quite diswomanized.

The poem was not included in Swinburne's collected works, but has been recently republished in a limited edition with engravings by John Buckland-Wright, one of them showing the finished cow standing on a table, Pasiphaë dressed as in Evans' reconstruction of Minoan costume, and Daedalus stroking his beard and holding a blueprint of his model in side and rear elevations.

What had been merely titillating to Swinburne becomes an existentialist parable to Henry de Montherlant, whose drama *Pasiphaé* was published in 1928. Here the act of love with the bull is the act of choice, free from all codes and principles, by which the individual creates his own morality. 'Today', says Pasiphaë, 'I am going to do a deed that I desire.' She has reached a state in which everything she has heard or read is forgotten: *toute la vie, tout l'univers, annulés*'. She has fought against the current, now she lets the current take her. Like her father, the sun, she will love and embrace everything. Her nurse, who represents conventional morality, tells her that she is already free, there is no need to assert her freedom by defying the law. But the chorus, representing the author (who in a footnote quotes Montaigne in support) asserts that nothing is unnatural or unhealthy; the only unhealthy thing about any desire is the belief that it is unhealthy. Pasiphaë sees this act as the realization of her true self; it is not happiness, not even pleasure, which she wants: it is the accomplishment of her own desire. 'I can say to myself—what I desired, I have done . . . I am what I am, and I do not wish to be other.' It is a philosophy that rejects the judgement of others: *Il n'est pas nécessaire que personne approuve*. To the chorus it is the absence of morality which conveys dignity, a dignity denied to men but achieved by *des bêtes, des plantes et des eaux*. *Pasiphaé* was republished in 1944 with illustrations by Matisse, and again four years later with illustrations by Cocteau. By this time what we might call the 'Minotaur revival' was in full swing.

It is perhaps unfair to begin an account of this with G. F. Watts. No one had less idea of rejecting conventional morality than Watts; *Ill. 222* conformity ran in his veins like blood. *The Minotaur* was painted in three hours, in a mood of furious indignation after reading W. T. Stead's articles on prostitution in the *Pall Mall Gazette*, 'The Maiden Tribute of Modern Babylon'. Watts knew the theory that the Minotaur was an aspect of Baal, and so by a series of rather confused associations chose it to represent vice and brutality. Leaning over the battlements of Knossos, it waits for its tribute, crushing a little bird under its hoof. A commentator, writing soon after Watts' death, expresses the message: 'He felt constrained to further the cause by presenting to the eye the embodiment of the cruelty and power of vice in this horrible form, so that everyone who saw it might not only abhor it, but seek to remove it off the face of the earth, in the spirit of Theseus, and slay it.' (This picture of Theseus as a crusader in the cause of sexual purity could surely have occurred only to a late Victorian.) Oddly enough, however, what appeals to us today is the pathos which Watts, consciously or unconsciously, put into the painting. By turning the head away, he avoids the problem of showing emotion on a bovine face, but he also forces us to imagine the emotion that we feel to be appropriate. And the whole pose of the animal body, gazing with dreadful awareness into the distance, suggests a helplessly crippled spirit, a human intelligence imprisoned in dumbness.

It is just this feeling which seems to have obsessed the most brilliant artist to touch the theme, Picasso. Picasso first became interested in the subject when he was commissioned by Albert Skira to provide illustrations to Ovid's *Metamorphoses*. This was published in 1931. In 1933 Skira founded a new literary and artistic magazine which he called *Minotaure*, and Picasso drew a picture of the Minotaur for the cover of the first issue. As was so often the case, his imagination went on playing round the idea, and in the same year he did a series of eleven etchings showing the Minotaur in various unprecedented situations—drinking with artists, sleeping, making drowsy or ferocious love to naked girls. In three etchings the Minotaur is killed in an arena by a youth with a sword, surrounded by curious, pitiless eyes. What had sparked off these associations in Picasso's mind was his memories of the bull-ring. The Minotaur is a symbol of animal strength defeated by cunning, and also of animal innocence defeated by a cruelty that it does not understand. Four later etchings in the same series, made in 1934, are extraordinary visions of a blind Minotaur, feeling his way with a stick and led by a little girl with a bunch of flowers or a lamp—strange works which almost identify the Minotaur with Oedipus at Colonus.

Skira's *Minotaure* went on for twelve more issues, coming to an end only in 1939. It published work by practically every avant-garde writer of the day, and the cover of each issue was designed by an eminent artist as a variation on the Minotaur theme, although the reason for its name was left a mystery. The cover of issue No. 2 was by Derain (a bull's head against Tarot cards); No. 7 by Miró (a bull's head); No. 10 by Magritte (a draped figure with a bull's skull); No. 11 by Max Ernst (a green bull's head); and No. 12—13, published together, contained a labyrinth by Diego Rivera showing Theseus and Ariadne as primitive Catalan nudes, the yellow thread twisting in and out, cells or hollows in the tunnel filled with bones, and in the centre the Minotaur bent back in the agony of death.

Ill. 222. Right, G. F. Watts' *The Minotaur* exhibits a vein of almost Surrealist imagination for which no other works of this artist prepare us. Intended by him as a straightforward symbol of bestiality and vice, the Minotaur seems now a far more ambiguous denizen of the unconscious than the artist himself ever suspected.

Ill. 225

Ill. 224

Ill. 223

Ill. 226

Ill. 227

Ill. 228

The subject continues to attract artists, especially those with Surrealist sympathies, such as André Masson. And, as one might almost expect, it had an early fascination for the first film makers. *The Minotaur* was released by the American company Vitagraph in 1910. It is a fascination that still holds—at least until 1961, when the Italian director Amadio made *Teseo contro il Minotauro*. But probably the only example in the medium to be of more than passing value is *Phaedra* by Jules Dassin; the star is Melina Mercouri, the story is brought up to date and given a modern setting, and Hippolytus is killed in a car crash.

The story of Daedalus and Icarus has been so far ignored in this chapter, since it relates only indirectly to Theseus himself.

Ill. 223. Picasso's Minotaur etchings from the *Vollard Suite* have no simple explanation. Here the blind, suffering monster, isolated from the surrounding world, follows a little girl with a dove, which in Picasso's work represents peace.

Ill. 224. Dying Minotaur, another etching from the *Vollard Suite*. Twisted in pain, the bull-like Minotaur dies amid a circle of cold human faces.

It has, however, formed the starting point for a highly interesting exploration of the half-mythical Minoan world by the English artist and writer Michael Ayrton. In paintings, drawings and works of sculpture he has attempted to master his 'obsession', for to Ayrton, Daedalus and Icarus represent the two principles of creative life, the one rational and earthbound, the other aspiring and heroic. First in a short work combining drawings, poems and prose, *The Testament of Dedalus*, and then in a full-length novel, *The Maze-Maker*, an imagined autobiography of Daedalus, the whole parable is fully worked out. Its basic idea is the contrast between the technician and the hero, symbolized up to a point by the two divine principles of the mother or earth goddess (Gaia) and the sky god

247

MINOTAURE

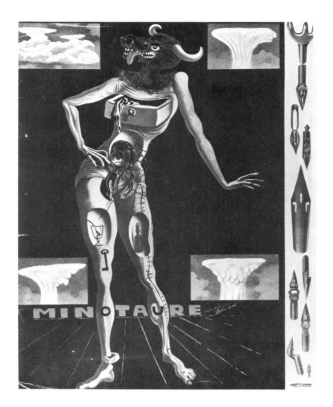

Ills. 225—228. Four covers from Albert Skira's avant-garde periodical *Minotaure*. Left: the first issue, by Picasso—the Minotaur armed amid a collage of lace and corrugated paper. Above left: the eighth issue, by Dali—the Minotaur stands like an art-nude with a gory bull's head. His chest is an open drawer with a cloth hanging out, his loins a lobster, one thigh a glass with a spoon in it, the other a medicine bottle. There is a border of pen nibs. Above right: the tenth issue, by Magritte. This Minotaur is a romantic, draped figure with a bull's skull. Around him are one of Magritte's diminishing torsoes fitting inside itself, a pair of feet with laces like boots and a trumpet in flames. Right: the last issue, by Rivera. In the centre of the labyrinth, amid the skulls and bones of its victims, the Minotaur lies in the agony of death.

(Apollo). Daedalus, the craftsman, by nature a creature of earth, worships Apollo with a sort of grudging admiration—Apollo who persecutes him and kills his son and yet represents light, order and reason. Icarus, a less complex character, is simply in love with Apollo, and uses his father's invention of wings to attempt physical union, an act of presumption for which Apollo burns him into nothing. (This demonstration of mystical heroism, which is beyond Daedalus' understanding, is described in language taken from Einsteinian physics, the hint being that Icarus reaches the speed of light; modern applications spring to mind.)

In spite of all its symbolism, the basic story is told in fundamentally realistic terms. Daedalus grows up in mainland Greece, amid petty chieftains whose homage is to Apollo, but who spend their time fighting over trifles and cultivating the ideal of heroism at its crudest. Crete, where he arrives as the lover of a Minoan princess, is the opposite—a land of culture and peace, worshipping the mother and able to appreciate Daedalus' genius as a creator. Minos, representing contemplative wisdom, orders him to construct the Labyrinth as a place to which he can retire 'to sit in judgement upon himself'. But Pasiphaë's monstrous lust brings catastrophe. The making of the cow and her encounter with the bull are described with considerable panache. The Minotaur is born and Minos imprisons it in the Labyrinth, immuring himself next to it, along with Ariadne, Daedalus and Icarus. It is from here, on the day when an earthquake strikes Knossos, that the two latter escape on wings—one to perish in the sun, the other to land exhausted at Cumae in Italy.

The gods of *The Maze-Maker* are treated at two levels. Superficially Daedalus accepts the whole mythological pantheon of capricious deities who have to be placated by sacrifice, though being a rationalist he reserves his opinion on the details. At another level he sees the gods as symbols of natural forces which are real and which he, as a technician, has to recognize. At Cumae he meets the Sybil, a prophetess through whom Apollo and Gaia are united, symbolized by a spectacular volcanic copulation.

At Cumae Daedalus also encounters a subterranean race of metal workers—Virgilian Nibelungs—who worship Gaia but help him build a temple to Apollo in expiation of his own and his son's *hubris*. Below ground, cut off from normal sensations, he has a hallucination in which he meets the Minotaur, understands its half-human thoughts, and in a vision sees that it too is an aspect of the heroic. All this, as he knows, is within himself: every man's brain is a labyrinth and the Minotaur that it contains is ambivalently bestial and divine.

Other more mundane examples of the heroic life, Heracles and Theseus, receive scant respect from Daedalus. Theseus, in fact, makes only the briefest of appearances in the book, and killing and treachery are 'his principal demonstration of power'. 'Altogether, my kinsman Theseus was a notable hero, not of the foolish sort like Icarus, but of the better lasting and less simple type whose deeds are praised for qualities anyone would despise except in a hero or perhaps a god.'

The story of the youths and maidens, we learn, is all a fable. Theseus came to Crete to take part in the funeral games of Androgeos, and there beat Minos' bodyguard Taurus. 'That is as near as Theseus got to fighting the Minotaur.' But he pretended to have killed the Minotaur, and seduced both Ariadne (whom Daedalus loved) and Phaedra. 'Therefore I shall say no more of Theseus.'

One consequence of the novel was to identify Ayrton even more closely with his protagonist; he became a maze-maker himself. For an American millionaire, Armand G. Erpf, he has built a vast brick *Ill. 229* and stone maze in the Catskill Mountains, New York. Mr Erpf finds in it 'spiritual truth'.

Ayrton's work is a personal statement, but it makes fluent use both of current anthropological study and of Sir Arthur Evans' excavations. These have already been discussed at sufficient length in earlier chapters of this book, but they must be mentioned again here for the effect they had upon artists and writers. Many, it is true, continued to use the Theseus story simply as a convenient framework for their ideas, but others were impressed by its possible actuality and went to the archaeologists to learn more. One of the best English illustrators of the 1930s, Edmund Dulac, who specialized in scenes from Classical mythology, gave his Knossos the 'horns of consecration' and stumpy red columns reconstructed by Evans, and his Ariadne the bright patterned skirt found on figurines.

Interest in Theseus as a possibly real historical figure inspired in the 1940s and 1950s two complete 'autobiographies' of him, from childhood to death—one by the South African novelist Mary Renault, the other by André Gide. They represent almost diametrically opposite points of view, yet both are serious attempts to recreate actual events.

Renault takes two fairly long novels to tell the story. Relying as much on *The Golden Bough* as on *The Palace of Minos*, she knits fact and speculation skilfully together, filling in the gaps with ingenious discretion. If, in spite of so much care, her picture fails to be totally plausible, it is chiefly because she adopts the style and many of the values of romantic fiction.

Her Theseus is a heroic king who lived at the time of the destruction of Knossos by the earthquake and its subsequent conquest by mainland Greeks. Mycenaean Greece, she assumes, had until recently practised sacrificial king-killing either as an offering to the earth goddess (the old deity of the Minoans) or as a sacrifice to Zeus (the new deity of the Dorians and of Theseus).

In *The King Must Die*, after most of the youthful adventures described by Plutarch, Theseus offers himself as one of the victims to go to Crete. Knossos and Cretan civilization are vividly described, and the sacrifice to the Minotaur is reasonably enough interpreted as being enforced performance of the bull dance, or bull-leaping, as represented in the frescoes. Ariadne, who falls in love with Theseus, is the high priestess of the old cult of the mother goddess. Theseus manages to stay alive at Knossos by his skill in bull-leaping until the palace is overwhelmed by an earthquake (which Theseus by a mysterious instinct is able to sense before it happens), and he leads a revolt of the bull dancers against Minos. The Minotaur is a human son of Queen Pasiphaë by an adulterous love affair, who is in the act of being anointed king and wearing the bull mask when killed by Theseus.

Ariadne leaves with him for Athens, but on Naxos she becomes involved in the bloodthirsty rites of Dionysus (here themes from the *Bacchae* are neatly integrated into the story) and Theseus leaves her in disgust.

The character of Theseus is built up to fit the premises of his reconstructed life: 'A light-weight' (I quote Renault's note at the

Ill. 229. The most recent labyrinth in the world: Michael Ayrton's maze built in 1966 for Armand G. Erpf in the grounds of his home in the Catskill Mountains, New York. 'You have to be indirect,' Mr Erpf is quoted as having said. 'The way to attain something is to go away from it. The maze is a spiritual truth.'

end of the book), 'brave and aggressive, physically tough and quick; highly sexed and rather promiscuous; touchily proud, but with a feeling for the underdog; resembling Alexander in his precocious competence, gift of leadership and romantic sense of destiny.'

Her other book, *The Bull from the Sea*, covers Theseus' life from his return to Greece to his old age. He conquers Crete (his marriage to Phaedra, his second Cretan princess, being 'a dynastic necessity') and brings the whole of mainland Greece under his rule. He fights the Amazons (warrior-priestesses of Artemis) and marries Hippolyta, the great love of his life. Phaedra's attempted seduction of Hippolytus is given a religious motivation—she is trying to restore the old religion of the earth goddess. Hippolytus' death happens amid another earthquake (also sensed in advance by Theseus) and it is a black bull from the sea—another of Poseidon's bulls—which makes his horses panic. All these details lend a satisfying unity to the saga. Theseus learns the truth from his own and Phaedra's son Akamas, and he strangles Phaedra with his own hands, leaving a fake suicide note confessing that her accusation of Hippolytus had been false.

In his old age, Theseus, disillusioned and pessimistic, suffers a stroke, has a dream in which he sees himself in spirit leading the Greeks at Marathon, and voluntarily ends his life by throwing himself (like Aegeus) from a cliff on Scyros.

André Gide's short novel *Tésée* is on the surface a slighter work but in reality has far more to it. Gide's Theseus intended his autobiography for Hippolytus, but he is dead—which enables Theseus to include a franker discussion of his sexual experiences than he would have done: 'he was extraordinarily prudish'. The narrative follows Plutarch closely, even to the thicket of asparagus in which he makes love to Perigone. At Knossos, Evans' descriptions are cleverly woven into the action: 'Among so much that was exquisite, I felt like a savage.'

After a banquet at which he sees Ariadne (who falls in love with him) and Phaedra (whom he prefers), Queen Pasiphaë takes him aside and explains how the Minotaur came to be born. She had seen Zeus in the bull (or thought she had), just as Minos' mother Europa had seen Zeus in *her* bull. 'And if ever, after the birth of the Minotaur, I noticed the king knitting his brows, I had only to say "What about your mother?".' He could only admit that it was a natural mistake.' She pleads with Theseus to be merciful and not kill the poor beast.

Ariadne sends for him, explains the secrets of the Labyrinth and goes to bed with him. He is bored with her sentimentality. He never (he now claims) made her any promises, and anyway he was not her first lover: 'This disposed of any scruples I might later have had about leaving her.'

Minos is an interesting character. Gide equates him and his brother Rhadamanthus with the legendary judges of the underworld.

Being a judge, Minos tries to *understand* everything, tolerantly letting things happen as long as he knows why.

Theseus also meets Daedalus, who explains that he designed the Labyrinth on the principle not that the Minotaur *could* not get out, 'but that he wouldn't *want* to get out'. For this purpose he keeps narcotic drugs burning all the time, sapping the will power. The real labyrinth is in the mind—a vivid picture of the drug addict. Icarus is presented as an addict, his intellect lost in metaphysical speculation. Theseus' only chance of not succumbing is to keep hold of Ariadne's thread, 'the tangible symbol of duty' between people; the only question being, how far away from her will Ariadne let him go?

His memory of the fight with the Minotaur is dim, but he remembers it as young, beautiful . . . and an idiot.

He deceives Minos about his connection with Ariadne by pretending to take her young brother Glaucus as a lover—a relationship approved of at the Cretan court. They escape by taking Phaedra disguised as Glaucus, and on Naxos he abandons Ariadne in her favour. 'She threatened me with a long poem which she proposed to write on the subject of this infamous desertion. I told her at once that she could not do better.' The story of the wedding with Bacchus, he has to confess, is only 'a way of saying that she found consolation in drink'.

Theseus returns to Athens and reorganizes it as a sort of totalitarian meritocracy (what Gide's translator John Russell rightly calls 'a modified Stalinism'). The episode of Phaedra and Hippolytus saddens him: 'I should have foreseen it, for he was very like me.' The book ends with his encounter with the aged Oedipus at Colonus, whom he admires as his superior. He learns the wisdom to be gained through suffering, though he cannot follow Oedipus' path himself. His destiny is practical and active, its aim and justification being the founding of Athens.

Gide's Theseus is a genuine man of the twentieth century, which is perhaps why he seems so much more convincing a Mycenaean than Miss Renault's. But indeed there has to be a Theseus for every age and for every artist. A legend like this seems after all to combine two elements—a historical event or series of events, which can partially be laid bare by archaeology; and a symbolic pattern springing from the unconscious. How that combination happens is mysterious, and the workings of the imagination which have been the subject of these chapters must certainly have a bearing upon it. But it means that Theseus is as much an archetypal symbol as a Bronze Age chieftain. The 'quest' turns out to be endless. Through myth, history becomes a mirror in which we see ourselves.

Conclusion

Anne G. Ward

OUR ENQUIRY INTO THE NATURE OF THESEUS has carried us a long way in both temporal and geographical terms, from the remote obscurities of the Bronze Age Aegean to the twentieth century, when acceptance of the values of the myth is perhaps broader and insight into its significance more profound than at any other time since it was first given a written literary form by the Classical Greeks. The facts have been marshalled and debated, but if, in the end, we return to the question of the historical reality of Theseus, who has been all things to all men since the earliest days of the Greek world, we are left with that bugbear of the prosecuting counsel, circumstantial evidence. The only verdict we can conscientiously return is 'not proven'. The conscientious legal verdict, however, notoriously often fails to carry total conviction, and where Theseus is concerned, circumstantial evidence is strong enough to raise persistent and insuperable doubts. Although there is no concrete proof of the existence of a Bronze Age King Theseus of Athens actually performing the feats attributed to him by the later Attic mythographers, we have seen that many of these exploits, or something too suspiciously like them to be lightly dismissed as mere coincidence even in the case of the most fantastic of all, are matters of sober archaeological record.

Although many Mycenaean elements were assimilated into the daily lives of the Dark Age Greeks and their successors, the downfall of the Bronze Age kingdoms was so complete that only the haziest memories can have survived. The story-tellers seized avidly on these traditions and, in the absence of any historical records to restrain the flights of their imagination, wove them into the myths which were adopted with such enthusiasm by their Classical descendants. If the real truth about the Labyrinth and the Bull of Minos was remembered at all, it was probably dismissed as a mere fairy-tale by the more intellectually disposed members of the community, and the story handed down by generations of simpler and more credulous folk must have been based on little more than a confused notion of something very tremendous to do with bulls which used to happen in a maze at Knossos in the old days 'when Theseus was king'. The purveyors of sailors' yarns and old wives' tales were, indeed, nearer the truth than the rationalizing mythographers of later years—nearer the truth than they realized, for the rediscovery of the Labyrinth has produced indisputable evidence for many of the most bizarre elements in the tale.

It is a strange and slightly ironic fact that we, several thousand years later, are in a position to know considerably more of the truth about Theseus than his nearer scions in the age of Pericles. Exactly how much of the legend they actually believed is hard to estimate. The saying, 'Not without Theseus', has a distinctly blasé ring, and the deliberate cynicism with which statesmen manipulated the details of the hero's life as a subtle comment on their own descent and achievements is far from suggesting profound reverence, but if their audience had been equally sceptical about the story there would have been little or no point in such publicity. They would hardly have troubled to invoke the name of Theseus if it had not been a powerful influence among the public at large.

In this age, a thousand years after his putative lifetime, Theseus probably enjoyed a greater ascendancy over the lives of a large number of people than he had ever done before, or was ever to do again. Wherever the Athenian citizen went he met with the hero's likeness, from the painted masterpieces of the Stoa Poikile and the carved reliefs of the temple of Hephaestus to the supreme glories of the Parthenon metopes and the great golden shield of the goddess herself. Even in the modest surroundings of the citizen's own home his wife might be dreaming of her dress for the next Oschophoria procession—one of the very few occasions when she might emerge from her domestic seclusion and appear with any éclat in public—and the very slave who brought his wine (perhaps in a cup painted with the death of the Minotaur) may have been planning to call upon the protection of Theseus' name to avert the consequences of his latest mischievous escapade.

As the Classical period progressed Theseus was gradually transformed into a very real presence, and by virtue of the politicians' manoeuvres what had once been no more than a good story became a potent instrument of domestic and international propaganda. The city's hero was the city's pride, and the former could not have been doubted without seriously undermining the latter.

By the time Athens fell and it was no longer in anyone's interest to keep Theseus before the people as a living presence, the story was so firmly entrenched in popular imagination that it had an enduring life of its own. Although from the great days of Rome onwards everyone probably regarded the details of the myth as entirely fictitious, they were so appealingly picturesque, so romantic, so dramatic and so colourful that exponents of all the major arts have, at one time or another, found tangible inspiration in the hero's vicissitudes. Without the evidence buried for so many centuries in the mound at Knossos, the artists and thinkers of each age were at liberty to choose the elements that sympathized best with their own preoccupations, and to invest the Theseus of their creation with the qualities, usually incongruous but never irrelevant, which mirrored their own day. It says much for the story's universal appeal that there has never once been a time when Theseus has been neglected as having nothing to offer to the arts.

Whatever the factual truth may be, the world's perennial acceptance of this most human and fallible of heroes has invested him over the course of the centuries with a deeper reality than one man's historical lifetime could ever have achieved. His vindication lies in his enduring function as a source of creative inspiration, and to us he is as real as the artistic masterpieces from the François Vase to the paintings of Picasso to which his story has given rise, as meaningful as the nuances of the word 'democracy', and as vital as the labyrinthine convolutions of the human mind.

Bibliography

Abbreviations *A. J. A.* American Journal of Archaeology
B. C. H. Bulletin de Correspondence Hellénique
B. S. A. Annual of the British School at Athens

General Bibliography

Convenient texts of all the major authors have been published in the standard collections (e. g. the Loeb Classical Library, with parallel English version), and translations of most of them are readily available (in Penguin Classics, Everyman Library, etc.).

AGARD, W. R., 'Theseus, a National Hero', *Classical Journal*, Vol. 24, p. 84 ff., 1928.

ÅLIN, P., 'Das Ende der mykenischen Fundstätten auf dem griechischen Festland', *Studies in Mediterranean Archaeology*, Vol. I, Lund 1962.

ALLBAUGH, L. G., *Crete : A Case Study of an Underdeveloped Area*, Oxford University Press, London 1953; Princeton University Press, Princeton 1953.

ARIAS, P. E. and HIRMER, M., *A History of Greek Vase Painting*, Thames and Hudson, London 1962; Abrams, New York 1962.

BANTI, L., 'Myth in Pre-classical Art', *A. J. A.* 1954.

BEAZLEY, J. D.: I *Attic Black-figure Vase-painters*, Oxford University Press, London and New York 1956. II *Attic Red-figure Vase-painters*, 2nd edn., Oxford University Press, London and New York 1963.

BOER, W. den, 'Theseus. The Growth of a Myth in History', *Greece and Rome* 16, pp. 1—13, 1969.

BOSSERT, H. T., *The Art of Ancient Crete*, Zwemmer, London 1937.

BURTON BROWN, T., *The Coming of Iron to Greece*, Wincle 1955.

CHADWICK, H. M., *The Heroic Age*, Cambridge University Press, Cambridge and New York 1912.

CHILDE, V. G., *The Dawn of European Civilization*, Routledge and Kegan Paul, London 1957; Knopf, New York 1958.

COOK, A. B., *Zeus*, Cambridge University Press, Cambridge 1914—40; Biblo and Tannen, New York 1914—40.

DEMARGNE, P., *Aegean Art*, Thames and Hudson, London 1964; Golden Press, New York 1964.

DIODORUS SICULUS, ed. C. H. Oldfather (Loeb), Heinemann, London 1933 et seq.; Harvard University Press, Cambridge, Mass. 1933—35 et seq. (see esp. IV. 59—63).

DÖRPFELD, W., 'Das alte Athen vor Theseus', *Rheinisches Museum für Philologie*, 1896.

DUGAS, C., 'L'Évolution de la légende de Thésée', *Revue des Études Grecques* 56, pp. 1—24, 1943.

DUGAS, C. and FLACELIÈRE, R., *Thésée : Images et Récits*, de Boccard, Paris 1958.

EDMONDS, J. M., *Lyra Graeca* (Loeb), Heinemann, London 1922—27; Putnam, New York 1922—27 (for Alcman, Bacchylides, Sappho, Simonides and Stesichorus).

ELLIADI, M. N., *Crete, Past and Present*, Heath Cranton Ltd., London 1933.

EVANS, Sir A. J., *The Palace of Minos at Knossos*, Macmillan, London 1921; Biblo and Tannen, New York 1921.

EVELYN-WHITE, H. G., *Hesiod, The Homeric Hymns and Homerica* (Loeb), rev. edn., Heinemann, London 1936; Harvard University Press, Cambridge, Mass. 1936 (for *Kypria*, *Nostoi*, as well as Hesiod).

FARNELL, L. R., *Greek Hero Cults and Ideas of Immortality*, Oxford University Press, London and New York 1921.

FESTA, N., *Mythographi Graeci* iii (2), Teubner, Leipzig 1902 (for Palaephatus).

FINLEY, M. I., *The World of Odysseus*, Chatto and Windus, London 1956; Viking Press, New York 1956.

FORBES, R. J., *Metallurgy in Antiquity*, Brill, Leiden 1950; Heineman, New York 1964.

FORSDYKE, Sir J., *Greece before Homer. Ancient Chronology and Mythology.* Max Parrish, London 1956; Norton, New York 1957.

FRAZER, Sir J. G., *Pausanias's Description of Greece*, Macmillan, London 1898.

GRAHAM, J. W., *The Palaces of Crete*, Princeton University Press, Princeton and London 1962.

GRANT, M., *Myths of the Greeks and Romans*, Weidenfeld and Nicolson, London 1962; Mentor Books, New English Library, New York 1964.

HALL, H. R., *The Civilization of Greece in the Bronze Age*, Methuen, London 1928.

HARRISON, J. E. and VERRALL, M. de G., *Mythology and Monuments of Ancient Athens*, Macmillan, London 1890.

HIGGINS, R. A., *Minoan and Mycenaean Art*, Thames and Hudson, London 1967; Frederick A. Praeger, New York 1967.

HILL, I. T., *The Ancient City of Athens*, Methuen, London 1953; Harvard University Press, Cambridge, Mass. 1953.

HOOD, M. F. S., *The Home of the Heroes*, Thames and Hudson, London 1967; McGraw-Hill, New York 1967.

HUTCHINSON, R. W., *Prehistoric Crete*, Penguin, Harmondsworth and New York 1962.

Jacoby, F., *Fragmente der griechischen Historiker*, Berlin 1923 et seq. (for Demon, Hellanicus, Cleidemus, Paion, Parian Marble, Pherecydes and Philochorus).

Kantor, H. J., 'The Aegean and the Orient in the Second Millennium B. C.', *A. J. A.* 1947.

Kerényi, C., *The Heroes of the Greeks*, Thames and Hudson, London 1959; Grove Press, New York 1959.

Lesky, A., *A History of Greek Literature*, Methuen, London 1966; T. Y. Crowell, New York 1966.

Lorimer, H. L., *Homer and the Monuments*, Macmillan, New York 1951.

Luce, J. V., *The End of Atlantis*, Thames and Hudson, London 1969.

Marinatos, S. and Hirmer, M., *Crete and Mycenae*, Thames and Hudson, London 1960; Abrams, New York 1960.

Mylonas, G. E., *Mycenae and the Mycenaean Age*, Oxford University Press, London 1966; Princeton University Press, Princeton 1966.

Myres, J. L., *Who were the Greeks?*, Cambridge University Press, Cambridge 1930; University of California Press, Berkeley 1930.

Nilsson, M. P.: I *Minoan-Mycenaean Religion and its Survival in Greek Religion*, 2nd edn., Gleerup, Lund 1950. II *The Mycenaean Origin of Greek Mythology*, University of California Press, Berkeley and Los Angeles 1932.

Oxford Classical Dictionary, entry under 'Theseus'.

Pendlebury, J. D. S., *The Archaeology of Crete*, Methuen, London and New York 1939.

Plutarch, *Lives*: I ed. B. Perrin (Loeb), Heinemann, London 1914; Putnam, New York 1914. II ed. R. Flacelière and others, Budé, Paris 1957.

Radermacher, L., *Mythos und Sage bei den Griechen*, Leipzig 1938.

Rose, H. J.: I *Primitive Religion in Greece*, Methuen, London 1925. II *A Handbook of Greek Mythology*, 6th edn., Methuen, London 1958; Dutton, New York 1959.

Schefold, K., *Myth and Legend in Early Greek Art*, Thames and Hudson, London 1966; Abrams, New York 1966.

Scholes, K., 'The Cyclades in the Later Bronze Age: A Synopsis', *B. S. A.* 1956.

Seznec, J., *The Survival of the Pagan Gods*, trans. B. Sessions, Bollingen Series, New York 1953.

Simpson, R. Hope, *A Gazetteer and Atlas of Mycenaean Sites*, Institute of Classical Studies, University of London 1965.

Singer, C. and others, *A History of Technology*, Vol. I, Oxford University Press, London and New York 1954.

Snodgrass, A. M., *Arms and Armour of the Greeks*, Thames and Hudson, London 1967; Cornell University Press, New York 1967.

Stais, V., *The Mycenaean Collection of the National Museum, Athens*, 1926.

Steuding, H., article s. v. 'Theseus' in W. H. Roscher, *Ausführliches Lexikon der griechischen und römischen Mythologie*, Vol. V, cols. 678—760, Teubner, Leipzig 1916—24.

STUBBINGS, F. H., *The Rise of Mycenaean Civilization* (Cambridge Ancient History II, fasc., Chapter XIV), Cambridge University Press, Cambridge and New York 1963.

TAYLOUR, Lord WILLIAM, *The Mycenaeans*, Thames and Hudson, London 1964; Frederick A. Praeger, New York 1964.

THOMAS, H. L., 'Near Eastern, Mediterranean and European Chronology', *Studies in Mediterranean Archaeology*, Vol. XVII, Lund 1967.

THOMSON, J. O., *History of Ancient Geography*, Cambridge University Press, Cambridge and New York 1948.

VERMEULE, E., *Greece in the Bronze Age*, University of Chicago Press, Chicago and London 1964.

WEBSTER, T. B. L.: I *From Mycenae to Homer*, 2nd edn., Methuen, London 1964; Barnes and Noble, New York 1964. II 'The Myth of Ariadne from Homer to Catullus', *Greece and Rome* 13, pp. 22—31, 1966. III *The Tragedies of Euripides*, Methuen, London 1967.

WILLETTS, R. F., *Aristocratic Society in Ancient Crete*, Routledge and Kegan Paul, London 1955; Hillary House, New York 1955.

ZERVOS, CH.: I *L'Art de la Crète Néolithique et Minoenne*, 1956. II *La Naissance de la Civilisation en Grèce*, 1962.

Special Bibliographies

CHAPTERS 1, 2

APOLLODORUS, ed. Sir J. G. Frazer (Loeb), Heinemann, London 1921; Putnam, New York 1921.

ASHMOLE, B. and YALOURIS, N., *Olympia. The Sculptures of the Temple of Zeus*, Phaidon, London and New York 1967.

BACCHYLIDES: I ed. B. Snell, 8th edn., Teubner, Leipzig 1961. II ed. Sir R. C. Jebb, Cambridge University Press, Cambridge 1905.

BOTHMER, D. von, *Amazons in Greek Art*, Oxford University Press, London and New York 1957.

BROMMER, F., *Vasenlisten zur griechischen Heldensage*, 2nd edn., Elwert, Marburg/Lahn 1960.

CALLIMACHUS, *Aetia, Iambi, Hecale and other fragments*, ed. C. A. Trypanis (Loeb), Heinemann, London 1958; Harvard University Press, Cambridge, Mass. 1958.

COSTE-MESSELIÈRE, P. de la, 'Thésée à Délos', *Revue Archéologique* 28, pp. 145—56, 1947.

EURIPIDES, *Hippolytos*, ed. W. S. Barrett, Oxford University Press, London and New York 1964.

FLACELIÈRE, R., 'Sur quelques passages des Vies de Plutarque I: Thésée-Romulus', *Revue des Études Grecques* 61, pp. 67—103, 1948.

HERTER, H.: I 'Theseus der Ionier', *Rheinisches Museum für Philologie* 85, pp. 177—91, 193—239, 1936. II 'Theseus der Athener', ibid. 88, pp. 244—86, 289—326, 1939.

HESIOD, for fragments, MERKELBACH, R. and WEST, M. L., *Fragmenta Hesiodea*, Clarendon Press, Oxford 1967.

KINKEL, G., *Epicorum Graecorum Fragmenta*, Teubner, Leipzig 1877 (for *Minyas* and *Theseis*).

KUNZE, E., *Archaische Schildbänder (Olympische Forschungen II)*, de Gruyter, Berlin 1950.

MIRÉ, G. de and COSTE-MESSELIÈRE, P. de la, *Delphes*, École Française d'Athènes, Paris 1957.

THOMPSON, H. A., 'The Sculptural Adornment of the Hephaisteion', *A. J. A.* 66, pp. 339—47, 1962.

THOMPSON, S., *A Motif-Index of Folk-Literature*, rev. edn., Indiana University Press, Bloomington, Ind. 1955—58.

CHAPTERS 3—7

ARMSTRONG, E. A., 'The Crane Dance in East and West', *Antiquity* 1943.

BANTI, L., *Il Palazzo Minoico di Festòs II*, Rome 1951.

BARNETT, R. D., 'Early Shipping in the Near East', *Antiquity* 1958.

BLEGEN, C. W., 'The Palace of Nestor Excavations', *A. J. A.* 1953—66.

BRANIGAN, L., 'Copper and Bronze Working in Early Bronze Age Crete', *Studies in Mediterranean Archaeology*, Vol. XIX, Lund 1968.

BRONEER, O.: I 'Excavations on the North Slope of the Acropolis in Athens, 1933—34', *Hesperia* 1935. II 'A Mycenaean Fountain on the Athenian Acropolis', *Hesperia* 1939. III 'The Dorian Invasion: What Happened at Athens', *A. J. A.* 1948.

BUXTON, L. H. D., 'The Inhabitants of the Eastern Mediterranean', *Biometrika*, 13, 1920.

CASKEY, J. L., 'Excavations at Lerna', *Hesperia* 1954—59.

CHAPOUTHIER, F. et al., 'Fouilles executées à Mallia', *Études Crétoises* 1922.

DAUX, G., 'Marathon, Grotte de Pan, Chronique des Fouilles en 1958', *B. C. H.* 1959.

DESBOROUGH, V. R. d'A., *The Last Mycenaeans and Their Successors*, Oxford University Press, London and New York 1964.

EVANS, Sir A. J.: I *Scripta Minoa*, Oxford University Press, London and New York 1909, 1952. II *The Shaft Graves and Bee-hive Tombs of Mycenae*, Macmillan, London and New York 1929.

FURNESS, A., 'The Neolithic Pottery of Knossos', *B. S. A.* 1953.

FURTWÄNGLER, A., *Die antiken Gemmen*, Leipzig and Berlin 1900.

FURUMARK, A., *The Chronology of Mycenaean Pottery*, Stockholm 1941.

GALLET de SANTERRE, H., *Délos Primitive et Archaïque*, Paris 1958.

HANSEN, H. D., 'Prehistoric Skyros', *Studies Presented to D. M. Robinson*, St. Louis 1951.

HOLLAND, L. B., 'The Hall of the Athenian Kings', *A. J. A.* 1939.

HOOD, M. F. S. and JONG, P. de, 'Late Minoan Warrior Graves', *B. S. A.* 1952.

HYDE, W. W., *Ancient Greek Mariners*, Oxford University Press, New York 1947.

JACOVIDES, S. E., 'Ἡ Μυκηναϊκὴ Ἀκρόπολις τῶν Ἀθηνῶν', Athens 1962.

KARO, G., *Die Schachtgräber von Mykenai*, Munich 1930—33.

LACEY, W. K., *The Family in Classical Greece*, Thames and Hudson, London 1968; Cornell University Press, New York 1968.

LENDLE, O., 'Das Kretische Stiersprungspiel', *Marburger Winckelmann-Programm* 1965.

MARINATOS, S., 'La Marine Créto-Mycénienne', *B. C. H.* 1933.

MYLONAS, G. E.: I *Ancient Mycenae*, Routledge and Kegan Paul, London 1957; Princeton University Press, Princeton 1957. II with K. KOURO-NIOTES 'Excavations at Eleusis', *A. J. A.* 1933.

ORMEROD, H. A., *Piracy in the Ancient World*, Hodder and Stoughton, London 1924; Argonaut, Chicago 1924.

PERSSON, A.: I *Royal Tombs at Dendra near Midea*, Oxford University Press, London and New York 1932. II *New Tombs at Dendra near Midea*, Oxford University Press, London 1942.

SEAGER, R. B., *Explorations in the Island of Mochlos*, Boston and New York 1912.

SCHLIEMANN, H., *Mycenae and Tiryns*, John Murray, London 1878.

SCHLOCKER, G., 'Kampfspiel an der Silberküste', *Atlantis* 1963.

STUBBINGS, F. H., *Mycenaean Pottery from the Levant*, Cambridge University Press, Cambridge and New York 1951.

THOMSON, H. A., 'Activities in the Athenian Agora: 1959, the Eleusinion', *Hesperia* 1960.

VENTRIS, M. and CHADWICK, J., *Documents in Mycenaean Greek*, Cambridge University Press, London and New York 1956.

VICKERY, K., *Food in Early Greece*, University of Illinois Press, Urbana, Ill. 1936.

WARD, A. G.: I 'The Cretan Bull Sports', *Antiquity* 1968. II *Minoan and Mycenaean Jewellery*, London University Thesis, 1963.

WELTER, G., *Troizen und Kalaureia*, Mann, Berlin 1941.

WIDE, S., 'Aphidna in Nordattika', *Athenische Mitteilungen* 1896.

XANTHOUDIDES, S., *The Vaulted Tombs of Mesara*, Hodder and Stoughton, London 1924.

CHAPTER 8

DEUBNER, L., *Attische Feste*, Berlin 1932.

DINSMOOR, W. B., 'The Sculptured Frieze from Bassae', *A. J. A.* 60, 1956.

HARRISON, E. B., 'The Shield of Athena Parthenos', *Hesperia* 35, 1966.

HERTER, H.: I 'Theseus der Ionier', *Rheinisches Museum für Philologie* 85, 1936. II 'Theseus der Athener', ibid. 88, 1939. III 'Theseus und Hippolytos', ibid. 89, 1940.

Jeffery, L. H., *B. S. A.* 60, 1965 (on the Painted Stoa).

Johansen, K. F., *Thésée et la danse à Délos*, Copenhagen 1945.

Mallwitz, A. and Schiering, W., 'Die Werkstatt des Pheidias', *Olympische Forschungen*, de Gruyter, Berlin 1964.

Morgan, C. H., *Hesperia* 31, pp. 221—35, 1962 (Hephaesteum frieze).

Schefold, K., 'Kleisthenes', *Museum Helveticum* 3, 1946.

CHAPTERS 9—11

Bush, J. N. D.: I *Mythology and the Renaissance Tradition in English Poetry*, Oxford University Press, London 1932; University of Minnesota Press, 1932. II *Mythology and the Romantic Traditon*, Oxford University Press, London 1937; Harvard University Press, Cambridge, Mass. 1937.

Dizionario Letterario Bompiani delle Opere e dei Personaggi, Milan 1947—66.

Matthews, W. H., *Mazes and Labyrinths*, Longmans, London and New York 1922.

Saxl, F., *Verzeichnis Astrologischer und Mythologischer Illustrierter Handschriften*, Vols. I and II, Vienna 1915, 1927, Vol. III, London 1953.

List of Illustrations, Maps and Tables

The contributors and publishers are grateful to the many official bodies, institutions and individuals mentioned below for their assistance in supplying illustrative material.
Abbreviations : NMA National Museum, Athens; AMH Archaeological Museum, Heraklion.

21 Theseus, Pirithous and Heracles in Hades, from a shield relief from Olympia, c. 580—570 BC. G. Jones after Schefold.

22 Plan of the Agora at Athens in the 2nd century AD. Photo: by courtesy of the American School of Classical Studies at Athens.

23 Chronological table illustrating the historical, artistic and literary background to the growth of the Theseus legend. G. Jones.

24 The island of Dia, seen from the north coast of Crete. Photo: Ronald Sheridan.

25 Theseus fighting the Minotaur, from a fragment of a shield relief from Olympia, c. 600 BC. Photo: by courtesy of the Deutsches Archäologisches Institut, Athens.

26 Theseus fighting the Minotaur, from a shield relief from Olympia, c. 600 BC. G. Jones after Schefold.

27 Theseus fighting the Minotaur, watched by Ariadne, from a gold ornament from Corinth, 7th century BC. G. Jones.

28 Ship scene from a Geometric bowl from Thebes, late 8th century BC. Photo: by courtesy of the Trustees of the British Museum.

29 Theseus with Athenian youths and maidens, detail of the top band of side B of the François Vase, made by Ergotimos and painted by Kleitias, c. 570 BC. Museo Archeologico, Florence. Photo: Scala.

30 Theseus fighting the Minotaur with Athena, Ariadne and the Athenian youths and maidens looking on, from a band-cup

by Archikles and Glaukytes, painted c. 540 BC. By courtesy of the Staatliche Antikensammlungen und Glyptothek, Munich. Photo: Kohlroser.

31 Man and a centaur, from an Attic Geometric neck-amphora, c. 700 BC. Photo: by courtesy of the National Museum, Copenhagen; Department of Oriental and Classical Antiquities.

32 Theseus capturing the bull of Marathon, from a black-figure amphora by the Painter of Würzburg. Photo: by courtesy of the Bibliothèque Nationale, Paris.

33 The abduction of Helen by Theseus and her rescue by the Dioscuri, from a proto-Corinthian aryballos, c. 680 BC. Musée du Louvre, Paris. G. Jones.

34 The abduction of Helen by Theseus and her rescue by the Dioscuri, from a proto-Corinthian aryballos, c. 680 BC. By courtesy of the Musée du Louvre, Paris. Photo: Maurice Chuzeville.

35—38 Details of Sciron, Theseus and the bull of Marathon, Theseus and the Minotaur and Theseus and Antiope from the metopes of the Athenian treasury at Delphi, c. 510 BC. Photos: by courtesy of the Ecole Française d'Athènes.

39, 40 Heracles freeing Theseus from the throne of rock in Hades, from a red-figure lekythos. Photos: by courtesy of the Staatliche Museen, Berlin.

41 Theseus killing the Minotaur, from a black-figure amphora from Vulci. Photo: by courtesy of the Trustees of the British Museum.

42 Theseus dragging the dead Minotaur from the Labyrinth, watched by Athena, from a red-figure cup by Aison. Photo: by courtesy of the Museo Arqueologico Nacional, Madrid.

43—45 Three views of a red-figure lekythos showing Theseus, Ariadne and Athena. Photos: by courtesy of the Soprintendenza alle Antichità della Puglia, Taranto.

46 Theseus with Amphitrite beneath the sea, from a kylix painted by the Panaitios Painter and signed by the potter Euphronios, c. 500—490 BC. Musée du Louvre, Paris. Photo: Phaidon Press.

47 Theseus and Pirithous carrying off Antiope, from a red-figure amphora by Myson, c. 500 BC. By courtesy of the Musée du Louvre, Paris. Photo: Maurice Chuzeville.

48 View of the cliffs near the reputed site of Sciron's lair. Photo: Ronald Sheridan.

49 Dionysus sailing in a boat, from a black-figure kylix by Exekias, mid-6th century BC. Staatliche Antikensammlungen Glyptothek, Munich. Photo: Phaidon Press.

50 Late Helladic terracotta snake excavated at Mycenae. Photo: by courtesy of Lord William Taylour.

51 Chronological table of the Aegean cultures in the Bronze Age. G. Jones.

52 Gold pendant with appliqué and granulated ornament, two bees, from Mallia, 1700—1550 BC, height 4.6 cm. AMH. Copy-

right © George Rainbird Ltd. 1968. Photo: Dimitrios Harissiadis.

53 Late Minoan chest (*larnax*), from Vasilika Anogeia, 1400—1350 BC, length 1.23 m. AMH. Photo: Peter Clayton.

54 Engraved gold double-axes from Arkalochori, 1550—1450 BC. AMH. Photo: A. G. Ward.

55 Plan of the palace at Knossos and the surrounding area. GJ after Pendlebury.

56 Aerial view of the palace at Knossos. Photo: Royal Hellenic Air Force.

57 Plan of the palace at Knossos. G. Jones after Demargne.

58 Remains of the viaduct at Knossos. Photo: Ronald Sheridan.

59 The central court of the palace at Knossos. Photo: Ronald Sheridan.

60 A kamares cup from the Middle Minoan II period. AMH. Photo: Ronald Sheridan.

61 A large storage jar (*pithos*) from Mallia, 1450—1400 BC. Photo: A. G. Ward.

62 Flat 'pilgrim flask' with octopus design (Marine style), from Palaikastro, 1500—1450 BC, height 28 cm. AMH. Photo: Josephine Powell.

63 Jug painted with reeds (Floral style), from Phaistos, 1550—1500 BC, height 29 cm. AMH. Photo: Ronald Sheridan.

64 The fresco known as 'La Parisienne', from the palace at Knossos, 1550—1450 BC. AMH. Photo: A. G. Ward.

65 Fresco showing the two-tailed bull, from Tiryns. Photo: Marburg.

66 Fresco of a dancing lady, from the palace at Knossos, 1550—1450 BC. AMH. Photo: Ronald Sheridan.

67 The Queen's Megaron in the palace at Knossos. Photo: Ronald Sheridan.

68 Gold signet ring showing a group of dancing women, from Isopata near Knossos, 1500—1400 BC, width 2.6 cm. AMH. Photo: Josephine Powell.

69 Ivory and gold representation of a snake goddess, *c.* 1600 BC, height 16 cm. Photo: by courtesy of the Museum of Fine Arts, Boston; Gift of Mrs. W. Scott Fitz.

70 Gold signet ring with intaglio design of two goats mating, from Crete, 1700—1550 BC, diameter of bezel 1.7 cm. By courtesy of the Trustees of the British Museum. Photo: Ronald Sheridan.

71 Gold pendant with profile heads with traces of inlay, from the so-called 'Aegina Treasure', 1700—1550 BC, length 10.8 cm. By courtesy of the Trustees of the British Museum. Photo: Ronald Sheridan.

72 Gold flower from a tomb at Volos, 15th century BC. NMA. Photo: Ronald Sheridan.

73 The duck-hunter gold pendant, from the 'Aegina Treasure', 1700—1550 BC, height 6 cm. By courtesy of the Trustees of the British Museum. Photo: Ronald Sheridan.

74 Gold and carnelian hoop earring, from the 'Aegina Trea-

sure', 1700—1550 BC. By courtesy of the Trustees of the British Museum. Photo: Ronald Sheridan.

75 The Grand Staircase at the palace at Knossos 1550—1430 BC. Photo: Ronald Sheridan.

76 The throne room at the palace at Knossos, after 1450 BC. Photo: Peter Clayton.

77 A fresco fragment showing a cushioned stool from the palace at Knossos. AMH. Photo: Ronald Sheridan.

78 Bath-shaped larnax, from Pachyammos, 1400—1350 BC, height 48 cm. AMH. Photo: Peter Clayton.

79 Drains at Knossos. Photo: Peter Clayton.

80 Section of the queen's lavatory at the palace at Knossos. G. Jones after Hutchinson.

81 Bronze lamp with chain. G. Jones after Evans.

82 Portable charcoal brazier for heating Cretan room. G. Jones after Evans.

83 Stone pedestal lamp, 1600—1500 BC. AMH. Photo: Ronald Sheridan.

84 Three-handled bronze cauldron from a Late Minoan house at Tylissos. AMH. Photo: Josephine Powell.

85 Rock crystal lamp in the form of a duck, from Grave Circle B at Mycenae, 1550—1500 BC, length 13.2 cm. NMA. Photo: Ronald Sheridan.

86 Bronze cup with ivy-leaf ornaments, from Mochlos, *c.* 1550 BC, height 6.5 cm. G. Jones after Evans.

87 Miniature gold scales, from Shaft Grave III, 1550—1500 BC. NMA. Photo: Ronald Sheridan.

88 Ivory cosmetic box (*pyxis*) with the figures of a charging bull and an acrobat, from the cemetery at Katsamba, the ancient port of Knossos, Late Minoan I. AMH. Photo: Ronald Sheridan.

89 Terracotta model sedan chair from Knossos, from the Middle Minoan period. AMH. Photo: Ronald Sheridan.

90 Ship, from a stirrup jar from Skyros, Late Helladic III. G. Jones after Vermeule.

91 Seal stone with ship, Middle Minoan. By courtesy of the Trustees of the British Museum. Photo: Ronald Sheridan.

92 Early Minoan clay model of a ship, from a tomb at Mochlos, Crete. AMH. Photo: Ronald Sheridan.

93 Linear B tablet from Knossos, Late Minoan. After Evans.

94 Plan of the Early Helladic 'House of the Tiles' at Lerna in the Argolid. G. Jones after Caskey.

95 Grave Circle A at Mycenae. Photo: Peter Clayton.

96 Bronze dagger blade inlaid with gold, silver and niello showing a lion hunt, from Shaft Grave V at Mycenae, 1550—1500 BC, length 23.8 cm. Photo: NMA.

97 Interior of the so-called 'Treasury of Atreus' at Mycenae, with door into side chamber, 1300—1250 BC. Photo: Alison Frantz.

98 Plan of the so-called 'Treasury of Atreus' at Mycenae, 1300—1250 BC. G. Jones after Hood.

99 Gold 'tea-cup' embossed with marine scene, from Dendra, *c.* 1400 BC, diameter 17.3 cm. NMA. Photo: Ronald Sheridan.

100 Seal ring with intaglio of a hunting scene, from Shaft Grave IV at Mycenae, 1550—1500 BC, width 3 cm. NMA. Photo: by courtesy of the Deutsches Archäologisches Institut, Athens.

101 The hearth in the great hall of the 'Palace of Nestor'. View from behind the hall with oil store in the foreground. Epano Englianos, near Chora, accepted site of ancient Pylos, 13th century BC. Photo: Alison Frantz.

102 Obsidian chalice, from Zakro, 1500—1450 BC, height 30.5 cm. AMH. Photo: by courtesy of Professor N. Platon.

103 Gold signet ring showing a procession of daemons bringing votive gifts to a goddess, from Tiryns, 1500—1400 BC, width 5.6 cm. Photo: NMA.

104 Gold signet ring showing two worshipping women, from Mycenae, 1500—1400 BC. NMA. Photo: by courtesy of the Deutsches Archäologisches Institut, Athens.

105 Reconstructed view of the citadel at Mycenae from a painting by Alton S. Tobey. Photo: by courtesy of Mrs. A. J. B. Wace.

106 Map of the Aegean. G. Jones.

107 The stone near Troezen known as the 'Theseus Rock'. Photo: Ronald Sheridan.

108 Bronze Age sandals worn by a soldier on the 'Chieftain Cup', from Hagia Triada, 1500—1450 BC. AMH. Photo: Peter Clayton.

109 A sword hilt embellished with lions and spirals in gold, from Grave Circle B, Mycenae, 16th century BC. NMA. Photo: Ronald Sheridan.

110 The road from Corinth to Athens. Photo: Ronald Sheridan.

111 The whole story of Theseus' exploits from Troezen to Athens and from Marathon to Crete, from an Attic red-figure kylix by the Codrus Painter, found at Vulci, 440—430 BC. By courtesy of the Trustees of the British Museum. Photo: John Freeman.

112 Gold ring from Mycenae showing a youth kneeling at a tree-shrine in the presence of two larger-than-life female figures. Photo: by courtesy of the Deutsches Archäologisches Institut, Athens.

113 Plan of Mycenaean Athens showing the Acropolis and the immediately surrounding area. G. Jones after Vermeule.

114 Group of tombs on the slopes of the Areopagus near Athens. Photo: by courtesy of the American School of Classical Studies at Athens.

115, 116 A spring chamber sunk through the rock at Athens. Photo: by courtesy of the American School of Classical Studies at Athens.

117 Part of a fortification wall which once encircled the whole top of the Acropolis. Photo: Ronald Sheridan.

118 The dromos of the Bronze Age tomb at Marathon. Photo: by courtesy of the Greek Archaeological Society, Athens.

119 The massive stucco 'horns of consecration' crowning the south façade of the palace at Knossos. Photo: Ronald Sheridan.

120 A section of the Admiralty Chart of Crete showing the coastline round Amnisos. Reproduced from BA chart No. 2536b with the sanction of the Controller, H M Stationery Office and of the Hydrographer of the Navy.

121 Ruins of the harbour town of Amnisos. Photo: Peter Clayton.

122 Plan of the Middle Helladic houses at Lerna. After Vermeule.

123 View of the palace at Knossos. Photo: Josephine Powell.

124 A reconstruction of the palace at Knossos, by Chr. Mathioulakis and N. Gouvoussis, Athens. Photo: Green Studio, by courtesy of J. V. Luce.

125 Rhyton in the form of a bull's head, serpentine with shell inlay, from Knossos, 1500—1450 BC. The horns are restored. AMH. Photo: A. G. Ward.

126 A modern impression from a lentoid seal, bull-leaping scene, from Crete, 1550—1500 BC. Photo: by courtesy of the Ashmolean Museum, Oxford.

127 A Minoan ivory figurine, picked out with gold, from Crete, c. 1550 BC, height 13.3 cm. Photo: by courtesy of the Ashmolean Museum, Oxford.

128, 129 A modern form of the Cretan bull sports as performed at Dax in France. Photo: Richard.

130 Reconstruction of the 'Grandstand' fresco from the palace at Knossos. By courtesy of the executors of Sir Arthur Evans' estate. Photo: Gregg International Publishers.

131 Bronze statuette of a bull and acrobat, 16th century BC, height 11.1 cm. By courtesy of the Trustees of the British Museum. Photo: Ronald Sheridan.

132 Ladies watching the bull sports, fresco from the palace at Knossos. AMH. Photo: Peter Clayton.

133 The bull-leaper fresco from the palace at Knossos. AMH. Photo: Ronald Sheridan.

134–136 Plans of the central courts and surrounding areas at Knossos, Phaistos and Mallia. J-C. Peissel.

137 A fresco fragment showing a woman behind a hurdle at the palace at Knossos. G. Jones after Evans.

138 Post-holes at Mallia. Photo: A. G. Ward.

139 The 'Priest-King' fresco from the palace at Knossos, 1550—1450 BC. This is largely restored, but the crown, the torso and most of the left leg are original. AMH. Photo: Ronald Sheridan.

140 A modern impression from an agate flattened cylinder from Priene, bull drinking at a cistern, c. 1600 BC, length 2.1 cm. Photo: by courtesy of the Ashmolean Museum, Oxford.

141 A niche on the north side of the central court at Phaistos with a diamond-shaped pattern. Photo: Ronald Sheridan.

142 Gold cup showing a bull being caught peacefully by means of a decoy cow and tethered by a hind leg, from Vapheio, 1500—1450 BC, diameter 10.8 cm. NMA. Photo: Ronald Sheridan.

143 Gold cup showing the capture of a bull in a hunting net, from Vapheio, 1500—1450 BC, diameter 19.8 cm. NMA. Photo: Ronald Sheridan.

144 Painted limestone sarcophagus found in a tomb at Hagia Triada, c. 1400 BC, showing a trussed bull awaiting sacrifice in a shrine, length 137 cm. AMH. Photo: Ronald Sheridan.

145 Ivory relief of a warrior armed with a figure-of-eight shield and boar's-tusk helmet, from Delos, 1400—1200 BC, height 13 cm. Delos Museum. Photo: Phaidon Press.

146 Remains of a Mycenaean building known as 'Building Gamma', on Delos. Photo: by courtesy of the Ecole Française d'Athènes.

147 Traditional Greek dancers at the Daphni wine festival. Photo: Ronald Sheridan.

148 A gold cup of distinctive Mycenaean design found at Rillaton in Cornwall. By courtesy of the Trustees of the British Museum. Photo: Peter Clayton.

149 A copper ingot from a ship which sank c. 1200 BC off the coast of Turkey at Cape Gelidonya. University Museum, Philadelphia. Photo: by courtesy of George F. Bass.

150 Late Bronze Age bronze figurine found at Tiryns representing a native Syrian god. Photo: by courtesy of the Deutsches Archäologisches Institut, Athens.

151 Lid from Knossos with the cartouche of the Seventeenth-Dynasty Hyksos King Khian, found at Knossos. AMH. Photo: Peter Clayton.

152 Late Helladic clay tablet from Pylos bearing the name of Theseus in Linear B in the fifth line. Photo: by courtesy of Carl W. Blegen, Department of Classics, University of Cincinnati.

153 Wappenmünzen bearing the image of an ox, c. 530—520 BC. NMA. Photo: Peter Clayton.

154 Athena with Theseus in a chariot, from an Attic red-figure kylix, 490—480 BC. Photo: by courtesy of the Metropolitan Museum of Art; Purchase, 1953, Joseph Pulitzer Bequest.

155 The 'Crane Dance', from a Geometric hydria from Analatos. Photo: NMA.

156 Theseus fighting Sciron, Cercyon and the bull of Marathon, from a red-figure kylix signed by the Chachrylion Potter. Photo: by courtesy of the Soprintendenza alle Antichità d'Etruria, Florence.

157 Acamas, Demophon and Aethra, from a red-figure crater. Photo: by courtesy of the Trustees of the British Museum.

158 Demos and Democratia, from the top section of a stele. Photo: by courtesy of the American School of Classical Studies at Athens.

159 A view of the temple of Hephaestus overlooking the Athenian Agora. Photo: by courtesy of the American School of Classical Studies at Athens.

160 Theseus fighting the centaurs, from the west frieze of the temple of Hephaestus, Athens. Photo: by courtesy of the American School of Classical Studies at Athens.

161 Theseus struggling against the Pallantids, from the east frieze of the temple of Hephaestus, Athens. Photo: by courtesy of the American School of Classical Studies at Athens.

162 Dinos showing Theseus fighting the Amazons. Photo: by courtesy of the Trustees of the British Museum.

163 A restored tholos tomb at Pylos. Photo: Alison Frantz.

164 Skeleton in a Mycenaean chamber tomb on the north slopes of the Areopagus. Photo: by courtesy of the American School of Classical Studies at Athens.

165 Theseus killing a centaur, from the Foundry Painter's vase from Vulci. By courtesy of the Staatliche Antikensammlungen und Glyptothek, Munich. Photo: Kohlroser.

166 Theseus in the palace of Poseidon, from an Attic red-figure kylix, 490—480 BC. Photo: by courtesy of the Metropolitan Museum of Art; Purchase, 1953, Joseph Pulitzer Bequest.

167 A potsherd (ostrakon) bearing the name of Cimon, son of Miltiades. Photo: by courtesy of the American School of Classical Studies at Athens.

168 Acamas and Demophon leading their horses, from a neck-amphora by Exekias, from Vulci. Photo: by courtesy of the Staatliche Museen, Berlin.

169 Theseus slaying the Minotaur and Heracles fighting the river deity Achelous, from a Corinthian bowl, 7th century BC. Photo: copyright A. C. L. Brussels.

170 Heracles fighting the Cretan bull, from a black-figure vase. Photo: by courtesy of the Trustees of the British Museum.

171 Heracles fighting the Amazons, from a black-figure amphora from Vulci. Photo: Museo Civico Archeologico, Bologna.

172 Theseus fighting the bull of Marathon, from an Attic red-figure kylix by the Codrus Painter, found at Vulci, 440—430 BC. By courtesy of the Trustees of the British Museum. Photo: Ronald Sheridan.

173 Theseus fighting the Amazons, from an Attic crater. Museo Etrusco Gregoriano, Rome. Photo: Alinari.

174 The Strangford shield, a fragment of a marble copy of Phidias' gold and ivory statue of Athena. Photo: by courtesy of the Trustees of the British Museum.

175 Impression of a carnelian intaglio, showing Zeus seated on his throne, after the colossal gold and ivory statue by Phidias at Olympia, c. 435 BC. Cabinet des Médailles, Paris. Photo: Phaidon Press.

176 Cup bearing the name of Phidias. Photo: by courtesy of the Deutsches Archäologisches Institut, Athens.

ing with Ariadne. Campana Collection, Musée du Louvre, Paris. Photo: Giraudon.

208 Jacob Jordaens: *Bacchus and Ariadne*. Photo: by courtesy of the Museum of Fine Arts, Boston; Maria T. B. Hopkins Fund.

209 Guido Reni: *Bacchus and Ariadne*. By courtesy of the Galleria della Accademia Nazionale di San Luca, Rome. Photo: Gabinetto Fotografico Nazionale, Rome.

210 A 16th-century Italian majolica plate showing the story of Phaedra and Hippolytus. By courtesy of the Victoria and Albert Museum, London. Crown Copyright. Photo: John Freeman.

211 An 18th-century Beauvais tapestry, showing Bacchus and Ariadne, from a set of 'Loves of the Gods', woven from designs by François Boucher, *c*. 1754. Photo: by courtesy of the Metropolitan Museum of Art; anonymous gift, 1922.

212 A drawing by Brunck of Phaedra, from an edition of Racine's *Phèdre*, 1942. Photo: by courtesy of the Bibliothèque Nationale, Paris.

213 Nicolas Poussin: *Theseus Raising the Stone*, to find his father's sword. Musée Condé, Chantilly. Photo: Giraudon.

214 Annibale Carracci: *The Triumph of Bacchus and Ariadne*. Palazzo Farnese, Rome. Photo: Alinari.

215 Giambattista Tiepolo: *Bacchus and Ariadne*. Photo: by courtesy of the National Gallery of Art, Washington, D.C.; Timkin Collection.

216 Cornelis Mebeecq: *Bacchus and Ariadne*. Photo: by courtesy of the Rijksbureau voor Kunsthistorische Documentatie, the Hague.

217 A reconstruction of the Labyrinth from Fischer von Erlach's *Entwurf einer historischen Architektur*. Photo: John Freeman.

218 Canova: *Theseus Triumphant*. Photo: by courtesy of the Victoria and Albert Museum, London. Crown Copyright.

219 Antoine Louis Barye: *Theseus*. By courtesy of the Musée des Beaux-Arts, Bordeaux. Photo: A. Danvers.

220, 221 Two scenes from the 1969 Sadler's Wells production of Richard Strauss' *Ariadne auf Naxos* showing Ariadne (Elizabeth Fretwell) and Zerbinetta (Jenifer Eddy) and Ariadne and Bacchus (Alberto Remedios). Photos: by courtesy of the Sadler's Wells Trust.

222 G. F. Watts: *The Minotaur*. Photo: by courtesy of the Tate Gallery, London.

223 Picasso: *Blind Minotaur*, etching from the *Vollard Suite*. Photo: © S.P.A.D.E.M., Paris.

224 Picasso: *Dying Minotaur*, etching from the *Vollard Suite*. Photo: © S.P.A.D.E.M., Paris.

225 The cover of the first issue of *Minotaure*, by Picasso. By courtesy of Editions d'Art Albert Skira. Photo: John Freeman.

226 The cover of the eighth issue of *Minotaure*, by Salvadore Dali. By courtesy of Editions d'Art Albert Skira. Photo: John Freeman.

227 The cover of the tenth issue of *Minotaure*, by René Magritte. By courtesy of Editions d'Art Albert Skira. Photo: John Freeman.

228 The cover of the twelfth/thirteenth issue of *Minotaure*, by Diego Rivera. By courtesy of Editions d'Art Albert Skira. Photo: Phaidon Press.

229 A maquette of the brick and stone maze built by Michael Ayrton for Mr Armand G. Erpf in the Catskills, New York, U.S.A. Photo: by courtesy of Michael Ayrton.

Acknowledgements

The editor and publisher would like to thank the following publishers for permission to quote from the cited works: Collins, London, *The Correspondence between Richard Strauss and Hugo von Hofmannsthal,* translated by Hans A. Hammelmann and E. Osers; Penguin Books, Harmondsworth, Euripides, *Hippolytos,* translated by P. Vellacott, and Thucydides, *History of the Peloponnesian War,* translated by Rex Warner; Routledge and Kegan Paul, London, and Bollingen Series xx, Princeton University Press, Princeton, C. G. Jung, *Symbols of Transformation,* translated by R. F. C. Hull; Secker and Warburg, London, and Alfred A. Knopf, New York, Thomas Mann 'Freud and the Future' in *Essays of Three Decades.*

Index

Numbers in *italic* refer to illustrations and their captions.